Enemies of the State

The American Ways Series

General Editor: John David Smith,
Charles H. Stone Distinguished Professor of American History
University of North Carolina at Charlotte

From the long arcs of America's history, to the short timeframes that convey larger stories, American Ways provides concise, accessible topical histories informed by the latest scholarship and written by scholars who are both leading experts in their fields and polished writers.

Books in the series provide general readers and students with compelling introductions to America's social, cultural, political, and economic history, underscoring questions of class, gender, racial, and sectional diversity and inclusivity. The titles suggest the multiple ways that the past informs the present and shapes the future in often unforeseen ways.

Current Titles in the Series

How America Eats: A Social History of U.S. Food and Culture, by Jennifer Jensen Wallach

Popular Justice: A History of Lynching in America, by Manfred Berg

Bounds of their Habitation: Race and Religion in American History, by Paul Harvey

National Pastime: U.S. History through Baseball, by Martin C. Babicz and Thomas W. Zeiler

This Green and Growing Land: Environmental Activism in American History, by Kevin C. Armitage

Wartime America: The World War II Home Front, Second Edition, by John W. Jeffries

Enemies of the State: The Radical Right from FDR to Trump, by D. J. Mulloy

ENEMIES OF THE STATE

The Radical Right in
America from FDR to Trump

D. J. Mulloy

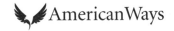

ROWMAN & LITTLEFIELD
Lanham • Boulder • New York • London

Published by Rowman & Littlefield
A wholly owned subsidary of The Rowman & Littlefield Publishing Group, Inc.
4501 Forbes Boulevard, Suite 200, Lanham, Maryland 20706
www.rowman.com

Unit A, Whitacre Mews, 26-34 Stannary Street, London SE11 4AB

British Library Cataloguing in Publication Information Available

Library of Congress Cataloging-in-Publication Data Available

ISBN: 978-1-4422-7651-2 (cloth : alk. paper)
ISBN: 978-1-4422-7652-9 (electronic)

♾™ The paper used in this publication meets the minimum requirements of
American National Standard for Information Sciences—Permanence of Paper for
Printed Library Materials, ANSI/NISO Z39.48-1992.

Printed in the United States of America

"It's rough out there / High water everywhere . . . "

—Bob Dylan, "High Water (For Charley Patton)"

For my students and for my teachers.

Contents

Acknowledgments

THIS BOOK ORIGINATED IN A CONVERSATION at the annual meeting of the Organization of American Historians in a rain-swept Rhode Island in April 2016. My sincere thanks to the American history editor at Rowman & Littlefield, Jon Sisk, and to the general editor of the American Way series, John David Smith, for that conversation and for their unstinting support and enthusiasm for this project. I would also like to thank assistant editor Kate Powers for her considerable assistance in seeing the book through to publication and everyone else at Rowman & Littlefield, especially associate editor Hannah Fisher, who made it possible. Adam Crerar, David Monod, and Peter Woolstencroft took time out of their busy schedules to cast their expert eyes over the manuscript, for which I am very appreciative. A list of the authors whose work I consulted in writing the book can be found in "A Note on Sources" at the book's end. I thank them all. History is an always ongoing discussion about the past, and I am deeply grateful to be able to contribute to it. My parents have remained steadfast in their support for more than forty years now. I do not take that for granted. Finally, I would like to thank my wonderful wife, the novelist Pamela Mulloy, and my amazing daughter, Esme, a budding social historian, for allowing me to escape so regularly to my office in the attic over the past few months and for not complaining too much about the strange music so often emanating from there.

Introduction

HOW DID WE GET HERE, many people are currently asking themselves—with a billionaire political outsider in the White House and a broader climate in which a fervent hostility to government, especially the federal government, seems to provide the very raison d'être for much of the politics taking place across the country? This book argues that to make sense of these contemporary developments we need to understand the longer history of the radical right in the United States—in all its many and varied forms—going back at least to the days of the Great Depression, the New Deal, and the extraordinary political achievements of Franklin D. Roosevelt. The book therefore provides a concise history of the American radical right from the 1930s through to the surprise election of Donald Trump in 2016 and his first year in office.

It examines a wide range of fascinating—and frequently controversial—groups and figures, including the American Liberty League, Huey Long, Father Charles Coughlin, Joe McCarthy, J. Edgar Hoover, the John Birch Society, Citizens' Councils, George Wallace, Barry Goldwater, Richard Nixon, Ronald Reagan, Phyllis Schlafly, Pat Robertson, militia groups, and the Tea Party. But it also considers the key role that big business and the extremely rich have played in supporting the radical right throughout this period, as well as the close, if sometimes fractious, relationship that has existed between members of the radical right and the Republican Party. In doing so, I make the case that the history of the radical right cannot and should not be seen in isolation from broader historical trends and developments. Hence, among the significant events and issues covered in the pages that follow are the "great debate" over America's entry into the Second World War, the Cold War, southern resistance to the civil rights movement, the rise of the religious right, the Great Recession of 2008, and the election of Barack Obama as the nation's first African American president.

What exactly do I mean by the term "radical right"? Its origins can be traced back to the 1950s, to the attempt to account for the apparent "lapse" in the American political system represented by McCarthyism.

In 1955 a group of prominent academics published a series of essays on the phenomenon called *The New American Right*. Included among them were Seymour Martin Lipset's "The Sources of the 'Radical Right'" and Richard Hofstadter's "The Pseudo-Conservative Revolt." It was these two essays—supplemented by another Hofstadter essay called "The Paranoid Style in American Politics," in 1964—that did much to both define the radical right and establish its chief characteristics. The fundamental difference between "moderate conservatives" and "pseudo-conservatives," these Columbia University professors argued, was that the former were usually willing to negotiate and compromise in order to achieve their political goals. They believed in "constitutional processes, civil liberties, and due process," and generally accepted "the past within limits." Whereas the latter—those on the radical right—wanted to "turn the clock back" and had a tendency toward political extremism, conspiracy theories, paranoia, and a "dense and massive irrationality."

The key distinction in Lipset and Hofstadter's analysis was between "genuine" conservatism and its more "radical" variant, but the term "radical right" is also widely used to separate the racist right—usually labeled the "extreme right"—from other right-wing groups that fall outside of the political mainstream. (To add to the complexity, another term, the "far right," is also sometimes used to denote both the radical right *and* the extreme right. And that is before we add in other commonly used descriptors, such as the religious right, the nationalist right, and most recently—as discussed in chapter 6—the alt-right.) In its everyday use, "radical" can have both negative and positive connotations, depending on the context in which it is used. One can be praised for being radical in the sense of wanting to bring about much-needed fundamental change and criticized for being *too* radical, if it is felt that the change being sought goes too far, is dangerous, or runs counter to previously established societal norms. Indeed, a group can be celebrated and condemned for its radicalism at the very same time, depending on the perspective of those observing it. American history is replete with examples of this, including the Radical Republicans, who tried to secure the rights of freed slaves in the South in the aftermath of the Civil War, and the radical left of the 1960s, in groups such as the Black Panther Party for Self-Defense or Students for a Democratic Society. (The word "radical" comes from the Latin *radix* and means "pertaining to roots." Politically, it has tended to be used to refer to those who have wanted to bring about significant change—to pull something up by the roots and drastically alter it—and until the middle of the twentieth century, it was more usually associated with the left than with the right.)

In this book, I use "radical right" to describe various right-wing groups and movements that, since the 1930s, have been driven by a deep suspicion of the federal government and its role in American society. This hostility to what is often referred to as "big government" contains a number of political assumptions about the place of the state in American life, the promise of the "free market," individual liberties, freedom, taxation, "traditional" values, federalism, patriotism, and even the nature of the constitutional system itself. It is an expression of political philosophy but also of political identity, and it is firmly rooted in American history. Indeed, anti-statism is as old as the nation itself, evident in the Declaration of Independence, for instance, and manifested in various forms, from Shays Rebellion and the Whiskey Rebellion at the end of the eighteenth century, through the rise of Jacksonian democracy and the agitations of the Copperheads during the Civil War. But in its modern incarnation, it is most closely associated with the American right's reaction to the enormous impact that FDR's New Deal reforms had on the United States—on its economy, on its politics, and on all levels of society—as the nation sought a way out of the Great Depression.

The New Deal was a very much a watershed moment in American history, with the federal government inserted into the lives of Americans in ways that were previously unimaginable. It was also profoundly consequential in purely political terms, not least because of the establishment of Roosevelt's New Deal electoral coalition—composed of labor unions, blue-collar workers, white southerners, farmers, intellectuals, and members of various ethnic and racial groups—which made the Democrats the dominant political party, at least at the presidential level, for almost the next fifty years. Not surprisingly, turning back this tide of liberalism became the overriding aim of both the radical right and mainstream conservatives, and it began as early as 1934.

Similarly, it is also important to point out that while an explicit and unabashed racism may clearly mark out one's membership in the extreme right, this does not mean that racial stereotypes and notions of white supremacy have played no part in the ideology of the radical right or of American conservatism as a whole. On the contrary, although often expressed in more coded form, in euphemism and through what has come to be called "dog-whistle politics"—an approach that can be traced back to the "southern strategy" of the Republican Party, beginning in the early 1960s—racism is frequently evident on the radical right and within conservatism more broadly, up to and including the presidency of Donald Trump. In addition, we should not ignore the fact that avowedly racist groups such as the Silver Shirts, the Black Legion, the Ku Klux Klan, or the National States' Rights Party—all discussed in this book—have also expressed more conventional and accepted right-wing beliefs, including a fervent opposition to the activities of the interventionist state and liberal welfarism. All of which is to say that the dividing lines between the extreme right, the radical right, and conservatism are much less robust than many people would like to believe. It is for all these reasons that the Republican Party—the official repository of mainstream American conservatism—features so prominently in the pages that follow. (It is also the case that the radical right has often seen the GOP as the most likely vehicle for the expansion of its political influence, another point that is important to recognize.)

Three other terms closely associated with the radical right also need some consideration. The first is demagoguery. From Huey Long and Father Coughlin, through Joe McCarthy and George Wallace, and onto President Trump, leaders of the radical right—if Trump is determined to belong to the radical right, which is not entirely clear, as we shall see— have often been accused of being demagogues. In the simplest sense, a demagogue is someone who appeals to popular desires and prejudices, rather than relying on rational argument. They are, as the novelist James Fenimore Cooper put it in 1838, a "leader of the rabble." A more sophisticated definition is provided by Michael Singer in his 2009 book, *Demagogues: The Fight to Save Democracy from its Worst Enemies*. In Singer's view, "true demagogues" meet four rules:

(1) They fashion themselves as a man or woman of the common people, as opposed to the elites; (2) their politics depends on a powerful, visceral connection with the people that dramatically transcends ordinary political popularity; (3) they manipulate this connection, and the raging popularity it affords, for their own benefit and ambition; and

(4) they threaten or outright break established rules of conduct, institutions, and even the law.

Just because someone is accused of demagoguery doesn't mean they actually are a demagogue, of course. This is because the term is also one of political abuse, a useful means of undermining an opponent. We certainly need to bear this in mind, but it is nonetheless striking just how often the term appears in discussions of the radical right.

Closely related to the concept of demagoguery is that of populism. Like demagogues, populists attempt to mobilize "the people" against "the elites," but determining who exactly are *the people* and who gets to speak for them is not necessarily a straightforward task. (The principal distinction between demagogues and populists, according to Singer, is that populists "play by the rules, but demagogues most often bully the rule of law.") It is also important to point out that there are many different varieties of populism: left-wing, right-wing, and even centrist. According to John Judis, for example, left-wing populists tend to "champion the people against an elite or an establishment," whereas right-wing populists "champion the people against an elite they accuse of favoring a third group," such as immigrants, ethnic minorities, or, as we will see in chapter 2, communists. Indeed, for the historian Michael Kazin, populism is "more an impulse than an ideology," a "persistent yet mutable style of political rhetoric."

In American terms, populism's roots are to be found in the short-lived but enormously influential left-wing People's Party, or Populist Party, formed in 1891 by leading members of the Kansas Farmers Alliance and the labor organization the Knights of Labor. The Populists railed against the "money powers," the railroads, and the "plutocracy" as they sought to reform capitalism and extend the powers of government to end "oppression, injustice, and poverty." (There was also an element of racism and nativist hostility to immigrants in some of their demands and rhetoric, it should be noted.) On the American right, the first major populist movements emerged during the 1930s, in the form of Father Coughlin's National Union of Social Justice and Huey Long's "share the wealth" clubs—both of which were accused by their opponents of being fascist. These were followed by George Wallace's American Independent Party in the 1960s and the presidential campaigns of Ross Perot and

Patrick Buchanan in the 1990s, but elements of populism—its "expressions, tropes, themes and images," to use Kazin's words—are evident in numerous other members of the radical right, including Joe McCarthy, Rush Limbaugh, Glenn Beck, the Tea Party, and Donald Trump.

The third term that we need to address is what has been called the "counter-subversive tradition" in American life. This too can be traced back to the very founding of the United States and is closely bound up with notions of American identity (and what Hofstadter called the "paranoid style" in American politics). Ever since the American Revolution, fears have been expressed that hidden enemies were a threat to the nation and that it was incumbent upon groups of motivated citizens to come together to both expose and thwart these subversive and sinister threats. These fears have not just been confined to the margins of American society. As Richard Curry and Thomas Brown pointed out in their 1972 book on the subject, "From George Washington to Richard Nixon, American presidents have uttered grim warnings against conspiracies. Fears of subversion are very much part of the mainstream of politics." As we shall see, this counter-subversive tradition has been an especially prominent feature of the radical right, and it has continued to find expression well into the twenty-first century, with the federal government itself often being accused of all manner of conspiratorial malfeasance. Interestingly, the historian David Brion Davis has attributed the persistence of these beliefs to the idea of American exceptionalism, to the notion that United States has a "special mission" in the world. There is, he says, "a striking correlation between fears of conspiracy and American aspirations to national greatness."

Finally, before setting out how the remainder of the book is organized, let me say a few words about its title. As is now hopefully clear, *Enemies of the State* is intended to capture the radical right's deep hostility to "big government" and the liberal state, but it also reflects the fact that many of the groups and individuals discussed in the six chapters that follow have themselves been frequently regarded as enemies of the state—as a threat to democracy and even as a potentially dangerous "enemy within," to continue with the idea of the counter-subversive tradition—and they have been routinely monitored, surveilled, and denounced precisely because of these concerns. I will leave it to my readers to decide whether such concerns are justified.

As for the rest of the book, chapter 1 provides an account of the New Deal and the extensive opposition it generated from a range of radical rightists, including the American Liberty League, Huey Long, Father Coughlin, and assorted domestic fascists such as Gerald Winrod's Defenders of the Christian Faith, William Dudley Pelley's Silver Shirt Legion, the Black Legion, and the German-American Bund. It also considers the Great Sedition Trial of 1944, in which thirty far-right activists were accused of being involved in a wide-ranging conspiracy to overthrow the U.S. government, as well as the broader "Brown Scare" over America's supposed fascist problem and the highly contentious debate between isolationists and interventionists concerning the nation's entry into the Second World War.

The anti-communist right of the early Cold War is the subject of chapter 2. While it details the dramatic rise and fall of Senator McCarthy, it does so by placing McCarthyism in the context of the domestic and international politics of the period, examining the key role played by the FBI, the House Committee on Un-American Activities, the American Legion, and other members of the broader anti-communist network during this time. Importantly, the chapter shows how the hunt for communist subversion was motivated, in large part, by a desire to undermine Roosevelt's successor, Harry Truman, and to undo the legacy of the New Deal. The John Birch Society, the most significant and formidable radical right-wing group of the 1960s, is also examined here, as are Dr. Fred Schwarz's Christian Anti-Communism Crusade and Reverend Billy James Hargis's Christian Crusade.

Chapter 3 assesses the radical right's opposition to the civil rights movement. From "massive resistance" and terroristic violence to subtler forms of protest centered on the advocacy of states' rights and apparent concerns about "law and order," some of the key groups and figures examined in this chapter include Strom Thurmond and the States' Rights Democratic Party, the Citizens' Council movement, the Birch Society, the Ku Klux Klan, George Wallace's American Independent Party, J. B. Stoner, and General Edwin Walker, as well as numerous local, state, and national politicians. It considers the various arguments that were used to justify the continuation of racial segregation in the South, including ongoing fears of communist subversion and objections to the overbearing and even "tyrannical" powers of the federal government, while stressing the lasting impact that massive resistance had on American politics and American society.

Ronald Reagan and the various elements of the New Right are the principal subjects of chapter 4. Reagan's remarkable transformation from Hollywood actor and New Deal–supporting Democrat to the apparent savior of American conservatism and scourge of "big government" is critically examined, as is the disappointment that many members of the New Right ultimately had in the Reagan presidency. The New Right was a broad-based coalition of grassroots activists, politicians, religious broadcasters, lobbyists, think tanks, and pressure groups, led by key figures such as Richard Viguerie, Paul Weyrich, and Phyllis Schlafly and supported by a wide-range of wealthy business leaders and their private foundations. Beginning in the early 1970s, it played a crucial role both in the "mainstreaming" of radical right-wing ideas and in the politicization of evangelical Christians, helping to draw the religious right into the orbit of the GOP through organizations such as Jerry Falwell's Moral Majority.

Chapter 5 explores the increasingly rightward shift of the Republican Party during the 1990s. It examines Newt Gingrich's Contract with America and the Republicans' long-running attempt to impeach Bill Clinton—which his wife, Hillary Clinton, famously claimed was the result of a "vast right-wing conspiracy"—as well as the presidential campaigns of the populist outsiders Pat Buchanan and Ross Perot. It also discusses how antigovernment sentiment, extreme rhetoric, and conspiratorial beliefs became increasingly prominent features of mainstream political life and considers the emergence of a startling new movement on the American radical right, the heavily armed citizens' militia movement.

Chapter 6 brings the story of the radical right into the early years of the twenty-first century by examining the sudden and dramatic appearance of the Tea Party and its attempt to both "take over" the Republican Party and "take back" the American nation. It considers whether the Tea Party is a genuinely grassroots political movement or an "astroturf" one—the creation of right-wing media outlets like Fox News in combination with members of the radical rich, such as the highly secretive Koch brothers—and also how much of its vehemently expressed opposition to the presidency of Barack Obama was motivated by racism. Donald Trump's startling election to the presidency, his enormously controversial first year in office, and his relationship with the Tea Party are also addressed in detail.

The book's conclusion assesses the overall significance of the radical right in modern American history and considers where Donald Trump can be situated within this history, returning us once again to questions of demagoguery, populism, racism, conspiratorial thinking, and the long-standing assault on "big government" in the United States since the 1930s.

1

Big Government on the March

FDR and the Roots of the Radical Right

DURING THE VERY DEPTHS of the Great Depression, on March 4, 1933, as part of his first inaugural address, Franklin Delano Roosevelt (FDR) famously declared that "the only thing we have to fear is fear itself—nameless, unreasoning, unjustified terror which paralyzes needed efforts to convert retreat into advance." Whether or not the new president actually believed that this was the only thing the nation had to fear, Roosevelt's persistent declarations of confidence in the American people and in the American system—"this great nation will endure as it has endured, will revive and will prosper," he further stated that March day—were powerful restoratives after the repeated failures and seeming indifference of the Hoover years. Crucially, and in stark contrast to his predecessor in the White House, Roosevelt also promised to mobilize the power of the federal government to help bring an end to the crisis and to implement his admittedly vaguely defined plans for a "New Deal" for Americans. The situation was akin to wartime, FDR said, and he would be asking Congress for "broad Executive power to wage a war against the emergency, as great as the power that would be given to me if we were in fact invaded by a foreign foe."

In many respects the accomplishments of the New Deal mark the beginning of modern American history. It is a period comparable to the wrenching changes brought on by the Civil War, with the federal government inserted into the economy and into society in ways that would have been unthinkable a generation before. In an address in Williamsburg, Virginia, in 1926, President Calvin Coolidge remarked that should the federal government "go out of existence, the common run of people would not detect the difference in the affairs of their daily life for a considerable length of time." It was not a comment that could be made by the late 1930s. The years from 1932 to 1945, during which time FDR served an unprecedented three terms in office, witnessed the redefinition and triumph of American liberalism, the establishment of a new Democratic Party electoral coalition, and the creation of the welfare state—followed in short order by that of the warfare state. Yet for all its successes, opposition to the New Deal and to Roosevelt was also significant, and it began early, within a year of his first inaugural address.

And for many of those on the American right during this time, it was the president and his new policies and programs that really needed to be "feared."

This chapter examines these opponents of FDR, people who believed that the New Deal would create a bureaucratic Leviathan, cripple the free enterprise system, destroy states' rights, undermine individual freedom, and put the nation on the road to communism, dictatorship, and tyranny. It is a grouping, as we shall see, that includes conservatives in Congress, big business, and various populists, nativists, and quasi-fascists. The chapter also examines how Roosevelt and others responded to the challenges posed by these groups. This is important because it is in the fierce contest between the administration and its right-wing opponents that we can find the roots of the "radical right" that would run—in various forms—throughout the rest of the twentieth century and on into the twenty-first century. We begin, though, with an overview of the Depression and of the New Deal

The scale of the crisis brought on by the Wall Street Crash of 1929 was both unprecedented and extraordinary. A quarter of the American workforce was unemployed by 1932 (some 11.5 million people), and those fortunate enough to remain in work often found themselves struggling by on reduced hours or reduced wages, as banks and businesses failed, savings were wiped out, and homes and farms were foreclosed upon. People starved, suicides increased, and the birth rate dropped. Many took to the road and to the rails in search of a fresh start, not least the "Okies" of Kansas, Oklahoma, and Texas, hastened on by drought and dust to the supposed "promised land" of California. Shantytowns, known as "Hoovervilles" in stinging rebuke to President Herbert Hoover, sprang up in dumps on the outskirts of towns and cities across the country. In the summer of 1932, thousands of World War I veterans marched on Washington to demand the immediate payment of a special "bonus" that Congress has promised them back in 1924, even though it wasn't due until 1945. The Senate refused to vote the veterans their relief, and the remnants of the Bonus Army were violently dispersed from the nation's capital by troops under the command of General Douglas MacArthur, their encampments torched in what, to many, seemed a horrible harbinger of the wider unrest that might yet be unleashed on the nation as a whole.

It wasn't true that Hoover, "the Great Engineer," had done nothing to end the Depression, as some of his critics charged, but it was certainly the case that he remained firmly wedded to the political and economic orthodoxies of an earlier age, mostly notably to laissez-faire economics and strictly limited government, as he attempted to deal with it. Hoover believed, for example, that the United States would be "plunged into socialism and collectivism" if the federal government provided direct unemployment relief and that it was really the role of state and local governments working in conjunction with private enterprise to find a way out of the crisis. In contrast, when he accepted the Democratic Party's nomination for president in 1932, Roosevelt had promised action, what he called "bold, persistent experimentation." "It is common sense to take a method and try it," he explained. "If it fails, admit it frankly and try another. But above all, try something." He was true to his word once in the White House.

The first hundred days of Roosevelt's first term passed by in a veritable blur of new federal initiatives, agencies, and programs. The Emergency Banking Act stabilized the nation's banking system and got money moving again. The Civilian Conservation Corps put people to work in the American countryside preventing floods, fighting pests, building bridges, and repairing fences, all in camps run by the War Department. The Agricultural Adjustment Act sought to drive up the prices of agricultural products by placing restrictions on output. The Glass-Steagall Banking Act separated commercial from investment banking and also created the Federal Deposit Insurance Corporation, by which the federal government guaranteed the savings of ordinary Americans. The Tennessee Valley Authority would build dams, control floods, and generate cheap hydroelectric power. A Public Works Administration and Civil

Works Administration were created—the latter of which, at its peak, employed 4,230,000 people, as 40,000 schools, 1,000 airports, and more than 500,000 miles of roads were either built or improved upon—and the National Industrial Recovery Act (NIRA) was passed. The NIRA allowed the administration to create work-relief agencies, but it also established national codes that were intended to regulate the prices, wages, hours, and conditions of work of hundreds of industries across the nation (all of which was watched over by the ubiquitous martial symbol of the Blue Eagle and its accompanying legend, "We Do Our Part").

Despite all of this activity, the problems of the Depression were far from solved, however, and as a result, a so-called second New Deal began in mid-1935. The National Labor Relations Act replaced the NIRA, which had recently been struck down as unconstitutional by the Supreme Court. The Wagner Act, as it was more commonly known (after Senator Robert Wagner [D-NY], who drafted it), threw the power of the state behind the right of labor to collective bargaining, empowering the National Labor Relations Board to supervise union elections and prohibiting "unfair labor practices" by employers, such as dismissing workers who joined a union. Its impact was dramatic: in 1930 only 10 percent of workers in the manufacturing sector belonged to a union; by 1940 that number was 30 percent. The Works Progress Administration put 8.5 million people to work at the cost of some $11 billion, including thousands of artists, musicians, actors, and writers, under projects such as the Federal Art Project, the Federal Music Project, the Federal Theater Project, and the Federal Writers Project. The Social Security Act established universal retirement, unemployment insurance, and welfare benefits for the poor and disabled. A Wealth Tax was initiated. And in 1938 the Fair Labor Standards Act, the last of the major New Deal reforms, was passed, banning child labor and establishing a federal minimum wage.

Opposition to the New Deal from the American right began in earnest during the summer of 1934, once the sense of immediate crisis had passed. In early July, for example, a radio address by Idaho Republican Senator William E. Borah denounced Roosevelt for attempting to "fasten a stranglehold system of bureaucracy upon the people." The Republican national chairman, Henry P. Fletcher, criticized the New Deal similarly as "government from above." It was predicated, he said, "on the proposition that the people can't manage their own affairs and that a government

Franklin D. Roosevelt prepares to give a radio address in 1938. His New Deal reforms of the 1930s provided a major spur to the development of the radical right in the United States. Library of Congress Prints & Photographs Division, Harris & Ewing Collection, LC-DIG-hec-47601.

bureaucracy must manage for them," and he feared that the economy itself was at risk of being destroyed by "an all directing State." Former president Hoover, in his 1934 book, *The Challenge to Liberty*, made the case that Roosevelt's program was a "new philosophy which must mark the end of liberty." Disaffected conservative Democrats like Alfred E. Smith, the party's presidential candidate in 1928; John W. Davis, who had run for the presidency in 1924; as well as numerous business owners, large and small, voiced similar complaints.

On August 15, 1934, a new conservative organization called the American Liberty League came into being. It had grown out of a remarkable exchange of correspondence the previous March between R. R. M. Carpenter, a retired vice president of the Du Pont corporation, and one of its current vice presidents, John J. Raskob, in which Carpenter had complained that "five negroes on my place in South Carolina refused work this spring saying they had easy jobs with the government. And a cook on my house-boat at Fort Myers quit because the government was paying him a dollar an hour as a painter." Raskob in reply had encouraged Carpenter to "take the lead in trying to induce the Du Pont and General Motors groups, followed by other big industries, to definitely organize to protect society from the sufferings which it is bound to endure if we allow communistic elements to lead the people to believe that all businessmen are crooks."

Wrapping itself in patriotism, rugged individualism, and the defense of the Constitution, the League was loftily committed, at least in principle, to the nonpartisan teaching of the "necessity of respect for the rights of persons and property" and of the "duty of government to encourage and protect individual and group initiative and enterprise." In practice, however, it was a huge propaganda machine set in almost perpetual motion against the "ravenous madness" of Roosevelt and the New Deal. In innumerable pamphlets, bulletins, leaflets, news conferences, radio programs, reports, and speeches, the League and its spokespersons railed against "that man in the White House" and his dangerous, immoral, and dictatorial schemes. Indeed, for many Liberty League pamphlets, it was usually enough to simply read the title in order to understand the message intended to be conveyed; to wit: "The President Wants More Power," "Will It Be Ave Caesar?" "New Labels for Old Poisons," "The Way Dictatorships Start."

The Liberty League could operate its extensive campaign against the New Deal because, simply stated, it was awash with money. In this respect the "big industries" that Raskob had seen as crucial in taking the lead in the organization had certainly come through. With the du Pont brothers, Irénée, Pierre, and Lammot, at the forefront of the operation, other key financial backers included the president of General Motors, Alfred P. Sloan; the chairman of General Foods, Edward F. Hutton; the steel magnate Ernest T. Wier; and the Texas cotton broker Will L. Clay-ton. Both Al Smith and John Davis became spokesmen for the League, and many other politicians, academics, bankers, financiers, corporate lawyers, and businessmen joined it. Jouett Shouse, who had led the Association Against the Prohibition Amendment, on which the Liberty League was modeled, was the organization's president.

The support of wealthy patrons was certainly a source of strength for the League, but it was also a major weakness. Even though it cost nothing to become a member, the organization was never able to create the mass movement it had set out to establish; at its peak in 1936, membership totaled only 124,856. Nor was it able to establish its planned Labor and Farm divisions. Indeed, its only two subsidiaries were composed of college students and lawyers. The League's nonpartisanship was also quickly exposed as a fiction. As the *New York Times* columnist Arthur Krock noted in January 1936, "Members of the League might be classed as the most conservative group in the country," and it "is dominated by Republicans." Nor did it seem to have any actual practical alternatives to the policies of the New Deal. (The best it could come up with was to suggest that the Red Cross be used to handle all direct relief.) What was worse, the League's constant stress on the value of rugged individualism and self-help betrayed a profound misreading of the humanitarian crisis unfolding all around it, making the organization and its millionaire backers an easy target for ridicule. The League was like a group committed to upholding only "two of the Ten Commandments," joked FDR shortly after its formation, and he virtually ignored the Republican Party and its official candidate, Alfred M. Landon, during the 1936 presidential election, preferring, it seemed, to campaign against the Liberty League instead. "The economic royalists complain that we seek to overthrow the institutions of America," he told a roaring crowd of more than one hundred thousand at the Democratic National Convention at Franklin Field in Philadelphia on June 27, 1936. "What they really complain of is that we seek to take away their power." "In vain they seek to hide behind the flag and the Constitution," he went on, turning the League's attempt to use the nation's patriotic imagery back against it.

The American Liberty League was not the only group of businessmen to inveigh against the New Deal. So too did the National Association of Manufacturers, the Chamber of Commerce, and many other organizations, as well as individual business owners, including the powerful agribusiness leaders of California, men like Harry Chandler, who was also the proprietor of the *Los Angeles Times*, and Joseph Knowland, publisher of the *Oakland Tribune*. William Randolph Hearst, the most successful newspaperman in the state, was an equally committed opponent of what

he required his journalistic employees to refer to as the "Raw Deal." Nor
did the financial backers of the League rely on it alone: they also supported a host of "masthead organizations" such as the Crusaders, Sen-
tinels of the Republic, Minute Men and Women of Today, the National
Conference of Investors, Women Investors of America, and the Farmer's
Independence Council—supposedly independent or genuinely grassroots
groups that were actually run, for the most part, by professional lobbyists
and publicists. In addition, the du Pont brothers, Alfred Sloan, and John
Raskob were also behind the ill-fated attempt to have the segregationist
Georgia Democrat Eugene Talmadge run for the presidency in 1936 as
part of his Southern Committee to Uphold the Constitution.

Such groups and their members were also responsible for much of the
highly personal and strikingly vicious abuse that was directed the president's way. "In their thesaurus of hate," the historian George Wolfskill
writes,

> Roosevelt was a "renegade Democrat," an "extravagant," "destruc-
> tive," "vacillating," "unprincipled charlatan." A "cripple," an "invalid"
> lacking physical stamina, a captive, psychologically, who was morally
> "weak," intellectually "shallow," unbelievably "gullible," a "dupe"
> (surrounded by "radicals," "crackpots," "quarterbacks," and "foreign-
> thinking brain-trusters, some of whom were better known in Russia
> than in the United States"). . . . From Newport to Miami, from Wall
> Street to Park Avenue, in country club locker rooms, the cathedral-
> like hush of bank offices, in board rooms and carpeted law offices, in
> hotel suites and cabin cruisers the broad stories passed: Roosevelt was
> an inveterate liar . . . a syphilitic, a tool of Negroes and Jews, a mad-
> man given to unprovoked gales of immoderate laughter, an alcoholic, a
> megalomaniac dreaming his dreams of dictatorship.

While directing most of their ire toward the administration in Washington, groups like the Liberty League were also concerned about the
rise of new "populist" movements like those associated with Dr. Francis
E. Townsend, Governor Huey "Kingfish" Long, and Father Charles E.
Coughlin (not to mention the activities of various socialist and communist
groups, of course). These movements were also of considerable concern to
Roosevelt, although for different reasons. The largely statist solutions to
the Depression proposed by Townsend, Long, and Coughlin may seem
to place them clearly on the left of the political spectrum, but this was not

necessarily how they were viewed at the time. Indeed, in the case of Long and Coughlin in particular, there were widespread fears that their activities portended the rise of fascism in the United States. As such, they form an important part of the story of the origins of the radical right during this period.

A retired Long Beach physician, Townsend proposed an Old Age Revolving Pension Plan, which would give every citizen aged sixty or over $200 a month, provided that the recipients agreed to spend that money within thirty days. As Townsend saw it, his plan would not only bring about a return of prosperity to the United States; it would also help "save America from radicalism." Intrigued by the simplistic but widely popular plan, by the end of 1934, more than two million people had joined his Townsend Clubs with the aim of seeing the plan put into operation. Even more popular than the Townsend Clubs were the Share-Our-Wealth clubs of Huey Long. Long, the former governor of Louisiana, who promised "every man a king, but no one wears a crown," had been elected to the U.S. Senate in 1930—although this hadn't prevented him from still running things back in Louisiana through his political flunky, Oscar "O. K." Allen. Long's proposal was that no individual be allowed to earn more than $1 million a year, with any amount over that taxed at 100 percent. All savings above a certain amount would also be seized (the exact figure varied from $1.7 million to $10 million), and the proceeds would then be redistributed to the rest of the population, with every citizen receiving a guaranteed income of $2,500. By 1935, Long claimed to have almost eight million people signed up to his clubs and, having turned against FDR, was contemplating running for the presidency himself in 1936, either as a Democrat or on a third-party ticket. He never got the chance. On September 8, 1935, the Kingfish was shot by the son-in-law of one of his political enemies in Louisiana. He died two days later.

In his 1935 book, *Forerunners of American Fascism*, Raymond Gram Swing spoke for many when he described Long as a man "ruthless, ambitious and indeed plausible enough to Hitlerize America." For others, he was simply a "pure species demagogue." Exactly the same fears and concerns swirled around the personality and politics of Long's contemporary, rival, and sometime associate, the "Radio Priest" Father Charles Coughlin.

Senator Huey Long, the political "Kingfish" of Louisiana, was a fierce critic of FDR. Some feared he might attempt to bring fascism to the United States. Library of Congress Prints & Photographs Division, Stereograph Cards, LC-USZ62-103627.

Born and raised in Canada, in 1926 Coughlin was sent to the small, poor Catholic community of Royal Oak, an industrial suburb of Detroit, where the Ku Klux Klan welcomed him by burning crosses on the front lawn of his Shrine of the Little Flower church. He took to the new medium of the radio in an attempt to build up his congregation, first simply by reading his regular sermons on the air but, after the Depression hit, expanding his repertoire to comment on more worldly matters, assailing the ineffectuality of the Hoover administration and denouncing the evils of communism and the greed and heartlessness of Wall Street in equal measure. Coughlin was a natural. He had, wrote the novelist Wallace Stegner, "one of the great speaking voices of the twentieth century . . . a voice made for promises." Only Roosevelt's mastery of the radio came close to rivaling the priest's. By the early thirties, with a national radio audience of more than thirty million and the ability to generate letters from his supporters in the hundreds of thousands, Coughlin was both a national celebrity and a real political force.

Coughlin's ideas drew on Catholic social-justice doctrines enunciated in Pope Leo XII's encyclical *Rerum Novarum* issued in 1891 and Pope Pius XI's *Quadragiesmo Anno* of 1931. But they also owed much to the Populist movement of the 1890s and its profound distrust of "the money powers," the banking industry, and pampered, effete, eastern plutocrats.

Initially hugely supportive of Roosevelt, by 1934, with the president now doing his best to keep the priest at distance personally and also refusing to implement some of his key polices such as the remonetizing of silver and the creation of a new national bank, Coughlin broke with the administration (although this was not necessarily clear to all of his followers) and created his own political organization, the National Union for Social Justice (NUSJ). No longer was it "Roosevelt or Ruin," as it had been in 1932. Now it was "Roosevelt *and* Ruin."

Coughlin also joined the ranks of those hurling personal insults at the president, who he began to denounce publicly as "the great betrayer and liar" and "Franklin Double-Crossing Roosevelt." On August 2, 1934, in a speech at New Bedford, Massachusetts, before a crowd of twelve thousand, Coughlin promised that just as he had ejected Hoover from the White House, so too would he now "take a Communist out of the chair once occupied by Washington." In another speech he declared that "we all know whom we're voting for if we vote for Mr. Roosevelt . . . the Communists, the Socialists, the Russian lovers, the Mexican lovers, the kick-me-downers." Teaming up with the Townsend movement, as well as Huey Long's former protégé and self-confessed "rabble rouser of the Right," Gerald L. K. Smith, for the 1936 election, Coughlin threw his and the NUSJ's support behind the third-party candidacy of the North Dakota congressman William Lemke. The choice was not a good one. Devoid of charisma, a poor public speaker, and often literally appearing second on the bill to Coughlin at his own rallies, Lemke went down to a humiliating defeat, receiving less than 900,000 votes (about 2 percent of the total cast). Landon received 16,679,683 (36.5 percent) and Roosevelt 27,750,866 (60.8 percent). In the electoral college, FDR's margin of victory was 523 to 8, as he won every state except Maine and Vermont.

Coughlin had promised to retire from the nation's airwaves, as well as from political life more generally, if he failed to deliver nine million votes for the Union Party in 1936. And for six weeks he did just that. Thereafter he returned to both. He also continued his increasingly rightward political trajectory. Indeed, by 1938, with the creation of a new Christian Front organization, declarations of Mussolini as the "Man of the Week" in his newspaper *Social Justice*, and the republication of anti-Semitic tracts like *The Protocols of the Elders of Zion*, he found himself firmly ensconced at the extreme end of the American political spectrum.

In the spring of 1942, the postmaster general banned *Social Justice* from the mails. That same year under pressure from the Justice Department, and with the intent of avoiding a damaging trial for sedition, Archbishop Edward Mooney of Detroit told Coughlin to "cease all public pronouncements for the duration of the war under penalty of defrockment." This time Father Coughlin's political career really was over.

Driven by events in Europe, fears that fascism was on the rise in the United States during the 1930s were not confined to concerns about the activities of Long, Coughlin, or their followers. Such fears pervaded American society at all levels. "Fordism is Fascism!" asserted the United Auto Workers union, as it struggled to organize the River Rouge plant of Henry Ford in Dearborn, Michigan, the largest automobile factory in the world. Congressional investigators claimed to have uncovered a fascist plot orchestrated by a Wall Street bondsman called Gerald McGuire to take over the U.S. government using unemployed veterans of the armed forces—placed, perhaps, under the command of General MacArthur. Sinclair Lewis's novel *It Can't Happen Here*, the cautionary tale of the fascist dictatorship of one Berzelius "Buzz" Windrip—a thinly disguised Huey Long—sold 320,000 copies in 1936 alone, while theatrical productions of the book ran in twenty cities nationwide at the same time. "If we ever have fascism in this country, it will come as a result of the activities of the economic royalists whose minds are closed against anything that has happened since 1870," the author soberly informed the press on the play's opening night. Huey Long was supposed to have similarly said that "when the United States gets fascism, it will call it anti-fascism." The Kingfish hadn't actually made the claim, but the argument was widely considered to be a prophetic one nonetheless. As one historian of the period has written: during the thirties "fascism could be found wherever one looked." Even the New Deal itself was charged as being fascist.

The pervasiveness of these fears reflected the innate analytical imprecision of fascism as a political concept, as well as its swiftly recognized value as a term of political abuse. It reflected the ominous "achievements" of Mussolini's Italy, Hitler's Germany, and, later, Franco's Spain. It reflected the continuing deep uncertainty the catastrophe of the Depression had caused and the loss of faith in existing institutions, existing solutions, and existing leaders. But it also reflected the fact there were some actual fascists, or at least some "quasi-fascists," active in the United

States throughout the 1930s. Indeed, by some estimates there were at least 120 such groups, with as many as 250,000 followers when added all together. Not a huge number of people in a nation of 128 million to be sure, and they were never a coordinated or even remotely plausible threat to the government of the United States. But they were noisy, and they were highly visible, and they were certainly troublesome. Indeed, as we shall see, in many respects the reaction they elicited is as important to the history of the American radical right as any of the ideas they sought to propagate. Among the most noteworthy of these quasi-fascists were Gerald B. Winrod's Defenders of the Christian Faith; the Silver Shirt Legion of William Dudley Pelley; and the secretive Klan off-shoot, the Black Legion. Ideologically speaking, all three exhibited a curious mélange of conservatism, religious belief, and nativism, to go along with their apparent fascist proclivities.

Gerald Winrod was a fundamentalist preacher from Wichita, Kansas. A gifted orator, he had created the Defenders of the Christian Faith in 1925 to advance his campaign against Darwinism and what he saw as the deep "moral sag" of American life—sexual impropriety, immodest fashion, and Hollywood depravity, all included. "Billows of immorality" were sweeping the land "like waves over the ocean . . . *everywhere animalism, animalism, animalism,*" he decried. Winrod was also the publisher of *The Defender*, which had a circulation of one hundred thousand by 1936, as well as *The Revealer*, which ran between November 1934 and January 1937 and which reflected his newfound concern about matters political. Like many other fundamentalists, chastened by the unedifying mid-decade experience of the Scopes "monkey" trial, the preacher had tended to stay away from national politics during the 1920s, but with the Bible as his prophetic guide, he had never stopped searching for signs of the impending Apocalypse, and in the New Deal he believed he had found them. As far as Winrod was concerned, for example, the NIRA's famous Blue Eagle, with seven feathers on one wing and ten on the other, recalled nothing so much as the horrifying Beast of seven heads and ten horns foretold in Revelation 13:1. Following a trip to Europe in 1934 to "study social, political, moral, economic and prophetic trends," Winrod added anti-Semitism, conspiracism, and an increasing admiration for the Nazis and Hitler to his heterogenic world view, joining the ranks of those for whom the New Deal was the "Jew Deal."

Toning down his anti-Semitism and playing up his economic conservatism, in 1938 Winrod ran for the U.S. Senate in Kansas on twin promises to "Keep Christian America Christian" and "To Keep America Safe for Americans." He dominated the early phase of the campaign to such an extent that Roosevelt was warned that this "raw and unashamed" fascist had a "fairly good chance" of winning. But, in the end, as local labor unions, prominent clergymen, leading Republicans, the press, and anti-extremist groups like the Friends of Democracy mobilized against him—the "Swastika Must Not Fly Over Kansas," vowed one anti-Winrod publication—he finished third, with 53,149 votes (about 20 percent of the total). Thereafter the infamous "Jayhawk Nazi" increasingly turned his attention to keeping the United States out of World War II.

The son of an itinerant Methodist preacher, William Dudley Pelley was born in Lynn, Massachusetts, in 1890, and he had a colorful, if not always very successful, career as a novelist, magazine journalist, screenwriter, and mystic, before forming the avowedly fascist Silver Shirts in 1933. Modeled on Hitler's SS, members wore shirts of silver gray, with a great scarlet "L" denoting Love, Loyalty, and Liberation stitched in silk over their hearts; blue corduroy knickers; long socks; blue ties; and a service hat. Comprising "the cream, the head, and the flower of our Protestant Christian manhood," the Silver Shirts, Pelley said, would "save America as Mussolini and his Black Shirts saved Italy, as Hitler and his Brown Shirts saved Germany." America needed saving, Pelley believed, because communist and Jewish conspirators acting through the New Deal were intent on the destruction of its freedom. As David Bennett has pointed out, the Silver Legion appealed mostly to people who lived in small communities and rural areas, where there were few actual Jews, but this apparent paradox simply made it all the easier to embrace "a misty yeoman ideology in which Jews were the sinister, symbolic nonproducers: bankers, businessmen and bond traders, parasites who grew nothing and made nothing except money," all of it a horrible corruption of the American Dream of "achievement through hard and productive work."

Officially Pelley disavowed violence, urging Silver Shirts to obey the law, but many of his "actionist boys" ignored the directive. In Salt Lake City local members kidnapped and beat a suspected communist, leaving him for dead. In Cleveland, a professor was threatened with "punishment" unless he ceased his communist teachings. And the San Diego Silver Legion not only advocated the violent overthrow of the Roosevelt administration, it also stockpiled arms and undertook military-style training in order to fend off a Bolshevik attack on City Hill that was being planned, it said, for May Day 1934. Spread across twelve states, although strongest in southern California, the organization had fifteen thousand members at its peak in 1934, declining to five thousand by 1938, before finally disbanding under government pressure in 1941.

More successful than the Silver Shirts, at least in terms of its size, was the Black Legion. Formed in Ohio in 1931, when renegade members of a local Ku Klux Klan donned black robes instead of white ones and instituted their own new initiation ceremony, the organization was centered in Ohio, Michigan, Indiana, and Illinois, where it appealed mostly to unskilled and semi-skilled workers set adrift by the enormity of the Depression. Armed and disciplined, with an estimated membership of between sixty thousand and one hundred thousand, the Legion, in the view of historian Peter Amann, was "the most formidable nativist organization around," its members sworn to wage a "holy war against Catholics, Jews, Communists, Negroes, and aliens." (Indeed, unlike Pelley, who welcomed Catholics into the Silver Shirts and praised Father Coughlin's *Social Justice*, members of the Legion plotted to assassinate the Radio Priest.) At the same time, however, in its opposition to the over-regulation of business, government relief, and trade unions, the organization also very much espoused the traditional conservative virtues of self-help and self-reliance.

The numerous crimes of the putatively secret organization inevitably brought it to the attention of the press, local authorities, the FBI, and even Hollywood. *Black Legion*, the motion picture starring Humphrey Bogart, was released by Warner Bros. in 1937; in it Bogart plays an auto worker and family man transformed into a brutal racist when he is passed over for a promotion in favor of a Polish colleague. Under the glare of such hostile publicity and with its members being routinely convicted of murder, arson, flogging, and kidnapping, the Legion was effectively moribund by 1938.

In propagating the idea of a Jewish-communist conspiracy against the United States—"Jewish Bolshevism" as it was often termed—Winrod, Pelley, and the other quasi-fascists were building on the sturdy foundations that had been laid by Henry Ford during the 1920s. Indeed, no one had done more in the American context to popularize such views. Beginning in 1920, first in his newspaper, the *Dearborn Independent*, and then in book form as *The International Jew*, Ford had used the notorious Tsarist forgery *The Protocols of the Elders of Zion* as the basis for his claims that a secret Jewish conspiracy was feverishly at work subverting the American nation as part of a much wider plot to destroy Christian civilization and to create a new world government. Ford poured an enormous amount of money into the enterprise, almost $5 million over the next seven years, during which time more than ten million copies of his book were pushed into circulation. Bolshevism was "the international program of the Protocols, which might be 'put over' by a minority in any country," Ford contended, while only "Jewish pens [were] trusted with Bolshevist propaganda." Adapting such arguments to the conditions of the 1930s, and incorporating advocates of the New Deal into them, was easily done, as Elizabeth Dilling more than demonstrated in *The Red Network* (1935) and *The Roosevelt Red Record* (1936). Harry A. Young's American Vigilant Intelligence Federation, founded in Chicago in 1927, was another major purveyor of conspiratorial anti-communist, anti–New Deal, and anti-Semitic tracts; as too was the German-American Bund.

In November 1935, the Bund, which had grown out of the remnants of an earlier organization called the Friends of the New Germany, came under the leadership of Fritz Julius Kuhn, who had fought in the German Army during the First World War and been a member of the Nazi Party since the 1920s. Its goal was to unite all German Americans, a population of some thirty million, into "one great, nation-wide, respect-commanding movement." This it clumsily and unconvincingly tried to do through the "Americanization" of National Socialism. Culminating, on February 20, 1939, in the bizarre—and, to many people, frightening—spectacle of twenty-two thousand Bundists gathered in Madison Square Garden to celebrate George Washington's birthday, the activities of the Bund during this period were also important because they seemed to provide self-evident confirmation of what had been widely suspected for some time: that a Nazi fifth column was operating freely on American shores.

The campaign against America's domestic fascists, which historian Leo Ribuffo has termed the Brown Scare, had begun as early as 1933, but it was

Members of the German-American Bund parade in New York on East 86th Street, October 30, 1939. Library of Congress Prints & Photographs Division, LC-USZ62-117148.

given a renewed and much more urgent emphasis by the prospect of war in Europe, and particularly by the Great Debate over whether or not the United States would intervene in it. The possibility of American entry into the war also further increased fears about the centralizing and "dictatorial" tendencies of the Roosevelt administration, fears that the president's ill-advised "court-packing" scheme, proposals to reorganize the executive branch, and plans to run for an unprecedented third term had done nothing to allay. Issues of loyalty, subversion, patriotism, and conspiracy were brought increasingly to the fore, as all sides in these debates laid claim to acting in the best interests of the nation while charging their opponents with being "un-American." The consequences would be long-lasting.

Many organizations participated in the Brown Scare, including the Non-Sectarian Anti-Nazi League, the Mobilization for Democracy, the Council Against Intolerance, the American Council Against Nazi Propaganda, and the Friends of Democracy, whose strategy of "pitiless publicity" was used so effectively to thwart Gerald Winrod's senatorial ambitions. Books with titles like *The Fifth Column in America* (1940) and *I Find Treason: The Story of an American Anti-Nazi Agent* (1941) were published. Popular journalists like Drew Pearson and Walter Winchell, along with major publications such as *Life* magazine and the *Saturday Evening Post*, issued frequent warnings about the dangers of domestic fascism—small-town, simple folk were "easy meat" for demagogues, explained *Life* in one typical 1939 feature, for example—while moviegoers were educated about the potential threat in the expertly produced *March of Time* newsreels narrated by the "Voice of Doom," Westbrook Van Voorhis.

From the local to the national level, official institutions and agencies sought both to expose and to rein in the activities of the far right. State legislatures passed laws requiring subversive organizations to be officially registered or banning the public display of masks and paramilitary regalia, and extremists were frequently investigated for tax evasion or other misuses of funds. In January 1935, for example, William Pelley was convicted of selling unregistered stock in North Carolina and of advertising his publishing arm, Galahad Press, even though it was an insolvent company. (He also lured students to his Galahad College by promising to find them well-paying jobs before, in a classic "bait-and-switch," trying to sell them bungalows instead.) More substantively, in 1942 he was charged with the dissemination of false information with the intent to impair the operations of the armed forces under the Espionage Act of 1917. During the trial Attorney General Oscar R. Ewing called Pelley "a traitor to your country, the arch-Quisling of America parading under a false flag of patriotism while you stabbed the U.S.A. in the back." No murderer, Ewing went on, "had a blacker heart than you, who tried to murder the country that nurtured you." Found guilty on all charges, Pelley was sentenced to fifteen years in prison.

One of the most notorious institutional components of the Brown Scare was the House Committee on Un-American Activities. Formed in 1938, the Dies Committee, as it was popularly known—after its chairman, the conservative Texas Democrat Martin Dies—investigated the activities of numerous domestic fascists, including the Silver Shirts and the German-American Bund, issuing seven reports and more than four thousand pages of testimony on the subject by 1942. Such statistics are a little misleading, however, because although generating enormous amounts of publicity, these inquires actually took up a relatively small amount of the committee's time, with fully three-quarters of its activities being aimed at uncovering communist conspiracies against the United States. To an extent this was justifiable, since to most Americans the threat posed by communism and fascism was equally serious. Indeed, especially after the Nazi-Soviet pact of 1939, the Soviet Union and Germany were widely regarded as indistinguishable totalitarian regimes: a combined and equally contemptible "Red fascism." But it was also political subterfuge. Reflecting both the resilience, as well as the resourcefulness, of conservatives in Congress, more often than not the real target of the committee's investigations was President Roosevelt and the New Deal.

Illinois Republican committee member Noah Mason believed that through the New Deal federal money had been "generously used to advance the cause of communism in the United States." Another committee member, the New Jersey Republican J. Parnell Thomas, made the case that as the fifth column was "synonymous to the New Deal, so the surest way of removing the fifth column from our shores is to remove the fifth column from the seat of government." Roosevelt and his cronies were "soft on communism," the committee constantly alleged, calling for the removal of key figures in the administration such as Secretary of the Interior Harold Ickes, Secretary of Labor Frances Perkins, and Works Progress Administrator Harry Hopkins, as it hunted for signs of Red influence in initiatives like the Federal Theater Project—which it helped to kill off in 1939—as well as in the labor movement. FDR was well aware of what was happening, of course, and he tried to moderate Dies, appealing to party loyalty, getting allies like Jerry Voorhis (D-CA) appointed to the committee, and suggesting that a more careful distinction between "liberalism" and "communism" might be in order, but his efforts went nowhere.

Having repeatedly expressed his hostility to both fascism and communism, Roosevelt was in a difficult position with respect to the Dies Committee. More than that, though, his own actions had contributed considerably to the Brown Scare that Dies and his colleagues were using for political cover. In 1935, for example, he had first authorized the FBI to begin a survey of pro-Nazi groups, and a year later he ordered a comprehensive investigation of "subversive activities in the United States, particularly Fascism and Communism" to be undertaken by both the FBI and military intelligence. Interpreting the agency's mandate as widely as possible, FBI Director J. Edgar Hoover never looked back. Within two years, and with Congress kept in the dark, the FBI's newly reconstituted General Intelligence Division had complied extensive dossiers on at least one hundred thousand dissidents. By 1939 the Bureau had become the nation's premier antisubversive government agency, charged, among other things, with preparing a "custodial detention index" of persons with "strong" Nazi or communist "tendencies" whose "presence at liberty in time of war or national emergency would constitute a menace." Not surprisingly, numerous domestic rightists such as Gerald Winrod were included on the list of those to be rounded up, and in May 1940, FDR added electronic surveillance to the FBI's considerable list of secret powers.

A series of new countersubversive laws were also passed in Congress, all contributing to the feverish atmosphere that was gripping the nation. The Foreign Agents Registration Act of 1938 required agents representing the interests of foreign powers in a "political or quasi-political capacity" to reveal the nature of their relationship—including any financial relationship—to the U.S. government. The Hatch Act of 1939—named for its sponsor, Carl Hatch (D-NM)—which the Dies Committee had been instrumental in bringing about, mandated the immediate dismissal of any federal employee found to be a member of a revolutionary or extremist group and also prohibited federal employees, including workers on federal relief projects, from taking part in political campaigns. Finally, the Alien Registration Act of 1940, or the Smith Act as it was better known—after its principal author, Congressman Howard W. Smith (D-VA)—required aliens to register with the attorney general and also made it a federal crime to "knowingly or willfully advocate, aid, advise, or teach the duty, necessity, desirability, or propriety of overthrowing or destroying any government in the United States by force or violence," as well as outlawing participating in the printing, writing, or circulation of material advocating such doctrines or in the organizing of groups with such purposes. The first sedition act passed in peacetime since 1798, "the Smith Act in effect outlawed ideologies that might be deemed 'un-American,'" wrote Geoffrey Smith.

In this climate, with the war in Europe the predominant political issue of the day, it was a relatively straightforward task for the Roosevelt administration, together with its interventionist allies, to tar its isolationist (or noninterventionist) opponents with the brush of extremism, associating them whenever possible with domestic fascism and the radical right. They were a "Trojan Horse," the president told radio listeners in one of his Fireside Chats in May 1940. (He was employing one of the more widely used metaphors of the time; Martin Dies also used it for the title of his 1940 book, warning about the dangers of communism already existing within the U.S. government: *The Trojan Horse in America*.) In another address Roosevelt characterized the America First Committee, the most significant isolationist group of the period, with close to 850,000 members in 450 chapters across the country, as "unwitting aids of the agents of Nazism." A Friends of Democracy pamphlet entitled *The America First Committee—The Nazi Transmission Belt* questioned whether the organization wasn't simply a "Nazi front," while Secretary of the Interior Harold Ickes assailed it for harboring anti-Semites and "appeasers." Walter Winchell called it the "America-Last Outfit," insisting that the audience at one of its rallies in New York consisted "mainly of members of the German-American Bund and various other groups which sympathize with or admire Hitler and Mussolini." Unsurprisingly, the FBI added many of its leading spokesmen and supporters, including Senator Burton K. Wheeler (D-MT), Senator Gerald P. Nye (R-ND), celebrity aviator Charles A. Lindbergh, and former ambassador to Great Britain Joseph P. Kennedy, to the list of those it was keeping under surveillance.

In truth, the America First Committee, which had been established by students at Yale University in the spring of 1940, contained a wide range of people with a wide range of different views on why America needed to remain out of the war, just as did other isolationist groups such as the National Committee to Keep America Out of Foreign Wars. They included: that it would only profit bankers and munitions makers; that it would endanger American democracy; that the Nazis were no real threat to the United States; that a negotiated peace was possible; that it would be a betrayal of long-standing American principles to remain aloof from the "entangling alliances" of European affairs; and that the financial and human costs would be too high—war would "plow under every fourth

American boy," as Senator Wheeler put it during the course of the debate of Roosevelt's Lend-Lease policy, for example. The problem was that although certainly warped by their own particular conspiratorial mindsets, many of the same arguments were being made by Father Coughlin, Gerald Winrod, Gerald L. K. Smith, as well as assorted Bundists and Silver Shirts, at exactly the same time. Indeed, as Alex Goodall has written, "The anti-interventionist movement offered an opportunity for down-at-the-heel domestic extremists to reintegrate themselves to the mainstream. They duly clutched at their newfound allies like an unpopular child finally allowed to join the ball game." The apparent overlap between the two groupings proved enormously detrimental to the forces of "responsible" isolationism.

Things came to a head in a 1941 speech by Charles Lindbergh. The first man to fly solo across the Atlantic—on May 21, 1927, in his plane the *Spirit of St. Louis*—Lindbergh was a bona fide American hero and one of the most popular men in the country. He had largely disappeared from public life following the kidnapping and brutal murder of his infant son in 1932, but he returned to the spotlight in 1939, deeply concerned about the state of world affairs, profoundly suspicious of New Deal liberalism, and an ardent admirer of the "efficiency" of Hitler's Germany. He quickly became one of the leading spokesmen for America First, its biggest draw, but in Des Moines on September 11, 1941, he did the noninterventionist cause irreparable damage when he claimed that the "three most important groups who have been pressing this country toward war are the British, the Jewish and the Roosevelt administration." Any apparent distinctions that might have been made between domestic extremism, isolationism, anti-Semitism, and pro-Nazism collapsed. As a writer in the liberal *New Republic* expressed it: "The thing that is dangerous about America First is that is has become the effective general staff of all the fascist, semi-fascist, and proto-fascist elements in America. It has become the focal point of anti-Semitism." The America First Committee never recovered, and the bombing of Pearl Harbor a few months later put an end to the Great Debate altogether.

The outbreak of war finally afforded FDR the opportunity to "clean up" some of the "vile publications" that had been hounding him for close to decade. (The president, noted his attorney general Francis Biddle sardonically, "was not much interested . . . in the constitutional right to criticize the government in wartime.") On July 21, 1942, a New York grand jury indicted twenty-eight German agents, Bundists, and other far-right agitators under the Smith Act. It took another two years and the addition of two more defendants for the case to actually come to court, but on April 17, 1944, *United States v. McWilliams*—aka The Great Sedition Trial—finally got under way. Among the accused were Gerald Winrod, William Pelley—dragged from the federal penitentiary at Terre Haute, Indiana, where he was serving out his time for his conviction under the Espionage Act—Elizabeth Dilling, and four former leaders of the German-American Bund. All thirty defendants were charged with conspiracy—both with each other and with Nazi Germany—to destroy democracy and establish "national socialist or fascist" governments in the United States and elsewhere. In addition, they were said to have cooperated in the spreading of "systematic propaganda" by claiming that the Roosevelt administration was dominated by plutocrats, radicals, and Jews and that the Axis powers were justly battling the combined threats of communism and Judaism, all of which was intended to impair the loyalty of America's armed forces.

The Great Sedition Trial, the culmination of the antifascist campaigns of the thirties and forties, was a political "show trial," with all that term implies. It was also not a very expertly handled one. Jury selection alone took a month, each of the defendants had their own attorneys who raised seemingly endless objections, and there was grandstanding and digression aplenty, as the judge, Chief Justice Edward C. Eicher, struggled to keep control of the proceedings. More fundamentally, the government's case was extremely weak; not surprisingly, since there was no "worldwide" Nazi conspiracy of which the defendants were all a part. To cap it all, after seven long months, Eicher had a heart attack and died. A mistrial was declared. Yet despite its understandable reputation as a "bizarre circus," the trial had served Roosevelt's purpose: the activities of the radical right in the United States had been effectively curtailed, at least for the time being.

Back in early 1935 FDR had told a newspaper reporter that he was "fighting Communism, Huey Longism, Coughlinism, [and] Townsendism," as he attempted to "save our system, the capitalist system" from "crackpot ideas." Ten years later the president could look back with considerable satisfaction. None of the four groupings he mentioned remained a threat to him, while other would-be challengers—the Liberty League, the quasi-fascists, the isolationists—had also been overcome. He had been reelected in 1936 and again in 1940 and 1944. New Deal liberalism and his new Democratic coalition seemed triumphant. And although he would not live to see it, the Second World War was almost won. Yet however successful the New Deal had been—and it was only the government's massive wartime spending ($350 billion) that finally ended the Great Depression—this did not mean that the forces of conservatism and the radical right had been vanquished forever from the American political scene.

The Liberty League, for example, was only the first in an ongoing series of efforts by business groups working in concert with conservative politicians to resist, and if possible turn back, the growth of government bureaucracy and the welfare state. And while the organization itself disbanded in 1940, the principles and beliefs that had animated it, not to mention the various tactics it had employed, did not simply disappear. Indeed, as Kim Phillips-Fein has pointed out, "Although the business opponents of the New Deal were defeated at the time, their ideas—and their money—would prove critical to the creation of a new conservative movement" in the years to follow.

Roosevelt wasn't even successful in purging the conservatives from his own party. In fact, back in mid-1937—in the wake of the court-packing fight and in the midst of the so-called Roosevelt Recession—these right-wing Democrats joined forces with like-minded Republicans to form a new "conservative coalition" in Congress, one that was extremely effective in stymieing any further New Deal initiatives. In December 1937, this bipartisan group, which was dominated by southern Democrats concerned particularly about the maintenance of the Jim Crow system of segregation in the South (discussed in detail in chapter 3), issued a ten-point "Conservative Manifesto." Among other things, it denounced sit-down strike action by labor unions, called for lower federal taxes and a balanced budget, defended states' rights, decried government regulation of private enterprise, and warned about the dangers of creating a permanently dependent welfare class. Its importance should not be underestimated. To quote the historian David Kennedy:

> The manifesto constituted a kind of founding charter for modern American conservatism. It was among the first systematic expres-

sions of an antigovernment political philosophy that had deep roots in American political culture but only an inchoate existence before the New Deal. . . . The crystallization of this new conservative ideology, as much as the New Deal that precipitated its articulation, was among the enduring legacies of the 1930s.

The radical right also reoriented itself in response to the New Deal. It too was concerned about what it saw as the dangerous expansion of federal authority, untamed government bureaucracy, and the creeping collectivization of American society. Indeed, as Alex Goodall has written, "Not least because they shared a hostility to Communist politics and the New Deal, the borders between the radical Right and mainstream conservatives were never entirely clear" during the 1930s. This was true even of quasi-fascists like Gerald Winrod and his Defenders of the Christian Faith. "When all is said and done," notes Peter Amann, Winrod's vocal opposition to Roosevelt, "aside from his increasingly strident anti-Semitism, was hardly distinguishable from the anti-New Deal tirades of perfectly respectable conservative Republicans." The extent to which a normative or "polite" anti-Semitism pervaded American society at this time should also be recognized; for most Americans, it would take the horrors of the Holocaust to finally discredit such attitudes, and even then not completely.

As they responded to New Deal, one of the most important changes that took place within the radical right—although this change was neither uniform nor fully complete—was its shift toward what David Bennett has called "inverted nativism," or "nativism turned upside down." Moving away from more traditional fears about "alien" immigrants and their "alien" ideas, groups such as the National Union of Social Justice and the Silver Shirts increasingly turned their attention inward, toward the American political establishment and to the white Anglo-Saxon Protestant elites who presumed to run it. (In part, this shift was made possible by the Immigration Act of 1924, which severely restricted immigration from Southern and Eastern Europe, the geographical source of much of the older nativist attitudes.) In particular, and most significantly of all, the federal government itself was now routinely identified as being the primary repository and chief incubator of "un-American" ideas and practices.

In this the radical right was tapping into the long-standing and deeply ingrained countersubversive tradition of American politics: the hunt for hidden enemies within. They were not its only practitioners during the Depression of course. In fact, as we have seen, at the very same time as members of the radical right labored to expose the secret conspirators lurking behind the New Deal, they themselves were suspected of being Nazi fifth-columnists dedicated to the destruction of American democracy. (The Dies Committee meanwhile managed to pursue both lines of inquiry simultaneously.) While numerous groups and institutions were involved in the campaign against America's domestic fascists, for Leo Ribuffo, "the most consequential decision of the Brown Scare" was FDR's "politicization" of the FBI. Indeed, as far as Ribuffo is concerned, the creation of the national security state is as much a Roosevelt legacy as the creation of the welfare state—although this version of "intrusive government" is one conservatives of all hues have seemed better able to reconcile themselves with. Ultimately, as we have also seen, the campaign against domestic fascism bled over into the war and drew in the isolationists. This too would have long-term consequences, setting the scene for the bitter and often highly divisive postwar debates on loyalty, subversion, and patriotism. Big government and liberalism might well be on the march, but McCarthyism was waiting fervently in the wings.

2

Wrestling the Octopus

Anti-Communism and the Radical Right

ON FEBRUARY 9, 1950, a hitherto largely obscure politician from Wisconsin called Joseph R. McCarthy gave a speech before the Ohio County Women's Republican Club in Wheeling, West Virginia. It was as part of the Republican Party's annual Lincoln Day celebration, and it was really a political chore for the junior senator, part of a speaking tour that would take him to Salt Lake City and Reno in subsequent days—albeit one that he hoped would help him get reelected in 1952. The subject of McCarthy's address was the Red Menace. The United States was losing the Cold War with the Soviet Union, the senator asserted; communism was on the march worldwide, and the hard-earned victories of the Second World War had been squandered. "The reason we find ourselves in a position of impotency is not because our only powerful potential enemy has sent men to invade our shores," he explained,

> but rather because of the traitorous actions of those who have been treated so well by this nation. It has not been the less fortunate or members of minority groups who have been selling this nation out, but rather those who have had all the benefits that the wealthiest nation on earth has had to offer—the finest homes, the finest college education, and the finest jobs in government we can give.

This was "glaringly true in the State Department," which was "thoroughly infested with Communists," McCarthy went on. "I have in my hand," he said, in a statement that would launch him to extraordinary levels of notoriety over the next four years, "205 cases of individuals who would appear to be either card-carrying members or certainly loyal to the Communist Party, but who nevertheless are still helping to shape our foreign policy."

McCarthy was speaking to the anxieties of the American nation at Wheeling, seeming to provide a simple, if frightening, explanation for its apparent vulnerability and weakness in an era of unprecedented strength and prosperity: its secret betrayal from within. McCarthy certainly did not invent the "communists-in-government" issue—as discussed in the previous chapter, it was a complaint that was widely used against the Roosevelt administration and the New Deal throughout the 1930s—but he did come to symbolize it more than any other person or institution. As a result, the senator's name has become synonymous with the whole period of the Red Scare that engulfed American life between 1946 and 1954.

Yet as important as McCarthy was to both the radical right and to the issue of anti-communism, it would be a mistake to focus on him alone. Therefore, while this chapter examines the precipitous rise and dramatic fall of Senator Joe McCarthy—as well as those who came after him in the form of the John Birch Society and other groups such as the Christian Anti-Communism Crusade and the Christian Crusade—it does so by placing his story in the context both of the domestic and international politics of the period and of the wider right-wing anti-communist network of which he was a part. As described by the historian Ellen Schrecker, this network consisted of a broad coalition of groups and individuals that included members of the Catholic Church, the American Legion, the Chamber of Commerce, the House Committee on Un-American Activities, J. Edgar Hoover's FBI, right-wing politicians of both major parties, conservative journalists, and an informal but influential association of former Communist Party members turned professional Red Hunters. "What differentiated these people from their fellow Americans was not their anticommunism, which most Americans shared, but its intensity," Schrecker points out. They were "zealous partisans who often made the eradication of the so-called Communist menace a full-time career" as they enlisted in "an ongoing crusade . . . whose main effect was to bolster right-wing social and economic programs." Crucially, as the new Democratic president, Harry S. Truman, endeavored to continue, and even extend, the policies of his predecessor—as the New Deal became the Fair Deal—so the charge that had been laid so frequently at Roosevelt's door, that he and his administration were "soft on communism," continued to be hurled at his successor, and for many of the same reasons, not the least of which was the desperate desire to halt the seemingly relentless march of big government.

A profound hostility to communism was already deeply rooted in the United States of course. The atheistic ideology of Marx and Lenin with its promises of a classless society, common ownership of the means of production, and the overthrow of capitalism had long seemed utterly horrifying to all those who cherished private property, free enterprise, Christianity, and democracy (for many, essentially the "American way"). This hostility became especially pronounced after 1919, when the Soviet government established the Comintern—also referred to as the Communist International or the Third International—with the intent of exporting its revolution to the rest of the world. Indeed, these events were key contributing factors to the first Red Scare of 1919–1920, an important precursor to the events of the forties and fifties, which had culminated in the rounding-up and deportation of thousands of foreign-born radicals, revolutionaries, and unionists.

During the 1930s, spurred on by the impact of the Great Depression at home and the rise of fascism abroad, the American Communist Party (CPUSA) grew in size from 7,500 to 55,000 members. There were also thousands of communist supporters or sympathizers—although opponents preferred the terms "dupes" or "fellow travelers" to describe them—to be found in civil rights' groups, refugee relief organizations, tenants' committees, peace groups, folk music clubs, and most of all unions, where communists were particularly valued for their dedication and organizational skills. Yet while communism—or at least the actions of certain communists—was gaining in respectability in left-wing circles, in broader American society and especially on the right, profound doubts still remained about the party, its supporters, and their underlying intentions and loyalties. Nor were these doubts allayed by the Soviet Union's eventual involvement on the Allied side during the Second World War. The party's secrecy, authoritarian structure, deceptive use of "front" groups, and, above all, clear commitment to the interests of a foreign nation—following the "Moscow line," as it was called, as amply demonstrated by the CPUSA's shifting politics during the Nazi-Soviet pact period—continued to make communism highly suspect, both as an ideology and as a domestic political movement: a clear threat in many people's eyes to the security and well-being of the United States. The onset of the Cold War served only to intensify these concerns.

On March 12, 1947, Truman, who had taken over the presidency following Roosevelt's death in 1945, set out the key terms of this new Cold War, when he appeared before a joint session of Congress. "At the present moment in world history nearly every nation must choose between alternative ways of life," he explained.

> One way of life is based upon the will of the majority, and is distinguished by free institutions, representative government, free elections, guarantees of individual liberty, freedom of speech and religion, and freedom from political oppression. The second way of life is based upon the will of a minority forcibly imposed upon the majority. It relies upon terror and oppression, a controlled press and radio, fixed elections, and the suppression of personal freedoms.

Numerous countries "have recently had totalitarian regimes forced upon them against their will," the president said, singling out the Eastern European nations of Poland, Romania, and Bulgaria for particular mention, and it would now be "the policy of the United States to support free peoples who are resisting attempted subjugation by armed minorities or by outside pressures." The president had not directly identified the Soviet Union as the nation's enemy in his address, but his intent was unmistakable, and the Truman Doctrine would help set the course of American foreign policy for the next forty-five years. The United States had committed itself to fighting communism around the globe; not just for the sake of international peace but also, crucially, in order to protect America's *own* national security.

The immediate issue at hand had been the deteriorating situation in Greece and Turkey. Drained by the enormous costs of the Second World War, in February the British government had informed the State Department that it could no longer provide economic or military support to these two countries. Fearful, in the words of one American official, that if Greece in particular "falls to communism, the whole Near East and part of North Africa as well is certain to pass under Soviet influence," the United States was clearly the only nation in a position to help, but persuading Congress to appropriate the $400 million in aid the president was asking for was not going to be easy. The only way to achieve it, the Republican chairman of the Senate Foreign Relations Committee, Arthur Vandenberg (MI), advised Truman, was for the president to "scare the hell out of the American people."

Truman was certainly successful in this respect. Congress approved the $400 million for Greece and Turkey in May and would follow it up with support for the much more extensive European Recovery Program—better known as the Marshall Plan, after its chief architect, Secretary of State George C. Marshall—the following year. But the Truman administration's scaremongering approach, with its alarmist rhetoric, Manichean analysis, and gloom-laden warnings, also had a profound impact on the domestic politics of the period. The creation of the Federal Employees Loyalty Program, signed into law by Executive Order 9835, on March 25, 1947, less than two weeks after the Truman Doctrine speech, illustrates the interconnections clearly enough.

The program required all civilian employees of the federal government to undergo background checks and to submit to a loyalty test. Dismissal could result if there were "reasonable grounds" to believe that the person being investigated was "disloyal to the government of the United States," and the criteria for establishing this disloyalty was extremely broad, ranging from treason and espionage to the newly introduced idea of being guilty of having a "sympathetic association" with groups deemed to be "totalitarian, fascist, Communist or subversive" by the attorney general. Although there were supposed to be legal safeguards in place, the system allowed informants to remain anonymous, and those being investigated often had no idea of what exactly they had done to make themselves suspect and therefore no real idea of how to defend themselves. During the course of the program, between 1947 and 1956, more than two million government employees were investigated by the FBI; 2,700 people lost their jobs; and another 12,000 resigned. The historian David Caute has gone so far as to describe the creation of the attorney general's list as the "most sinister and destructive departure" in postwar American politics.

Whether motivated by genuine concerns about national security, an attempt to stave off criticism from Republicans that the administration was "soft on communism," or intended to help generate support for his foreign policy, Truman's loyalty-security program also did an enormous amount to contribute to the widespread sense of anxiety that went to the heart of the second Red Scare. Indeed, rather than putting an end the "communists-in-government" issue, the program served only to magnify it, creating even more of a political opportunity for the radical right to exploit. In addition, having legitimated the use of political tests for employment in government, the practice quickly spread out to other areas of American life, to the defense and shipping industries, to schools and universities, to newspapers and police forces, to research laboratories, and to unions. Perhaps this shouldn't have been surprising with Truman's own attorney general, J. Howard McGrath (the person charged with overseeing the program from 1949 to 1952), pointing out that communists were "everywhere," "in factories, offices, butcher shops, on street corners, in private business," and each one carrying with them "the germs of death for society."

The members of the House Un-American Activities Committee (HUAC) needed no persuading in this regard. Although it had almost gone out of business during World War II, it was revived in 1945 and transformed into a new permanent standing committee of the House of Representatives. Forcefully equipped with the power of subpoena, HUAC was formally authorized to investigate subversive threats and "un-American propaganda" against the United States. It swiftly became a key institutional component of the anti-communist network, one, in the words of James T. Paterson, that "attracted some of the most reactionary and bigoted men in public life." Chaired by the New Jersey Republican J. Parnell Thomas, other members included the conservative Democrats John Rankin of Mississippi and John Wood of Georgia, as well as Republicans Karl Mundt of South Dakota and Richard Nixon of California (who had successfully red-baited FDR's old ally Jerry Voorhis to take his congressional seat in 1946). To a considerable extent, the newly revived committee simply continued the approach and methods of its predecessor. Just as the old Dies Committee had sought to undermine the Roosevelt administration, so its successor would try to bring down Truman. Indeed, as far as the historian Robert Griffith is concerned, it was Martin Dies and his colleagues who really established "the whole spectrum of slogans, techniques, and political mythologies that would later be called 'McCarthyism.'"

HUAC had a powerful ally in its crusade in the form of the FBI director, J. Edgar Hoover, who had turned against the Truman administration, frustrated by what he saw as the weakness of its approach to the domestic communist issue, particularly its unwillingness to support his plans for a new comprehensive "custodial detention program," similar to the ones he had developed in 1919 and 1939. On March 26, 1947, Hoover made this disquiet very public when he agreed to an unprecedented appearance before the committee. "The aims and responsibilities of the House Committee on Un-American Activities and the Federal Bureau of Investigation are the same," Hoover began: "the protection of the internal security of this nation." But if the FBI and HUAC were equally engaged in the good fight, the same apparently could not be said for Hoover's ostensible political masters. On the "necessity of alertness in keeping Communists and sympathizers out of government service," the FBI merely reported "facts," its director noted tartly; it was "up to the interested government department to make a decision." The "power of exposure" must be employed much more widely in order to counter the sinister ability of communists to "infiltrate and corrupt various spheres of American life," Hoover asserted, not just in government but in labor unions, in the motion picture industry, in churches, in school boards, and in a host of "liberal and progressive" causes. "Communism, in reality, is not a political party," declared the nation's most trusted authority on the subject. "It is a way of life—a malignant and evil way of life. It reveals a condition akin to disease that spreads like an epidemic, and like an epidemic a quarantine is necessary to keep it from infecting the nation."

According to Hoover, the film industry had been specifically targeted for communist infiltration since 1935. "The party is content and highly pleased if it is possible to have inserted in a picture a line, a scene, a sequence, conveying the Communist lesson, and more particularly, if they can keep out anti-Communist lessons," he explained to the committee. Responding swiftly to its cue, HUAC made its first foray to Hollywood in October of 1947.

The hearings began with "friendly witnesses" such as the actors Robert Montgomery; Gary Cooper; Ronald Reagan, who was also the president of the Screen Actors Guild; and Adolphe Menjou; as well as studio heads including Jack L. Warner, Louis B. Mayer, and Walt Disney. Asked as a "prominent person" in his field whether Congress should pass legislation

outlawing the Communist Party, Cooper seemed to both agree and dis-
agree, while conveying his almost total lack of expertise in the area, when
he replied: "I think it would be a good idea, although I have never read
Karl Marx and I don't know the basis of Communism, beyond what I
have picked up from hearsay. From what I hear, I don't like it because
it isn't on the level. So I couldn't possibly answer that question." (In 1952
Cooper would star in the iconic western *High Noon*, about a marshal,
Will Kane, who makes a lone stand against a gang of murderous outlaws,
which its left-wing screenwriter, Carl Foreman, intended as a cautionary
"parable about Hollywood and McCarthyism.") Menjou, a future member of the John Birch Society who made it a point to inform the committee
that "Mr. Edgar Hoover . . . is a very close personal friend of mine," was
much less circumspect. "I am a witch-hunter if the witches are Communists," he said. "I make no bones about it whatsoever. I would like to see
them all back in Russia." (It was a comparison that would be taken up
by the playwright Arthur Miller in 1953, in another cautionary tale about
the dangers of McCarthyism, *The Crucible*, his fictionalized account of the
Salem witchcraft trials of 1692–1693.)

The real stars of the show, though, were the "unfriendly witnesses,"
ten of whom refused to answer questions about their political affili-
ations—including "the $64 question": "Are you now or have you ever
been a member of the Communist Party?"—on the grounds that it vio-
lated their First Amendment rights. They were: Alvah Bessie, Herbert
Biberman, Lester Cole, Edward Dmytryk, Ring Lardner Jr., John Howard Lawson, Albert Maltz, Samuel Ornitz, Adrian Scott, and Dalton
Trumbo. Most of the "Hollywood Ten," as they became known, were
screenwriters, among the most talented and sought-after in the film
industry; the exceptions were Biberman and Dmytryk, who were directors, and Scott, who was also a producer. They were also highly active
politically. Indeed, all ten either were, or had been, members of the Communist Party. All of them were cited for contempt of Congress, and all
of them were sent to prison. Subsequent "unfriendly" witnesses would
learn to rely on the Fifth Amendment to avoid a similar fate.

Under severe pressure to do something about the now undeniable communist problem in their midst, in November studio bosses convened at the
Waldorf Astoria hotel in New York City to formulate a response. The Hollywood Ten had "impaired their usefulness to the industry," read the resultant

Waldorf Statement. They would be either suspended or fired, and they would not be rehired until they had been acquitted, purged themselves of contempt, or swore that they were not communists. The country as a whole was also put on notice that no communist would henceforth "knowingly" be employed in the film industry. The era of the Hollywood blacklist had arrived.

Seemingly unable to resist the glamour of Tinseltown, HUAC returned to Hollywood throughout the 1950s, but as useful as these hearings were in generating publicity for the committee and its allies, they paled in comparison to the case of Alger Hiss. In the summer of 1948, the committee had been hearing evidence from the "Red Spy Queen," Elizabeth Bentley, who identified several New Dealers as members of a spy ring that had been run by her former lover, Jacob Golos. To support her testimony, HUAC also called on Whittaker

The actor Lionel Stander, with cigarette hanging from his lips, testifying before the House Un-American Activities Committee in 1953; attorney Leonard Boudin is sitting next to him. Stander, who had helped to organize the Screen Actors Guild, was blacklisted by the film industry until the early 1960s. Library of Congress Prints & Photographs Division. Photographed by Walter Albertin. LC-DIG-ppmsca-24370.

Chambers, an editor at *Time* magazine and a former Communist Party member who had been trying to warn the U.S. government about spies in its midst for the previous ten years. Chambers named eight people, including Hiss, as being fellow communists during the 1930s. Hiss was a graduate of Johns Hopkins University and Harvard Law School who had worked as a clerk at the Supreme Court for Oliver Wendell Holmes and then for various New Deal agencies—most notably the Agricultural Adjustment Administration—before joining the State Department as an assistant to the secretary of state for the Far East and serving as part of Roosevelt's delegation at the Yalta conference at the end of the Second World War. In 1947 he left the State Department to become president of the Carnegie Endowment for International Peace. All of which is to say that Hiss was a quintessential establishment figure, an indisputable member of the liberal, government elite.

When Hiss appeared before the committee, he denied being a communist and challenged Chambers to repeat his allegations outside of Congress. Chambers obliged and Hiss sued for slander. In December 1948 Chambers led HUAC investigators to his Maryland farm and from the hollowed-out insides of a pumpkin dramatically produced microfilmed summaries of State Department documents, which, he said, Hiss had given him in 1937 and 1938. This raised the stakes considerably. The suggestion was no longer just that Hiss was a closeted communist but that he was an actual Soviet agent. Yet because the statute of limitations on espionage had run out, Hiss could not actually be charged with spying. A grand jury indicted him on two counts of perjury instead. The first trial ended in a hung jury, but on January 21, 1950, Hiss was convicted at the second attempt and sentenced to five years in prison.

The Hiss case was taken as a triumphant vindication for HUAC and for the entire right-wing, anti-communist network—"Mr. Hiss represents the concealed enemy we are all fighting and I am fighting," Chambers had told Nixon during his testimony before the committee. Not only did Hiss's conviction seem to confirm that spying was taking place at the very highest levels of the U.S. government, it also lent credence to another of the central—and most persistent—claims of the right: that the New Deal had been infected with communist ideas and communist agents from the very outset. "So we find this traitor hobnobbing through the years with the mightiest of the New Deal mighty," ran an excoriating editorial in the conservative *Chicago Tribune*, for example. The "guilt is collective," and it "spreads over the New Deal, which sponsored and protected this monstrous conspiracy against America," the paper asserted. Meanwhile HUAC's own Karl Mundt railed that for eighteen years the country had been run by "New Dealers, Fair Dealers, Misdealers, and Hiss dealers who have shuttled back and forth between Freedom and Red Fascism like a pendulum on a cuckoo clock."

Having dismissed the charges against Hiss at the outset of the case as a "red herring"—an unfortunate choice of words given the circumstances—Truman was both weakened and embarrassed by its final outcome, his administration made even more vulnerable to the charge that it was "soft on communism." Events overseas were hardly helping in this regard. In August of 1949 the Soviet Union had exploded its first atomic bomb, bringing the United States' nuclear monopoly to an abrupt and frightening end. Three months later Mao Zedong, having finally defeated the Nationalist forces of Chiang Kai-shek, proclaimed the creation of the People's Republic of China. In the eyes of his critics, not only had Truman been unable to protect the secrets of "the bomb"; he had also somehow managed to "lose" the largest country in the world to communism.

These, then, were the circumstances in which Senator Joseph McCarthy stood up to give his famous speech in Wheeling in February 1950, less than two weeks after the outcome of the Hiss case. Indeed, the "sordid events" of how Hiss had "sold out the nation which had given him so much" were still so fresh in everyone's minds, McCarthy said that night, that he saw no need to go over them all again in any detail, except to make the point that Hiss was not important "as an individual any more, but rather because he is so representative of a group in the State Department." So, just who was Joseph McCarthy? And how did he come to epitomize the anti-communist fervor of the radical right at this time?

In many ways McCarthy was a classic embodiment of the fabled American Dream. He was one of nine children from a modest Irish-Catholic family in east-central Wisconsin (in an area that had been strongly supportive of Father Coughlin). He was a chicken farmer, ran a grocery store, was a small-town lawyer, became a judge, served in the Second World War, and then finally, in 1946, became a U.S. senator. But in his rise to this position, McCarthy also displayed many of the unpleasant and unsavory tactics that would come to represent the "ism" that bore his name, not least his unwillingness to follow rules and a fondness for what one of his biographers, Richard Rovere, has called the strategy of "Multiple Untruth." When campaigning to become a circuit judge, for example, he lied about his rival's age to make him seem old and incapable, and once in office he was censured by the Wisconsin Supreme Court for abusing his judicial authority. He also exaggerated his war service, forging a letter of commendation and claiming combat injuries when he had actually fallen down some steps during a hazing ritual, all the while employing the self-promoting nickname of "Tail Gunner Joe" to enhance his "tough guy" persona. (The number of combat missions McCarthy claimed to have flown grew over time, from fourteen in 1944, to seventeen in 1946, and then thirty-two in 1951. The actual number was eleven, but the lies enabled him to be awarded the Distinguished Flying Cross, which required a minimum of twenty-five such missions. McCarthy's wartime work mostly took place on the ground and involved the briefing of pilots and the examination of high-altitude photographs.) It was a pattern of behavior that continued in the Senate, where he acquired a new nickname, the "Pepsi-Cola Kid," for his services to the sugar industry; flouted the institution's customs and procedures; and was the subject of numerous unflattering stories concerning his heavy drinking, gambling, and sexual liaisons.

Certainly, McCarthy was not regarded as any kind of expert on the Red Menace when he stood up to speak on the subject at Wheeling. It was the reaction to the speech that turned McCarthy from an obscure first-time senator desperately trying to get himself reelected to a household name, the leader of the new Red Scare, and a hero to the radical right. The reaction came both from the press—in an era of supposed objectivity and deference, journalists were not inclined to doubt the truthfulness of the senator's very specific charges ("I have here in my hand a list . . .")—and from the Truman administration itself. Given the pressure the administration was under both in terms of world events and from the GOP, and given McCarthy's poor reputation, he was an inviting target to attempt to fight back on. The State Department issued three denials of McCarthy's charges and asked for a copy of his list of names (which didn't exist), and on February 16, Truman himself said that there was "not a word of truth" in what the senator was saying. Truman and the Democrats had underestimated McCarthy and his extraordinary publicity-generating gifts, however. As he continued his speaking tour, he kept tantalizing the press about what he was going to reveal, and the fact that he claimed to have numbers—exact figures—made his allegations impossible to ignore. The absence of proof proved to be no deterrent at all. As McCarthy informed a local reporter in Milwaukee, he had a "sockful of shit" and he knew "how to use it." It is what he'd been doing his whole career.

On February 20, 1950, McCarthy took his case directly to the floor of the Senate, where he was questioned by the Senate majority leader Scott Lucas (D-IL) about the different numbers he had been using on the road—was it 205, 57, or 81 traitors he had identified? Both parties then called for a formal investigation of McCarthy's charges: the Republicans because they believed it would further undermine Truman; the Democrats because the claims were so obviously trumped-up that any sustained examination of them would surely only serve to discredit the GOP. But the results of the investigations of the Tydings Committee, a subcommittee of the Senate Foreign Relations Committee, chaired by the Democrat Millard Tydings of Maryland, in the end served only to further confirm just how much the whole "communists-in-government" issue had become embroiled in partisan domestic politics. The majority report issued by the three Democrats on the committee—which the two Republicans refused to sign—accused McCarthy of perpetrating a "fraud and a hoax" on the American people. "We have seen the character of private citizens and of government employees virtually destroyed by public condemnation on the basis of gossip, distortion, hearsay and deliberate untruths," it said. McCarthy and his allies in contrast dismissed the whole thing as a "whitewash." McCarthy himself called the report "a green light to the Red fifth column in the United States" and "a sign to the traitorous Communists and fellow travelers in our government that they need have no fear of exposure."

Afterward, Republican Party leaders such as Senator Robert A. Taft of Ohio encouraged their Wisconsin colleague to keep going—"Keep talking," Taft said; "if one case doesn't work, proceed with another"—and praised McCarthy for his courage and determination. "That fighting Irish Marine would give the shirt off his back to anyone who needs it—except a dirty, lying, stinking Communist. That guy he'd kill," claimed another admirer, Herman Welker, the newly elected Republican senator from Idaho.

Meanwhile, events at home and abroad continued to go against the Truman administration, all the while strengthening the hand of the anti-communist right. On June 25, 1950, for example, the Cold War suddenly turned hot when almost one hundred thousand North Korean troops marched across the 38th parallel into South Korea. "The attack upon Korea makes it plain beyond all doubt that Communism has passed beyond the use of subversion to conquer independent nations and will use armed invasion and war," Truman told the American people two days later. Within short order U.S. combat troops were actively fighting communism on the peninsula (although technically under the auspices of the United Nations). The war would drag on inconclusively for three years at the cost of more than thirty-five thousand American lives. The high-profile spying case of the Rosenbergs was also in the news at this time. In February of 1950, a British physicist called Klaus Fuchs had confessed to passing atomic secrets to the Soviet Union, which led to a number of arrests in the United States, including that of a New York engineer called Julius Rosenberg on July 18, only a few weeks after the outbreak of the Korean War, and his wife, Ethel, the following month. Unlike the other alleged co-conspirators in this "crime of the century," Julius maintained his innocence throughout his subsequent 1951 trial, but both he and his wife—who had been indicted only as a pressure tactic by the prosecution intended to force Julius to confess—were found guilty. They were executed by electric chair at sundown on June 19, 1953.

The passage of the Internal Security Act in September of 1950 also reflected badly on the Truman administration. Truman had not only opposed the bill—better known as the McCarran Act after its sponsor, the powerful chairman of the Senate Judiciary Committee, conservative Democrat Pat McCarran of Nevada—as an unnecessary attack on Americans' civil liberties; he had actually vetoed it, only to have his veto overwhelmingly defeated in Congress (the votes were 286 to 48 in the House and 57 to 10 in the Senate). The resultant law required all communist and other "subversive" organizations, including front groups, to register with the attorney general. It denied passports to members or past members of such groups, restricted their rights of travel, prevented them from working in defense-related industries, and even provided for their detention in concentration camps in the event of a "national emergency."

Then came the November mid-term elections. Overall the Democrats managed to hang on to their control of Congress, but there were some very notable casualties among the twenty-eight House seats and five Senate seats the party lost to the GOP in 1950, including Millard Tydings and Scott Lucas; losses that pointedly seemed to illustrate the dangers of speaking out against McCarthyism, while also boding ill for the upcoming 1952 elections.

It was the stalemate in Korea, or rather Truman's decision to fire General Douglas MacArthur for repeated acts of insubordination while trying to break that stalemate, that provided McCarthy with his next major issue. On the basis that there was "no substitute for victory," MacArthur, the commander of U.S. forces on the ground, had been pushing publicly for an expansion of the war into China, a strategy that the chairman of the Joint Chiefs of Staff, General Omar Bradley, dismissed as one that "would involve us in the wrong war, at the wrong place, at the wrong time, and with the wrong enemy." Having consulted with Bradley, as well as with Secretary of State Dean Acheson and Secretary of Defense George Marshall, and having repeatedly warned MacArthur about his conduct, Truman relieved the errant general of his command on April 11, 1951.

Initially McCarthy suggested that Truman might have been drunk when he fired MacArthur and that "the son of a bitch should be impeached," but on June 14 he took to the Senate floor—which was completely absent of Democrats who had decided to stage a boycott of the proceedings—to launch an extraordinary attack on the administration through the proxy figure of George Marshall. The U.S. secretary of defense had been serving the interests of the Soviet Union throughout his career, McCarthy alleged. It was Marshall who had let the Soviets gain control of Eastern Europe at the end of the Second World War and Marshall who had "sold out" China to communism. Indeed, as McCarthy saw it, a massive conspiracy had taken hold of the entire U.S. government, and Marshall was at the center of it. In one of the classic iterations of the counter-subversive tradition in American politics, he asked,

How can we account for our present situation unless we believe that men high in this government are concerting to deliver us to disaster? This must be a product of a great conspiracy, a conspiracy on a scale so immense as to dwarf any previous such venture in the history of man. A conspiracy of infamy so black that, when it is finally exposed, its principals shall be forever deserving of the maledictions of all honest men.

Truman did not seek reelection in 1952. Instead it was the governor of Illinois, Adlai E. Stevenson, who faced off against the Republican candidate, Dwight D. Eisenhower, the former five-star general and supreme commander of Allied Forces in Europe during World War II. Stevenson lost in a landslide, by 33.9 million votes to 27.3 million and by 442 electoral votes to 89. That Stevenson too would be "soft on communism" was, of course, a staple of the campaign against him, part of the GOP's overall K1C2 formula—"Korea, Communism, and Corruption." Richard Nixon, running as Eisenhower's vice-presidential candidate, for example, called Stevenson "Adlai the appeaser," suggesting that he possessed a "PhD from Dean Acheson's cowardly college of Communist containment." For his part, in a nationally televised address on October 27, McCarthy twice made the faux mistake of referring to the Illinoisan as "Alger" Stevenson. As ugly as the strategy appeared to many outside observers, it worked. What McCarthy and other Republicans called the "twenty years of treason" of the Roosevelt and Truman administrations were finally over.

This, though, changed the political landscape considerably. What continuing use was there for the "communists-in-government" issue with the Republicans in control of both Congress and the White House? What would McCarthy and his allies do now? The Republican Party leadership effectively tried to sideline the newly returned senator from Wisconsin by giving him the chairmanship of the exceedingly minor Committee on Government Operations. (The plum anti-communist positions of chair of HUAC and of the Senate Internal Security Subcommittee went to Harold Velde of Illinois and William Jenner of Indiana, respectively.) But once again McCarthy had been underestimated. Appointing himself chair of the Permanent Subcommittee on Investigations, which had the authority to examine "government activities on all levels," stacking it with loyal supporters like Karl Mundt, Everett Dirksen (R-IL), and Charles Potter (R-MI) and utilizing its extensive but hitherto little-used powers to call hearings, issue subpoenas, and make official reports, he made it clear that he was "not retiring from the field of exposing Communists." On the contrary, he had only "scratched the surface" of the matter, he said. To aid him in his ongoing crusade, McCarthy also hired the New York prosecutor—and virulent anti-communist—Roy Cohn as his chief counsel, as well as Cohn's good friend, the wealthy G. David Schine, as an unpaid "consultant," decisions that were to have fateful consequences for the senator.

If McCarthy had been something of a latecomer to the anti-communist cause in 1950, by the time he took over the Permanent Subcommittee on Investigations, he was exhibiting all the signs of the true believer, his monomania pushing him to the very heart of the larger anti-communist network. Information, tips, and money poured in from other anti-communist activists, from right-wing journalists, from organizations like the American Legion, from Hoover and the FBI, as well as from hundreds of government workers and members of the armed forces, participants in "the Loyal American Underground," as some of these secret informers referred to themselves. With a budget of $200,000, between 1953 and 1954, McCarthy's committee undertook a wide range of investigations of both people and institutions, none of which produced much evidence of any widespread communist infiltration of American life, but all of which continued to generate publicity for the senator and his cause. Among those called before it, for example, were the African-American poet Langston Hughes, the crime writer Dashiell Hammett, and the avant-garde composer Aaron Copland. In early 1953, the committee began investigating two programs of the State Department's International Information Agency, the Voice of America radio stations and its overseas library system, which culminated in the unedifying front-page spectacle of Cohn and Schine criss-crossing Europe as panicked government librarians removed suspect tomes from their shelves and even burned a few for the lack of space to store them.

As all of this was taking place, President Eisenhower remained conspicuous in his silence. This, though, was by design. While detesting McCarthy personally, Eisenhower was determined to deny him any more of the publicity he was clearly seeking. He would "not get down in the gutter with that guy," the president said, believing that he had learned a lesson that Franklin Roosevelt had failed to understand during his own demagogic dealings with Huey Long in the 1930s. If he was patient, eventually McCarthy would bring about his own demise, Eisenhower believed. The problem is that, while this can be taken as being representative of

Eisenhower's "hidden-hand" approach to the presidency—working quietly behind the scenes to bring about a desired result—it was a strategy that left the public initiative very much in McCarthy's hands. As critics of Eisenhower have pointed out, a little more political courage on the president's part might not have gone astray.

Nonetheless, McCarthy did begin to make mistakes. In June 1953 he appointed J. B. Matthews as the executive director of his subcommittee. Matthews, who had been a fellow traveler during the 1930s, had transformed himself into an almost legendary figure on the anti-communist right, largely through his extensive collection of Communist Party and front group literature, which he made available—sometimes for a fee—to his many political and corporate clients, including HUAC, McCarthy, and the Hearst newspaper corporation. Unfortunately for his new employer, however, he had just written an article called "Reds and Our Churches" for the right-wing magazine *American Mercury*, the lead paragraph of which stated flat out that "the largest single group supporting the Communist apparatus in the United States is composed of Protestant clergymen." The storm of protest the article elicited was such that even McCarthy was forced to back down. Matthews "resigned" from his new position on July 9.

Blocked from launching a probe into the supposed lax security arrangements of the CIA, McCarthy instead sought to investigate the extent of communist infiltration in the U.S. Army. He began with the Army Signal Corps at Fort Monmouth, New Jersey, but couldn't find any evidence of the spy ring he was hunting. Next, he took on the case of a military dentist called Irving Peress, who took the Fifth Amendment rather than answer the senator's questions and who after his appearance before the subcommittee was honorably discharged from the Army. McCarthy summoned Peress's commanding officer, General Ralph W. Zwicker, to explain why but lost his temper during the questioning, calling Zwicker "ignorant," a "disgrace," and not "fit to wear" his uniform. Furious at the treatment of one of its generals, on March 12, 1954, the Pentagon issued a damning report accusing McCarthy and Cohn of having threatened various Army officials in order to get preferential treatment for Cohn's friend—and presumed lover—G. David Schine. McCarthy responded by accusing the Army of blackmail and bribery and of simply trying to block his investigations, and a whole new set of hearings was convened to sort through the thicket of allegations and counter-allegations.

The importance of the Army-McCarthy hearings, as they were called and which lasted from April 22 to June 17, 1954, was that they exposed the American public at large to McCarthy's methods and tactics for the very first time, and the senator came across very poorly. He was his usual aggressive self; he badgered witnesses, was rude, relied on obviously

Senator Joseph McCarthy (center) addresses reporters in June 1954. The Army-McCarthy hearings would play a key role in the senator's downfall. Library of Congress Prints & Photographs Division, *U.S. News & World Report* Magazine Photograph Collection, LC-U9-394-9.

doctored photographs for evidence, and constantly interrupted the proceedings with points of order. All of this was extensively covered both in the press and on the national TV networks. Indeed, in the view of newspaper columnist Walter Lippmann, the hearings became something of a "national obsession." They culminated symbolically and dramatically—if not in actuality—on June 9 in an interchange between the Army's lawyer, Joseph R. Welch, and McCarthy over an associate in Welch's law firm called Fred Fisher. McCarthy believed Welch had broken an agreement they had reached that Welch would not raise the issue of homosexuality between Schine and Cohn if McCarthy refrained from mentioning Fisher's past association in the National Lawyers Guild, a communist front group. When McCarthy began accusing Welch of harboring a communist on his staff, Welch responded (in remarks he had prepared in advance should they be needed):

> Little did I dream that you could be so reckless and so cruel as to do an injury to that lad. . . . If it were in my power to forgive you for your reckless cruelty, I would do so. I like to think I am a gentleman, but your forgiveness will have to come from someone other than me. . . . Let us not assassinate this lad further, senator. You have done enough. Have you no sense of decency, sir, at long last? Have you left no sense of decency?

It was like the moment in *The Wizard of Oz*, when Toto pulls back the curtain to reveal the quotidian reality of the once mighty figure believed to be lurking behind, and McCarthy never recovered from it. As Senator Stuart Symington (D-MO), one of McCarthy's principal opponents during the hearings, told him as he tried to backtrack and find a way out of the mess he had created: "The American people have had a look at you for six weeks. You are not fooling anyone." According to Gallup polls, McCarthy's approval rating in January 1954 had been 50 percent; by the end of the hearings it had plummeted to 30 percent. But, of course, there were other factors at work. Even before the hearings began, Edward R. Murrow, perhaps the most respected newsman in the country, had used his primetime CBS documentary series *See It Now* to attack McCarthy—"His primary achievement has been in confusing the public mind between the internal and external threat of communism," Murrow had said—and many of the senator's former allies, including J. Edgar Hoover, had abandoned him, seeing him as more of a liability than an asset to the anti-communist cause. He had certainly outlived his usefulness to the GOP.

On December 2, 1954, McCarthy was officially censured by the Senate for his mistreatment of fellow senators and for his abuse of General Zwicker during the Fort Monmouth hearings. It was a relatively minor reprimand, and he could probably have avoided it altogether had he been willing to simply apologize for his behavior. This, though, had never been McCarthy's style. Defiant to the end, he declared that he "would have the American people recognize, and contemplate in dread, the fact that the Communist Party—a relatively small group of deadly conspirators—has now extended its tentacles to the most respected of American bodies, the United States Senate." The vote against him was 67 to 22. Descending into full-blown alcoholism, he died three years later, on May 2, 1957, of cirrhosis of the liver.

McCarthy's four-year crusade had certainly done an enormous amount of damage to the anti-communist cause—making it seem, at times, "nothing more than the ravings of a dangerous madman," in the view of Richard Gid Powers—but it had not destroyed it completely. Organizations like the American Legion and the Catholic Church continued to sponsor conferences to combat communism. The professional ex-communists continued to rail against the god that had failed them. HUAC and the FBI continued to issue warnings about the dangers of internal subversion. New organizations also began to emerge on the scene, the most important of which, in December 1958, was the John Birch Society (JBS).

The Birch Society was the brainchild of Robert H. W. Welch Jr., a retired candy manufacturer, former board member of the National Association of Manufacturers, and ardent supporter of both Robert Taft and Joe McCarthy. In 1952 Welch wrote a book called *May God Forgive Us*, in which he took the Truman administration to conspiratorial task for its "almost unbelievable combination of trickery, chicanery, and treason," which had led to the "loss" of China to communism. He followed that up two years later with *The Life of John Birch: In the Story of One American Boy, the Ordeal of His Age*, about a Baptist missionary and soldier who was killed by Chinese communists in August 1945. Welch regarded Birch as the first American casualty of World War III and received the blessing of Birch's parents to name his new Society after the fallen hero. Prominent among its founding members were: T. Coleman Andrews, a former commissioner of internal revenue of the United States; Colonel Laurence E. Bunker, the former personal aide of Douglas MacArthur; William J. Grede, the head of Grede Foundries in Milwaukee, Wisconsin; W. B. McMillan, president of the Hussmann Refrigerator Company of St. Louis, Missouri; Louis Rothenberg, onetime president of the Indiana Chamber of Commerce; Dr. Revilo P. Oliver, professor of classical languages and literatures at the University of Illinois; and, perhaps most notably of all, Fred C. Koch, president of Rock Island Oil and Refining of Wichita, Kansas; one of the wealthiest men in the state; and the father of Charles and David Koch, who would become two of the key financial backers of the twenty-first-century Tea Party movement and a host of other right-wing groups.

Headquartered in suburban Belmont, Massachusetts, the Birch Society was organized through a series of small local chapters, or clubs, of no more than twenty members each (critics would refer to them more sinisterly as "cells"). Annual dues were $24 for men, $12 for women, with a lifetime membership available for $1,000. Paid regional coordinators supervised the local volunteer chapter leaders, and above them stood the National Council and, ultimately, "The Founder" himself, as Welch liked to be known. At its peak, in 1965, there were an estimated one hundred thousand JBS members spread across the United States, from New Jersey to Texas to Oregon, although the movement was especially strong in Southern California. These Birchers were mostly white, middle-class, conservative-minded Republicans, both men and women, who, in the findings of one researcher, were profoundly "dissatisfied with government" and negatively inclined "toward Communists, symbols of the Left, and the eastern establishment."

The goal of the Society, as Welch explained in its founding document, *The Blue Book of the John Birch Society*, was "stopping the Communists, and destroying their conspiracy, or at least breaking its grip on our government and shattering its power within the United States." This, though, was not going to be easy given that the tentacles of the communist octopus were so extensive that they

> now reach into all the legislative halls, all of the union labor meetings,
> a majority of the religious gatherings, and most of the schools *of the*

whole world. It has a central nervous system which can make its tentacles in the labor unions of Bolivia, in the farmers' co-operatives of Saskatchewan, in the caucuses of the Social Democrats of West Germany, and in the class rooms of Yale Law School, all retract or reach forward simultaneously. It can make all of these creeping tentacles turn either right or left, or a given percentage turn right while the others turn left, at the same time, in accordance with the intentions of a central brain in Moscow. . . . The human race has never before faced any such monster of power which has determined to enslave it.

At a more prosaic level, the Society's targets continued to be those that had been animating the radical right ever since the 1930s: centralized power, the expansion of workers' rights, higher taxes, increased bureaucracy, and rising deficits—the "cancer of collectivism" in all its myriad forms. As Welch maintained: "The greatest enemy of man is, and always has been, government. And the larger, the more extensive that government, the greater the enemy."

At their monthly meetings, Birchers were encouraged to take part in letter-writing campaigns, to circulate petitions, to form study groups, to organize protests and demonstrations, and even to create their own front organizations to combat those of the communists—"little fronts, big fronts, temporary fronts, permanent fronts, all kinds of fronts"—all with the intention of "awakening" the apathetic or "brainwashed" American people to what was really going on around them. To aid in this endeavor, the Society published its own monthly magazine, *American Opinion*; ran an extensive network of libraries and bookstores; broadcast a weekly radio program called *Are You Listening, Uncle Sam?*; and operated its own book-publishing division and speakers' bureau.

The JBS did not come to widespread public attention until the summer of 1960, when Jack Mabley, a reporter with the *Chicago Daily News*, published two articles about the new "ultra-conservative" organization, describing it as secretive, authoritarian, and, not surprisingly, conspiratorial. The really big scoop, though, was that Mabley had obtained a copy of *The Politician*, a privately printed manuscript that Welch had been circulating to a few trusted colleagues and potential members of the Society since 1954. *The Politician* was an extended attack on Eisenhower and the "modern republicanism" he claimed to represent, but it also contained the truly astounding allegation that the president was actually "a dedicated, conscious agent of the Communist conspiracy" in the United States—a view Welch explained as being "based on an accumulation of detailed evidence so extensive and so palpable that it seems to me to put this conviction beyond any reasonable doubt." Nor was this all. Secretary of State John Foster Dulles; his brother, Central Intelligence Director Allen Dulles; and Supreme Court Chief Justice Earl Warren were all named as co-conspirators, and it was further suggested that Milton Eisenhower, the president's brother, was likely Eisenhower's boss within the CPUSA. As the North Dakota Republican Milton Young told the Senate, such allegations went "far beyond anything the late Senator Joe McCarthy ever thought of."

A flurry of articles followed in the nation's press, and there were extensive calls for some kind of official investigation of the Birchers. On July 7, 1961, California's attorney general, Stanley Mosk, issued the results of his particular inquires. The report's widely cited opening paragraph made for damning reading. "The cadre of the John Birch Society seems to be formed primarily of wealthy businessmen, retired military officers and little old ladies in tennis shoes," it began.

> They are bound together by an obsessive fear of "communism," a word which they define to include any ideas differing from their own, even though these ideas may differ even more markedly with the ideas of Marx, Engels, Lenin and Khrushchev. In response to this fear they are willing to give up a large measure of the freedoms guaranteed them by the United States Constitution in favor of accepting the dictates of their "Founder." They seek, by fair means or foul, to force the rest of us to follow their example. They are pathetic.

Other observers saw more sinister motivations behind the JBS. Indeed, just as with the Brown Scare of the 1930s, there were widely expressed fears that the appearance of the organization portended the rise of fascism in the United States. The Society's "militant words and thoughts are barely a goosestep away from the formation of goon squads," argued *Time* magazine. The Rabbinical Council of America warned about the "serious dangers" posed to the country by the "narrow Fascist-like and bigoted Birch Society," while the Wisconsin Congressman Henry Reuss (D) worried that what "the Society is up to sounds ominously like what the Nazis once were up to in Germany."

Overall, the reaction to the JBS was so strong—and mostly out of proportion to what the Society was actually doing—largely because it had emerged so soon after the travails of the second Red Scare. To many, McCarthyism (in all its aspects) had exposed the weakness of American democracy, its vulnerability to demagogic manipulation, and there was a widespread determination on that part of the nation's political elites in particular that there should be no repetition of the phenomena in the years to come. What's more, for those who felt they had failed to stand up sufficiently to McCarthyism the first time around, the JBS offered the opportunity for redemption; this time against a much weaker opponent. The new Democratic incumbent in the White House, John F. Kennedy, who had never spoken out publicly against McCarthy when he was in the Senate—in part because both his constituents and his father were solidly in support of the Wisconsin senator—certainly showed that he would be much more forthright than his two immediate predecessors had been in dealing with what he called the "discordant voices of extremism" at work in the nation.

Speaking at a fund-raising dinner at the Hollywood Palladium on November 18, 1961, for example, Kennedy explained that there "have always been those on the fringes of our society who have sought to escape their own responsibility by finding a simple solution, an appealing slogan, or a convenient scapegoat," those who believed that "it was not the presence of Soviet troops in Eastern Europe that drove it to communism but "the sellout at Yalta" or that it was "not a civil war that removed China from the Free World" but "treason in high places." Such "fanatics," he said, "convinced that the real danger is from within," looked "suspiciously at their neighbors and their leaders"; found "treason in our churches, in our highest court, in our treatment of water [a reference to the JBS's campaign against fluoridation]"; and equated "the Democratic Party with the welfare state, the welfare state with socialism, socialism with communism." Urging his fellow countrymen not to give in to such "counsels of fear and suspicion," Kennedy explained that "most Americans" well knew that the real peril came from the external threat of communism and that this threat could only be met though a bolstered military, strategic alliances, and increased international trade.

The JBS was not the only right-wing organization that remained concerned with the internal communist menace, however. Other members of the radical right of this period include: Dr. George S. Benson's Harding College, based in Searcy, Arkansas; Reverend Carl McIntire's American Council of Christian Churches; the Cardinal Mindszenty Foundation, run by Fred and Phyllis Schlafly; the Conservative Society of America; the Church League of America; Willis Carto's Liberty Lobby; the Life Line Foundation, sponsored by the Texas oil tycoon H. L. Hunt; and a host of smaller groups and one-man outfits with evocative names like the Freedoms Foundation at Valley Forge, Let Freedom Ring, and Moral Re-Armament. The two most notable, though, were Dr. Fred C. Schwarz's Christian Anti-Communism Crusade (CACC) and Reverend Billy James Hargis's Christian Crusade.

Schwarz, the son of a Pentecostal preacher and an Australian by birth, was a physician and psychiatrist. He moved to the United States in 1953, setting up the CACC initially in Waterloo, Iowa, before moving it, in 1958, to Long Beach, California. It also maintained regional offices in Houston, Seattle, San Francisco, Indianapolis, and Sydney, Australia. The organization's stated aim was to "combat communism by means of lectures in schools, colleges, civic clubs, servicemen's organizations and through radio and television broadcasts and by providing courses for missionaries and others to be used in Bible schools and seminaries and the holding of religious and evangelistic services in churches, and through the publication of books, pamphlets and literature." In 1957 Schwarz testified before HUAC on the subject of "International Communism (the Communist Mind)," which helped establish his expertise in the field, and in 1960 he published his best-known work, the mischievously titled *You Can Trust the Communists (To Be Communists)*, which went through ten hard-cover printings in 1960 alone, selling more than one million copies.

Also central to the spreading of the CACC's anti-communist word were its week-long Schools of Anti-Communism—lectures ran from nine in the morning until nine-thirty at night at the cost of $10—and its electrifying rallies; often complete with the anti-communist folk stylings of the Crusade's musical director, Janet Green, the "Joan Baez of the Right," as one historian describes her. (Her songs included "Commie Lies," "Fascist Threats," "Poor Left Winger," and "Comrades Lament.") One of the most successful of these rallies took place at the Hollywood Bowl in October 1961. Attended by approximately fifteen thousand Crusaders, the three-hour show was also watched by a televi-

sion audience estimated at four million. Seated on the stage were such
well-known figures as John Wayne, Ronald Reagan, Cesar Romero,
Ozzie and Harriet Nelson, and Jack Warner. As with so many other
radical right-wing groups—including the JBS—the CACC's backers
included wealthy businessmen like Patrick Frawley, whose companies
Technicolor Inc. and the Schick Safety Razor Company were the official sponsors of the Hollywood Bowl rally, along with the California-
based Richfield Old Company.

Billy James Hargis was born in Texarkana, Texas, in 1925. After graduating from high school, he attended Ozark Bible College at Bentonville,
Arkansas, before being ordained as a minister in the Disciples of Christ
Church in 1943. He subsequently received honorary doctorates from both
Gerald Winrod's Defender Seminary in Puerto Rico and Bob Jones University in Greenville, South Carolina. Hargis founded the Christian Crusade in 1951, and by the early sixties he had turned it into the largest and
most lucrative organizations on the Christian anti-communist right, with
a revenue of almost a million dollars a year. Its news magazine, *Christian Crusade*, reached more than one hundred thousand readers a month;
Hargis's sermons could be heard on 270 radio stations every week; and
the organization also produced a staggering array of pamphlets, films,
books, records, television shows, and tape recordings with titles such as
Communist America—Must It Be? (an LP), *The Real Extremists—The Far
Left* (a book), and *Communism, Hypnotism and The Beatles* (a pamphlet).
Although based in Tulsa, Oklahoma, the Christian Crusade held Anti-
Communist Leadership Schools around the country—speakers included
General Albert C. Wedemeyer, who had been highly critical of the Tru-
man administration's "loss" of China; the Mormon leader Ezra Taft
Benson; ex-FBI agent turned conservative radio personality Dan Smoot;
and prominent Birchers like Revilo Oliver—ran a summer Youth Anti-
Communist University in Manitou Springs, Colorado; and even staged
an Anti-Communist Congress at the 1962 Seattle World's Fair.

A passionate and persuasive orator, Hargis railed against all those he
believed had "betrayed" the United States, including the "liberals, welfare
staters, do-gooders and one worlders." He attacked the United Nations,
justified racial segregation as a "law of God," and considered all of the
nation's principal institutions—the churches, Congress, the Pentagon,
the Supreme Court, the unions, the media—to have been so thoroughly

infiltrated by communists that he expected the entire country to fall to them by 1974 unless something major happened to prevent it. "I have lived through liberalism since the days of Franklin Delano Roosevelt," he would lament in a typical sermon, "and I have seen my country go bankrupt economically; and I've seen our churches become apostate; and I've seen our schools emphasize internationalism instead of nationalism and even turn against the faith of our fathers." The "seeds of a dictator-ship" had been sown in Washington, he would declare to loud Amens and shouts of encouragement from the audience, and he was concerned, and he had a "*right* to be concerned," and as "long as he lived" he would "*express* that concern."

In the fall of 1961 Attorney General Robert Kennedy invited the lead-ers of the United Automobile Workers union and close confidants of the Kennedys, Walter P. Reuther and Victor G. Reuther, along with civil rights lawyer Joseph L. Rauh Jr., to advise the administration on how it should deal with groups such as the John Birch Society, the Christian Anti-Communism Crusade, and the Christian Crusade. Noting that these groups were stronger and "almost certainly better organized than at any time in recent history," the resultant Reuther memorandum (as it became known) called for "deliberate Administration policies and programs to contain the radical right from further expansion and in the long run to reduce it to its historic role of the impotent lunatic fringe." In practical terms, this meant turning the power of the state against them. The attorney general's subversive list should be expanded to include right-wing extremists, the memo recommended. The FBI should begin to infiltrate such groups; their tax-exempt status investigated by the IRS; and their radio and television broadcasting licenses revoked. Revealingly, though, the memo also recommended a substantial toning down of offi-cial anti-communist rhetoric. The radical right fed on charges of "trea-son, traitors, and treachery," it noted, and while every administration since the end of World War II had "maximized the Communist prob-lem," there was no longer any need to "dramatize the domestic Com-munist issue." Putting everything "in proper perspective" was likely to alleviate many of the problems being caused by the radical right and their supporters, the memo concluded.

As for leading figures in the emerging conservative movement of this time, it was really only Robert Welch's leadership of the JBS that seemed problematic, at least initially. In January 1962 a number of these figures, including William Buckley, the founder of the movement's flagship journal, *National Review*; the political philosopher Russell Kirk; and the director of the American Enterprise Institute, William Brody, met with the Arizona Republican Senator Barry Goldwater at the Breakers Hotel in Palm Beach, Florida, to sound out Goldwater on his willingness to run for the presidency in 1964. Following their discussion, Buckley penned a blistering attack on Welch in the February issue of *National Review*. While Welch's intentions were to be applauded, Buckley said, his conspiratorial beliefs were "disastrously mistaken" and he was fundamentally damaging the cause of anti-Communism with the "fog of confusion" that issued from his "smoking typewriter." Welch should either resign his leadership of the JBS or ordinary Birch members should rise up and remove him, Buckley believed. Senator Goldwater concurred. "We cannot allow the emblem of irresponsibility to attach to the conservative banner," he wrote in a letter published in the following issue of the magazine; "the best thing Mr. Welch could do to serve the cause of anti-Communism in the United States would be to resign."

Welch did not resign, however, nor was he forced out. In fact, following President Kennedy's assassination in November 1963, he and thousands of other Birchers worked tirelessly on Goldwater's behalf as he faced off against the Democratic Party's candidate, Lyndon Johnson, in the 1964 presidential election. Goldwater's defeat was overwhelming. Johnson won a record 61 percent of the popular vote (43 million to Goldwater's 27 million) and 90 percent of the Electoral College (486 to 52). The Democrats also gained thirty new congressmen and two new senators to give the party a two-thirds majority in both houses of Congress.

In the election's aftermath, moderate and conservative Republicans alike decided the time had finally come to oust all Birch members from the GOP—if only to "erase the stigmas" of Goldwater's candidacy, as William Scranton, the governor of Pennsylvania, put it. Buckley and his *National Review* colleagues went even further, attempting to excommunicate the Society from the whole conservative movement in a twelve-page special feature on the organization published in October 1965. "The false analysis and conspiratorial mania of the John Birch Society has moved beyond diversion and waste of the devotion of its members to the mobilization of that devotion in ways directly anti-conservative and dangerous to the interests of the United States," wrote Frank Meyer, one of *National Review*'s senior editors.

The heyday of the John Birch Society and of the other anti-communist groups on the radical right was over. This is not to say that the fear of communism or a hostility toward its practitioners disappeared from American life. Far from it. But from the mid-1960s onward, the focus would be much more squarely on the external threat the Soviet Union posed to the United States rather than questions of internal treachery and subversion. (This had been the preferred position of liberal anti-communists all along, it should be said.) The years of the second Red Scare and their aftermath had nonetheless had a deep and profound impact on American politics and American society. It was a period of sustained and widespread political repression in the United States, one that, as we have seen, was the product of many factors, involving many different players, but one in which the right-wing anti-communist network had played a crucial role. In the end, what distinguished McCarthy from the many other anti-communist activists of the period, including others in the Senate, was his audacity and unscrupulousness, his relentlessness, and his acute sense of drama. Yet for all this, as McCarthy's most perceptive biographer, David M. Oshinsky, has pointed out, in many respects the senator had been rather "self-contained" in the sense that he had demonstrated "no desire to lead a movement, to run for higher office, or to formulate a program that went beyond the simple exposure of Communists. . . . He was not a would-be dictator." Nor, for all his investigative energy, did he ever uncover a single communist agent operating in the United States.

What McCarthy had certainly helped to produce, though, was a very particular and highly influential understanding of what the radical right actually was: its motivations and key concerns. For Seymour Martin Lipset and his Columbia University colleagues in *The New American Right* (1955), for example, McCarthy and his followers "represented a form of extremism rather than a genuine effort to bespeak the conservative point of view." They were irrational, paranoid, and conspiratorial, not to mention a fundamental threat to America's democratic system. The emergence of subsequent radical right groups such as the John Birch Society, Christian Crusade, and the Christian Anti-Communism Crusade provided Lipset and his colleagues with the opportunity to update their findings. Not surprisingly perhaps, they found that the activities and beliefs of these groups simply confirmed their original analysis, as was made abundantly clear throughout their new work, *The Radical Right: The New American Right Expanded and Updated*, published in 1963.

The historian Richard Hofstadter had used the term "pseudo-conservatism" to describe the radical right in *The New American Right* and its follow-up, but in 1964, in an essay in *Harper's* magazine, he hit upon a much more evocative term. In their "heated exaggeration, suspiciousness and conspiratorial fantasy," McCarthy and the JBS both practiced the "paranoid style" of American politics, he argued. "The distinguishing thing about the paranoid style is not that its exponents see conspiracies or plots here and there in history, but that they regard a 'vast' or 'gigantic' conspiracy as *the motive force* in historical events . . . and what is felt to be needed to defeat it is not the usual methods of political give-and-take, but an all-out crusade," Hofstadter wrote. As we shall see in later chapters, this notion of the "paranoid style" would be applied regularly to other groups on the radical right in the years to come, from the New Right of the 1970s and 1980s, to the militia movement of the 1990s and the Tea Party and Trumpist right of the twenty-first century. Before we get to these groups, though, first we need to consider the issue of race and the radical right.

3

Resisting the Tide

Civil Rights and the Radical Right

DURING THE MONTGOMERY BUS BOYCOTT that began in December 1955, when Rosa Parks, a black seamstress and member of the National Association for the Advancement of Colored People (NAACP), refused to give up her seat to a white passenger, Martin Luther King Jr., memorably declared that "the arc of the moral universe is long, but it bends towards justice." King would repeat the phrase, which was coined by the nineteenth-century theologian and abolitionist Theodore Parker, frequently in the years that followed, including at the culmination of the Selma to Montgomery marches that helped lead to the passage of the Voting Rights Act of 1965. King's words have become part of the heroic legacy of the civil rights movement—invoked often by President Barack Obama during his time in office, for example—and they seem to speak to the inevitability of the triumph of the freedom struggle in the United States during the 1950s and 1960s, part of the endless forward march of American democracy. Success was not preordained, however, and it is sometimes forgotten just how widespread and fierce the opposition to the civil rights movement was during this period, especially in the South.

This chapter examines this opposition—what is often called "massive resistance"—as it relates to the radical right. It addresses a range of right-wing organizations, including Citizens' Councils, the Ku Klux Klan, the National States' Rights Party, the John Birch Society, and George Wallace's American Independent Party, but it also considers the crucial role played by numerous local, state, and national politicians in supporting—and often initiating—this resistance. Indeed, the term "massive resistance" originated with the Democratic Virginia Senator Harry F. Byrd.

Attacking the Supreme Court's 1954 decision in *Brown v. Board of Education of Topeka*, the senator argued that "if we can organize the Southern States for massive resistance to this order, I think that in time the rest of the country will realize that racial integration is not going to be accepted in the South."

The chapter also builds upon the themes developed in the previous two chapters. For while white supremacy and racial prejudice certainly drove opposition to the civil rights movement, concerns around the intrusiveness—and basic unconstitutionality—of the federal government's attempt to "impose" racial equality in the South, as well as the supposed communist influence on the movement, were also frequently expressed. As we shall see, by 1968, the actions—and interactions—of the federal government, the civil rights movement, and massive resistance had transformed American society and American politics in fundamental ways. We begin, though, in 1946.

In early December of that year, in response to widespread brutal acts of violence against African Americans in the South and under increasing pressure from the NAACP and other civil rights activists to do something about it, Harry Truman established a President's Committee on Civil Rights (PCCR). Composed of fifteen members, including union leaders, clergymen, two white southerners—who were quickly accused of "selling out" the region—and two blacks, Channing H. Tobias and Sadie T. Alexander, it was chaired by Charles E. Wilson, the head of General Electric. Having comprehensively reviewed the state of American race relations, the committee's 173-page report, *To Secure These Rights*, was released the following October. The PCCR recommended the introduction of legislation to eliminate the practice of segregation and discrimination in areas of employment, housing, education, public transportation, health care, and the armed services. It called for the federal protection of voting rights, the creation of a Commission on Civil Rights, a permanent Fair Employment Practices Committee, and an end to police brutality and lynching. Truman endorsed almost all of the committee's proposals in a special message to Congress on February 2, 1948.

Truman's apparent commitment to the cause of civil rights represented a dramatic shift from the policies of his predecessors. Although in practice the administration was extremely slow in following up its supportive words with meaningful action, for the first time since Reconstruction, the federal government seemed prepared to directly challenge what was still euphemistically referred to as the "southern way of life." The Democratic Party also then adopted a liberal civil rights plank at its 1948 convention, a decision that prompted thirty-five delegates from Alabama and Mississippi to walk out of the Philadelphia Convention Hall in protest. (The South had been solidly Democratic ever since Abraham Lincoln's Republicans had defeated the Confederacy. Indeed, the region formed a crucial part of FDR's New Deal electoral coalition because of this.)

Four days later, on July 17, 1948, in Birmingham, Alabama, six thousand supporters of the third-party States' Rights Democratic Party—better known as the Dixiecrats—met to select their own candidate for the upcoming election, the South Carolina governor, Strom Thurmond. The Dixiecrats did not expect to win the presidency, it should be said; their aim was simply to draw enough votes in the South to deny Truman and his Republican opponent, Thomas E. Dewey, any outright victory in the Electoral College, thus turning over the results of the election to the House of Representatives.

Racial fears and notions of white supremacy obviously underpinned the movement. In Thurmond's infamous view, for example, there weren't "enough troops in the army to force the southern people to break down segregation and admit the nigger race into our theaters, into our swimming pools, into our homes, and into our churches." But as Thurmond's biographer, Joseph Crespino, has pointed out, the party also "represented the most significant opportunity to date for conservative economic forces in the region to consolidate an anti-New Deal constituency." As a result, its leading backers and leaders were drawn largely from the ranks of wealthy businessmen, corporate lawyers, bankers, oil company executives, and textile manufacturers: people like Ben Laney and John Daggert of the Arkansas Free Enterprise Association, the Alabama lawyer Gessner McCorvey, and the wealthy New Orleans industrialist John U. Barr. Equally prominent in leadership positions were state and regional politicians concerned about their authority and powers coming under threat from Washington. Certainly, it was no coincidence that it was two governors—Thurmond and Fielding L. Wright of Mississippi—who headed the States' Rights ticket.

As a result, themes of anti-statism and anti-communism, laissez-faire economics, and limited constitutional government were all significant features of the "Dixiecrat revolt." According to the official platform of the States' Rights Democrats, for example, their national counterparts "denounced totalitarianism abroad but unblushingly proposed and approved it at home." Thurmond accused Truman of trying to impose a "police state in this country," while Alabama governor Frank Dixon attacked the "the unholy alliance of left-wingers, pseudo-liberals and radicals of as many hues as Joseph's coat" set loose upon the nation.

In a surprising upset, Truman defeated Dewey by 24,179,345 votes to 21,991,291 (49.6 percent of the popular vote to 45.1 percent). Thurmond received 1,176,125 votes (2.4 percent), and Henry Wallace, Truman's former vice president, who was running as the left-wing Progressive Party candidate, received 1,157,326 (2.37 percent). Thurmond won only four states, South Carolina, Mississippi, Alabama, and Louisiana—all in the Deep South—receiving 39 Electoral College votes to Truman's 303 and Dewey's 189. Interestingly, given the political calculations that had helped make Truman supportive of black civil rights in the first place—continuing black migration from the South to the North after the end of the Second World War and the potential of African-American voters to "swing" critical elections—the president won two-thirds of the overall black vote, helping him to crucial victories in California, Ohio, and Illinois.

In an article for *Family Weekly* in 1976 titled "How it Feels to Run for President and Lose," Thurmond wrote: "If I had been elected president in 1948, history would be vastly different. I believe we would have stemmed the growth of Big Government, which had begun with the New Deal and culminated with [Lyndon Johnson's] Great Society." Be that as it may, and despite its overwhelming failure, the formation and activities of the States' Rights Party during this time—it limped on, absent Thurmond's involvement, until the early 1950s—set an important precedent for the radical right's resistance to the expansion of civil rights in the South, laying the groundwork for the much more extensive "massive resistance" that followed.

The spur for this massive resistance was the Supreme Court's landmark decision in *Brown v. the Board of Education of Topeka* in 1954. The culmination of the NAACP's legal assault on Jim Crow, the case had begun back in 1950 when the civil rights group had first filed lawsuits on behalf of black parents in Virginia, Delaware, South Carolina, Louisiana, Kansas, and the District of Columbia, seeking to have their children admitted to white schools. (Led by Thurgood Marshall, the NAACP had already successfully chipped away at some elements of the "separate but equal" doctrine of *Plessy v. Ferguson*—the 1896 legal decision that underpinned segregation—in cases such as *Sweatt v. Painter* [1950], *McLaurin v. Oklahoma State Regents for Higher Education* [1950], and *Henderson v. United States* [1950].) On May 17, 1954, the newly appointed chief justice, Earl Warren, who had worked tirelessly to bring about a unanimous verdict in the case, finally issued the Court's decision. "In the field of public education," he declared, "the doctrine of 'separate but equal' has no place. Separate educational facilities are inherently unequal." It was a stunning victory for the civil rights movement. The entire legal basis for Jim Crow rule had been overturned.

Initially, at least in some parts of the South, the Court's decision was accepted, certainly not with enthusiasm but resignedly and relatively calmly. "When the Supreme Court speaks, that's the law," stated "Big" Jim Folsom, the governor of Alabama, for example, while Governor Frances Cherry of Arkansas promised that his state would "obey the law" just as it "always" had. "Segregation has been ruled out," the *Greensboro Daily News* soberly informed its readers, "and the responsibility now is to readjust to that reality," as numerous cities, especially in the Border States, began drawing up plans on how to go about desegregating their school districts.

Yet within short order, a fierce and frequently violent "white backlash" to *Brown*—and later to the broader civil rights movement—with thousands of participants, encompassing hundreds of new grassroots organizations, and involving political elites from the local to the state to the national level, swept first across the whole of the South before moving into northern states as well. In part this was a result of the failings of the Supreme Court. In order to obtain unanimity, Warren had agreed to the delay of its implementation ruling for an entire year, and when this was eventually handed down—on May 31, 1955, in a decision known as *Brown II*—it was vague and indecisive. Desegregation of the nation's school systems should be "prompt and reasonable," taking place with "all deliberate speed," the Court said, but no actual deadline was set; and much of the practicality of the process was deferred back to the federal district courts to determine. Because of this, *Brown II* provided an almost open invitation to committed segregationists for delay, inaction, and resistance.

But it also reflected the basic constitutional fact that the Supreme Court has few substantive enforcement powers of its own and is therefore forced to depend on the legislative and executive branches of government to support and implement its decisions. The nation's chief executive, President Dwight D. Eisenhower, made no real attempt to provide this support—primarily because he wasn't in agreement with the Court's position in the first place. Regarding the appointment of Warren as the "biggest damn fool mistake" he had ever made, Eisenhower tried to persuade the errant chief justice that all the opponents of desegregation were really concerned about was "to see that their sweet little girls are not required to sit in schools alongside some big overgrown Negroes." At root Eisenhower simply did not believe that the federal government should be "interfering" with the activities of the states in this way. "The Supreme Court decision [in *Brown*] set back progress in the South at least fifteen years," he informed one of his aides, and the "fellow who tries to tell me that you can do these things by force is just plain nuts."

Citizens' Councils were at the very forefront of the massive resistance to *Brown*. Inspiration for the formation of the Councils came from a Mississippi circuit court judge called Tom P. Brady. The former Dixiecrat had first attacked the Supreme Court's decision in a fiery address to the Greenwood chapter of the Sons of the American Revolution, which was expanded, published, and widely circulated as a ninety-page booklet called *Black Monday*. (The title was a reference to the day of the week *Brown* was decided, which Brady had borrowed from U.S. Representative John Bell Williams [D-MS]. The Court had driven "a knife into the heart of the U.S. Constitution," in Williams's view.) Forced now to choose between "SEGREGATION AND AMALGAMATION," Judge Brady called for the immediate creation, across the South, of "law abiding" resistance groups that would both defy the Supreme Court's ruling and spread "correct information" about the "imminent dangers" facing the nation.

The first person to translate Brady's words into action was Robert "Tut" Patterson, a Mississippi plantation manager. With the support of other prominent local figures, including the town's mayor and city attorney, Paterson established the inaugural Citizens' Council in Indianola, Mississippi, in July 1954. Thereafter, he and his fellow Councillors set out on a remarkably successful proselytizing mission to spread both Brady's message and the "Indianola Plan" across the rest of the South. Within two years Citizens' Councils could boast membership in the region of 250,000. The Councils were strongest in Mississippi, Alabama, Louisiana, South Carolina, and Virginia, especially within the "black belt"—those areas of the South where the white minority lived most closely with the black majority—but they operated in every southern state. Most of the organizations called themselves Citizens' Councils, although some preferred more distinguishing nomenclature: the Patrick Henry Group of Richmond, the Paul Revere Associated Yeoman of New Orleans, the Birmingham-based American States Rights Association, Louisiana's Southern Gentlemen, the Patriots of North Carolina, for example.

For the most part the Councils were composed of lawyers, doctors, farmers, businessmen, school teachers, and politicians, the economic and civic leaders of their local communities, people who went to great pains to emphasize their supposed respectability and reasonableness, deploring violence—at least publicly—and seeking to distinguish their activities from those of the Ku Klux Klan and other, more virulent and disreputable racists. This provided the Councils with an influence even beyond their impressive membership numbers, especially when it came to the policing of any potential dissent to their politics from within the white community itself. "Their ranks were the 'Jesuits' of the white supremacy creed, the cadres of massive resistance," as historian Numan V. Bartley puts it.

Heeding Brady's recommendation, much of the activity of the Councils was directed toward the "education" of their fellow citizens. Indeed, they unleashed a veritable tsunami of propaganda material on the South, including millions of pamphlets, tracts, posters, cartoons, newspapers, and booklets—"offensive by duplicating machine," as the *Delta-Democrat Times* of Greenville, Mississippi, described it—created radio and television programs; and sponsored speeches and other public forums, all in fervent and righteous support of the segregationist cause. In addition, Councillors and their allies initiated and helped to sustain economic boycotts against civil rights activists, directly suppressed the activities of the NAACP, limited African Americans' access to the ballot box, and supported the myriad attempts of state legislatures to prevent the implementation of *Brown*, as discussed in more detail below.

It's important to point out, though, that while the Citizens' Councils movement was frequently the driving force behind the South's resistance to desegregation, it was, at times, also a reactive one. There were significant bursts of activity and accompanying increases in Council membership after the initial *Brown* decision; again after *Brown II*—especially when the NAACP began the process of individually petitioning local school boards for integration—then again in the wake of the 1955 Montgomery bus boycott, the event that first brought Martin Luther King Jr. to widespread national attention; and following the riots that accompanied Autherine Lucy's attempts to become to the first African-American student to attend the University of Alabama in 1956, for example. But in between such high-profile events, when the Citizens' Councils had nothing so immediate to resist against or feel threatened by, there would often be lulls, and during such times, much to the consternation of the movement's leadership, interest would flag, finances declined, and new members became more difficult to recruit.

Despite their genuine grassroots nature, contributing considerably to the significance and strength of the Citizens' Councils was the extent to which they were supported by, and closely entwined with, the local and state political establishment; an interconnection that, according to sociologist Sara Diamond, meant the Councils in many respects functioned "as agents of a racist southern state apparatus" during the mid-1950s and early 1960s. This was particularly evident in Mississippi, especially after the election of long-standing Council member Ross R. Barnett to the governorship in 1960. Indeed, in the acerbic view of one contemporary observer, Leslie Dunbar, Barnett's inauguration suggested that the Magnolia State was "experimenting with a Soviet style government, with the Citizens' Council paralleling the state machine in emulation of a successful Communist Party."

At the national level, no member of the formidable congressional Southern Caucus actually joined a Citizens' Council, but this didn't indicate a lack of support from the South's senators and congressmen. Far from it. The now Democratic Senator Strom Thurmond of South Carolina, for example, encouraged all Council members to "have the intestinal fortitude to fight for the rights that are guaranteed them under the Constitution of the United States." During a rally in Montgomery, on February 9, 1956, at the height of the bus boycott in the city, Senator James O. Eastland (D-MS)—the very "Voice of the South," according to the

Citizens' Councils' own advertisements—told a cheering crowd of fifteen thousand that they were not required to obey the Supreme Court's ruling in *Brown* but instead were "obligated to defy it." A month later, on March 13, 1956, came the Caucus's Declaration of Constitutional Principles.

The Southern Manifesto, as it was better known, was signed by 19 of the region's 22 senators and by 82 of its 106 representatives. (The three senators who didn't sign were Estes Kafauver and Albert Gore Sr., both of Tennessee, and the senate majority leader, Lyndon Baines Johnson of Texas. All three were relatively liberal and also harbored hopes for the presidency.) Standing full-square behind both massive resistance and the efforts of the Citizens' Councils to enact it, the Manifesto attacked the "unwarranted decision of the Supreme Court" in *Brown* as a "clear abuse of judicial power."

Promising to "use all lawful means to bring about a reversal of this decision . . . and to prevent the use of force in its implementation," the Declaration accused the federal government of being intent on "destroying the amicable relations between the white and Negro races that have been created through 90 years of patient effort by the good people of both races." It also appealed "to the states and people who are not directly affected by these decisions to consider the constitutional principles involved against the time when they too, on issues vital to them, may be victims of judicial encroachment." Although some scholars have cast doubt on the significance of the Manifesto, seeing it as more symbolically than substantively important, for John Kyle Dyle, not only did it give "state and local intransigent segregationists the political cover to . . . stifle the civil rights movement within their communities across the South," but the "complete implementation of desegregation was effectively halted for years, as was meaningful federal civil rights legislation" as a result of its promulgation and support.

Despite the creation of would-be coordinating groups such as the Federation of Constitutional Government in July 1955 and the Citizens' Councils of America (CCA) in April 1956, the Citizens' Councils remained a fundamentally decentralized movement. As a result, as Neil McMillen has pointed out, it never developed "a systematic intellectual framework in which to operate." The justifications that were provided for the continuation of segregation—as well as the manner and style in which such arguments were made—varied according to the Citizens' Council that was making them; the part of the South from which they came; and the composition, experiences, and capabilities of their members. This same range of approaches was also evident in the rationalizations about Jim Crow that came from the region's elected representatives, whether at the local, state, or national level. Much also depended on the audiences that were being addressed, whether within the South or without, and whether they were sympathetic, skeptical, or outright hostile. Some appeals were crudely racist and populist in nature; others were sophisticated and more elite-oriented. Nonetheless, overall, from grassroots activists to the halls of Congress, three broad sets of argument against desegregation and in support of massive resistance can be identified.

The first of these centered on whites' supposed racial superiority to blacks, and hence the necessity of keeping the existing separation of the races firmly in place. Biological, historical, religious, sociological, and scientific "evidence" was variously deployed in support of this proposition. The CCA's official handbook for fifth and sixth graders explained the essential differences between the brain weights, eyes, lips, hair, skulls, ears, jaw shape, and noses of the two races, for example. Judge Brady's *Black Monday* booklet—the Citizens' Councils first official handbook—opined:

> You can dress a chimpanzee, housebreak him, and teach him to use a knife and fork, but it will take countless generations of evolutionary development, if ever, before you can convince him that a caterpillar or a cockroach is not a delicacy. Likewise, the social political, economic, and religious preferences of the Negro remain close to the caterpillar and the cockroach.

Disputing the "equalitarian dogma of modern science" in book called *Race and Reason* (1961), Carleton Putnam, a retired Delta Air Lines executive, made the case that "any man with two eyes in his head can observe a Negro settlement in the Congo . . . can compare this settlement with London or Paris, and can draw his own conclusions regarding relative levels of character and intelligence." The book sold 150,000 copies by 1969, including to Louisiana's State Board of Education for distribution to its school children. In Mississippi, Governor Barnett declared October 26, 1961, to be "Race and Reason Day." "The races of man are the handiwork of God, as is everything in nature," maintained a Mississippi Citizens' Council pamphlet. "If He had wanted only one type of Man, He would have created only one."

The second set of arguments in support of the South's resistance invoked a range of constitutional, states' rights, and limited government positions—some more novel than others—that rejected not just the specific reasoning behind *Brown* but judicial activism and the increasing centralization of government powers in Washington more generally. "May I say to you that when any court takes leave of the law and starts rendering edicts based on sociology, it is high time for all Americans to wake up," Williams J. Simmons, editor of the monthly newspaper *The Citizens' Council*, informed a Farmers-Merchants banquet in Oakland, Iowa, in February 1958:

> If any court can tell the people of Mississippi or Louisiana that they shall run their public schools according to the theories of certain social revolutionaries, then the court can tell the people of Iowa or Nebraska that they shall run *their* schools according to notions equally as radical. If our States' Rights are usurped with impunity, are yours safe?

What Simmons was referring to in his Iowa address was also what had led Senator Richard Russell Jr. (D-GA) and the other drafters of the Southern Manifesto to denounce *Brown* as an abuse of judicial power, which was the Supreme Court's use, in part, of sociological and psychological evidence—especially the work of E. Franklin Frazier, Kenneth Clark, and Gunnar Myrdal—to justify its finding that segregation created a permanent sense of inferiority and stigma in black children, thereby apparently allowing it to simply disregard several decades worth of legal precedent in the area. To the proponents of massive resistance, Warren's attempt to use the Court to promote "social justice" in this way was nothing more than "judicial tyranny."

The old legal notion of interposition was also resurrected. Drawing heavily on Thomas Jefferson, James Madison, John C. Calhoun, and other pre–Civil War thinkers, proponents of the theory maintained that each state possessed the right to "interpose" between its populace and the federal government when the state determined that its citizens' rights as guaranteed by the U.S. Constitution were being infringed. As one of its key promoters, James Jackson Kilpatrick, the editor of the *Richmond News Leader*, explained:

> This right rests in the incontrovertible theory that ours is a Union of sovereign States; that the Federal Government exists only by reason of a solemn compact among the States; that each respective State is a co-equal party to this compact; that if the compact is violated by the Federal Government, every State has a right to judge of the infraction; and that when an issue of contested power arises, only the States themselves, by constitutional process, may finally decide the issue.

Essentially, this meant that the states could simply refuse to implement a federal law when a majority of its (white) citizens disagreed with it. Not surprisingly, the Citizens' Councils and other defenders of segregation embraced the theory with gusto. By 1957 eight southern states had passed formal resolutions of imposition—Virginia, Louisiana, South Carolina, Arkansas, Alabama, Mississippi, Florida, and Georgia—while others such as Texas, Tennessee, and North Carolina simply expressed "support" for the doctrine.

The third set of arguments intended to resist *Brown* drew on anti-communism and the contemporary tensions of the cold war. *Is the Supreme Court Pro-Communist?* asked one widely distributed Citizens' Council pamphlet, authored by Senator Eastland, who as chairman of both the Senate Judiciary Committee and the Senate Internal Security Subcommittee was presumably well-placed to answer the question with a resounding "yes." Nor was the Supreme Court alone in the apparent attempt to "Sovietize the South." In another heavily promoted Council broadside, *The Ugly Truth About the NAACP*, Georgia attorney general Eugene Cook outlined how the civil rights group had "allowed itself to become part and parcel of the Communist conspiracy to overthrow the democratic governments of this nation and its sovereign states." The official motto of the Oklahoma Citizens' Council made things abundantly clear: "Our White Christian Civilization is the only barrier between Soviet Dictators and World Conquest," it maintained.

As George Lewis has pointed out, embracing conspiratorial anti-communism had a number of advantages for the proponents of segregation, allowing them to recast some of their older, more traditional arguments in a "new light" and "transforming what was perceived to be, in essence, a southern sectional problem of race relations into an American problem of national security." (From a different perspective, another historian, Mary Dudziak, has shown how the Cold War and national security concerns also put pressure on successive U.S. administrations to end segregation, lest the Soviet Union continue to "embarrass" the United States over the issue on the world stage.) It also allowed segregationists, especially those in the Deep South, to continue to perpetuate their much-cherished myth of the "contented Negro" and to blame all the racial unrest in the region on the work of "outside agitators."

Interposition may have been a legal and constitutional fiction—effectively allowing the South to relitigate if not actually refight the Civil War—but it was a very useful one. Not only did it permit states to declare *Brown* to be "null and void, and of no effect"—as many did—it also enabled them to pass a vast array of additional legislation to resist desegregation and fight the civil rights movement. This was obviously crucial. Argument and propaganda were one thing, meaningful action quite another.

With specific respect to *Brown*, for example, "freedom of choice" laws were passed to allow parents to select for themselves the school their children would attend, thereby creating a system of "voluntary segregation"; "pupil placement" laws empowered local school officials to decide where children would be educated not on the basis of race, but according to new criteria such as "the general welfare" (but of course the effect was the same); while other laws prevented the spending of any public monies on integrated schools. The states provided tuition grants to help white school children attend private schools, denied licenses to teachers who advocated for integration or fired them, and even authorized governors and local school boards to close down their public schools rather than integrate them. But the legislative onslaught went beyond the school system. A 1956 Louisiana law prohibited "all interracial dancing, social functions, entertainments, athletic training, games, sports or contests and other such activities." The same year, a Mississippi statute attempted to outlaw all dissent of any kind, making it illegal within the state—and punishable by a $1,000 fine and six months in prison—"to solicit, advocate, urge or encourage disobedience to any law of the State of Mississippi," as well as its "established traditions, customs, and usages."

The legal assault on the NAACP was particularly effective. Throughout the South, laws were passed banning public employees from belonging to the organization; governors were granted emergency powers to halt its activities; and various committees were established to investigate it, hunting for evidence of criminal law violations, tax evasion, and of course, communist infiltration such as Florida's Legislative Investigative Committee, Arkansas's State Sovereignty Committee, and Virginia's Legislative Committee on Offenses Against the Administration of Justice. Five states also passed laws requiring the NAACP to register and provide its membership lists to state authorities. As the historian Adam Fairclough has noted, this put the NAACP in an extremely invidious position. If the organization complied with the law and handed over its lists, as the NAACP did in Louisiana, then it lost most of its members "for the Citizens' Councils immediately published the lists, inviting whites to fire, boycott and intimidate those whose names appeared." But if it refused, as the NAACP did in Alabama, it would be found in contempt of court and banned from operating altogether (the organization was put out of action in the state from 1956 to 1964). Overall, between 1955 and 1957, NAACP membership in the South dropped from 128,000 to 80,000, as almost 250 branches were shut down; in Louisiana, membership fell from 13,190 to 1,698, following the disclosure of its lists, and 58 of its 65 branches ceased to operate.

Then there was violence. This had always been a crucial component of the maintenance of white supremacy in the South, but perhaps not surprisingly there was a noticeable increase in its deployment after the *Brown* decisions. In fact, of the eleven documented lynchings of African Americans that took place during the 1950s, eight happened in 1955. One of the most shocking occurred on August 28, 1955, in Money, Mississippi, when a fourteen-year-old boy called Emmett Till, who was visiting his relatives in the area, was brutally murdered by two white men, Roy Bryant and John Milam. Till's "crime" had been whistling at a white woman—Bryant's wife—in a grocery store. Recovered from the Tallahatchie River, where it had been dumped after been bound with barbed wire and tied to a cotton gin fan, Till's badly disfigured body was shipped back home to Chicago, where Till's mother, Mamie Bradley, insisted that it be displayed in an open casket. "There was just no way I could describe what was in that box. No way. And I just wanted the world to see," Bradley explained. In September 1955, an all-white jury acquitted Bryant and Milam of Till's kidnapping and murder. (The two men confessed to the murder in an interview with *Look* magazine in 1956. In 2017 Bryant's wife, Carolyn, finally revealed that Till had never made any physical or verbal advances toward her, as she had alleged back in 1955.)

Although much diminished in comparison to the 1860s and 1920s, the Ku Klux Klan also underwent a revival in the wake of *Brown*. One of the first post-*Brown* Klan rallies took place in Sumter County, South Carolina, in June 1955, and within three years there were almost forty thousand Klansmen operating across the South, albeit in twenty-seven different—and highly antagonistic—factions, including the Gulf Ku Klux Klan, Knights of the Ku Klux Klan of the Confederacy, the Association of the Alabama Knights of the Ku Klux Klan, the Independent Knights of the Ku Klux Klan, the Original Ku Klux Klan of the Confederacy, and so on. There were so many different groups in operation that William J. Griffin, Dragon of the Associated Florida Klans, admitted that the "old countersigns and passwords" no longer worked; "Klansmen are strangers to each other," he lamented. This didn't prevent individual groups or individual Klansmen from perpetrating numerous acts of violence in defense of white supremacy, however.

The Southern Regional Council, an Atlanta-based civil rights agency, documented 530 cases of suspected Klan violence between 1955 and 1959. In January 1957, following the success of the Montgomery bus boycott, the Klan bombed four black churches and several black homes in the city. It set off another twenty-seven bombs across the South in 1959, and its acts of violence continued on into the 1960s. On September 15, 1963, four Klansmen exploded a bomb at the 16th Street Baptist Church in Birmingham, Alabama, which killed four young girls and injured twenty-two others. Speaking at the girls' funeral, Martin Luther King told the assembled crowd that these "unoffending, innocent and beautiful children"—Addie Mae Collins, Cynthia Wesley, Carole Robertson, and Carol Denise McNair—were "the victims of one of the most vicious and tragic crimes ever perpetuated against humanity." In 1964 Klansmen shot and killed Lemuel A. Penn, a black school administrator from Washington, D.C., as he drove through Georgia on his return from Army Reserve duty at Fort Benning. That same year three young civil rights workers—Michael H. Schwerner, aged twenty-three; Andrew Goodman, aged twenty; and James E. Chaney, aged twenty-one—were murdered by the Klan in Mississippi during a Freedom Summer project designed to help register black voters in the area.

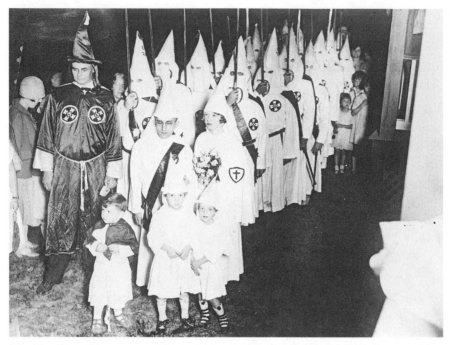

The Ku Klux Klan renewed its activities during the 1950s and 1960s in opposition to the civil rights movement and desegregation, although this "third Klan" was never as large, extensive, or respectable as it was during its second incarnation during the 1920s (pictured here). Library of Congress Prints & Photographs Division. LC-DIG-npcc-27617.

Other far-right extremists were also willing to engage in violence in defense of Jim Crow. The most notable of these was J. B. Stoner, "perhaps the most violently fanatical racist spawned by massive resistance," in the view of historian Clive Webb. Stoner was born into a well-to-do family in La Fayette, Georgia, in 1924. He attended the exclusive McCallie School in Chattanooga and became a lawyer. But his real passion was for politics, especially racist politics. In 1942, aged just eighteen, he rechartered a dormant chapter of the Klan in Chattanooga—the polio Stoner had contracted as a two-year-old, which left him with a lifelong limp, kept him out of service during the Second World War. He became an avid supporter of the rabidly racist Senator Theodore G. Bilbo of Mississippi, and he also attended the inaugural meeting of the States' Rights Democratic Party in 1948. Stoner was also a virulent anti-Semite. In another version of the "outside agitator" theory, he regarded Jews as being the "real masterminds" behind the civil rights movement because blacks lacked the intelligence and enterprise to challenge white supremacy themselves. "Of course, the niggers want it," he stated, "but they don't have the brains or the power to do it."

Having been thrown out of a number of Klaverns for his "extremist" views, in August 1958 Stoner helped found a new organization, the National States' Rights Party (NSRP), based first in Jeffersonville, Indiana, and then in Birmingham, Alabama. Like the quasi-fascist groups prevalent in 1930s (discussed in chapter 1), which in many ways it resembled, the NSRP was organized along military lines. Members were supposed to wear a uniform of white shirt and black trousers, a black tie, and an armband displaying the party emblem, a thunderbolt over a Confederate battle flag. While many of its leaders were, like Stoner, from the professional middle classes, the party aimed its recruitment activities at blue-collar workers, disaffected union members, and rural and small-town youth. By 1963, the NSRP claimed to have thirty-six chapters in thirteen states, although external estimates suggest that overall party membership never exceeded five hundred people. Yet, as Clive Webb has pointed out, the influence of the NSRP was much greater than its small number of members suggests. By the late sixties, its newsletter, *The Thunderbolt*, had a circulation of twenty-five thousand, "the largest readership of any far-right publication in the United States," for example, and its "use of direct action tactics ensured that the NSRP had an impact on the political scene out of all proportion to the actual number of its members."

Like other segregationist organizations, the NSRP invoked a range of religious, biological, historical, political, and constitutional arguments to justify its position. In particular, the party portrayed itself as patriotic inheritors of the ideals of the founding fathers, defending states' rights as one of the defining features of American governance, with Stoner riding across the South like some latter-day Paul Revere "awakening and uniting our people" (in the words of the September 1965 issue of *The Thunderbolt*). Five members of the NSRP were indicted for the October 1958 bombing of Hebrew Benevolent Congregation Temple in Atlanta, Georgia—with dynamite believed to have been supplied by Stoner—but juries twice cleared them. In 1977 Stoner himself was charged with another violent attack, the 1958 bombing of the Bethel Baptist Church in Birmingham. Convicted in 1980, he was sentenced, after an exhaustive appeals process, to ten years in prison in 1983. He served three and a half years. Following his parole, Stoner ran for lieutenant governor of Georgia in 1990, receiving thirty thousand votes, 3 percent of the total.

While the Citizens' Councils formally eschewed such extremism and violence, they gave these practices at least tacit endorsement by failing to work actively against them. All segregationists shared the same ultimate goal, after all: the continued subjugation of black Americans. Indeed, in the view of liberal journalists like Atlanta's Ralph McGill and Greenville's Hodding Carter, the Councils were best understood as "a scrubbed up cousin of the Klan," "a hoodless Klan," "an uptown Klan," or a "country-club Klan." The historian Wyn Craig Wade also makes the point that while the Councillors certainly saw themselves as the elite of militant segregationists, an important knock-on effect of their organizational structure was to leave the Klan "nothing but the violent-prone dregs of Southern white society." Furthermore, not only did the Klan and the Councils work in unofficial tandem, but each provided support to, and were in turn supported by, the racist southern power structure. The states often simply refused to prosecute those who committed acts of violence against civil rights workers, for example, and even when they did, southern juries rarely convicted the "alleged" perpetrators, especially in the Deep South. The activities of federal agents in the region were routinely blocked as well. "Invariably, when atrocious acts of violence break out we run into an iron curtain of silence," J. Edgar Hoover informed President Eisenhower when he asked the FBI director about the problem. "The difficulties which our agents face at times are almost indescribable," he confessed.

Eisenhower was finally, although very reluctantly, compelled to use the federal government's powers to check the forces of massive resistance by the crisis that erupted at the Central High School in Little Rock, Arkansas, during the summer and fall of 1957. Revealing hitherto untapped demagogic skills, the governor of Arkansas, Orval Faubus, precipitated the crisis when he ordered troops from the state National Guard to prevent nine black children who had been assigned to Central High from entering the school. Faubus had a previous reputation as a moderate on racial issues, but he was in a close battle for reelection and also under significant pressure from grassroots groups such as the Capital Citizens' Council and the Mothers' League to prevent desegregation from taking place. For three weeks the children were stopped from attending school by the Guard, as angry mobs of whites hurled racial abuse at them. In an attempt to defuse the situation, Eisenhower met with Faubus at his summer retreat in Rhode Island, extracting a promise from the governor that he would cause no further problems. Reneging on the deal, however, Faubus withdrew the National Guard troops, with the result that on Monday, September 23, when the children were finally able to take their places at Central High, large-scale violence seemed the likely result. To prevent this, Eisenhower federalized the Arkansas National Guard and dispatched 1,100 army paratroopers into Little Rock. The paratroopers stayed until November, the now federalized guardsmen for the whole of the school year.

It was not a sudden conversion to the cause of civil rights that had motivated Eisenhower to act. Faubus's "insubordination" had offended his military sense of honor, the events at Little Rock were causing embarrassment to the United States around the world, and, above all, the president recognized the fundamental constitutional issues that were at stake. To not have acted, he said, would have been to "tantamount to acquiescence in anarchy and the disillusion of the union." Nor, to be sure, did Eisenhower's intervention represent an unalloyed victory for the civil rights movement—Faubus closed all the schools in the city for the 1958–1959 academic year rather than implement their desegregation, and he won his reelection in 1958 and then again for three more terms after that—but it was a significant step nonetheless: the first time since Reconstruction that federal troops had entered the South in order to protect the civil rights of African Americans.

This assertion of federal authority was also evident in the passage of the Civil Rights Acts of 1957 and 1960. The laws were modest, both in terms of their scope and in their actual impact: the 1957 Act created a Civil Rights Commission with powers of subpoena and a civil rights division within the Justice Department; the 1960 Act authorized federal courts to appoint voting referees to help blacks register and introduced penalties for anyone who obstructed voter registration. But they laid the groundwork for future legislation and also clearly signaled the extent of the powers available to the federal government, should it choose—or should it be compelled—to use them. Much to the alarm of the segregationists, as well as to opponents of big government more generally, the process Truman had begun in 1948 was now a lot closer to being real-ized, as the whole issue of black civil rights moved toward the very center of American political life.

The most important factor in achieving this shift of emphasis—so that civil rights and racial equality were regarded as significant issues of national concern, rather than some purely regional consideration—was the actions of civil rights activists themselves. The next phase of the civil rights movement began on February 1, 1960, when four freshmen from North Carolina A&T College in Greensboro, North Carolina—Ezell Blair Jr., David Richmond, Franklin McCain, and Joseph McNeil—organized a sit-in at the segregated lunch counter of their local Woolworth department store. Their protest grew like wildfire. Within two months, fifty-four sit-ins were taking place in fifteen cities across nine southern states, and within the year they had spread out to the rest of the South and even into some northern states. In total, it is estimated that seventy thousand people, many of them young black students, took part in these demonstrations, challenging segregation not just at lunch counters and restaurants, but also at parks, churches, swimming pools, beaches, libraries, and other facilities. The cost could be high. The protestors were met with frequent acts of violence and abuse, and many were jailed—approximately 3,600 in 1960–1961 alone. Out of the experience also came a new civil rights organization, the Student Nonviolent Coordinating Committee (SNCC).

The sit-ins were followed by the "freedom rides," which were largely prompted by the fact that the Supreme Court and other federal courts continued to rule in favor of desegregation and against the various obstructionist measures of southern legislatures attempting to avoid or delay the process. Organized by James Farmer and other members of the Congress of Racial Equality (CORE), the plan was for activists, white and black, to travel on buses into the South to test whether interstate bus facilities had actually been desegregated as the Supreme Court had ruled they should be in *Boynton v. Virginia* (1960). As they had anticipated, the "freedom riders" were met with violence. In Anniston, Alabama, for example, a mob of whites slashed the tires of the bus, smashed its windows, and fire bombed it, as the police stood idly by. In Birmingham, Klansmen beat the protestors with impunity. But the rides continued. Volunteers from SNCC joined those from CORE, and after a year of intense struggle, the Interstate Commerce Commission finally prohibited all interstate bus and railroad companies from using segregated transport facilities.

Not all civil rights protests were successful, however. For instance, the massive, almost year-long protests in Albany, Georgia, that took place between October 1961 and August 1962, involving the combined forces of the NACCP, SNCC, the Southern Christian Leadership Conference (SCLC), and thousands of local people, left the city just as deeply segregated when they ended as when they had begun. Tensions were also increasingly evident within the civil rights movement itself, over issues of class, generation, race—as more and more white students got involved in the "freedom struggle"—and also about the methods that were best suited to bring about equality in American society. Nonetheless, considerable progress was certainly being made. Thanks in large part to the extraordinary courage, dedication, and sacrifice of ordinary black Americans, the civil rights issue was finally becoming the focal point of the nation's politics, just as the leaders of the movement had set out to make it.

Other elements of the radical right also had to contend with these developments, including the movement's standard-bearer, the John Birch Society (JBS). Not surprisingly, the Birchers tended to regard the activities of the civil rights movement largely through their already firmly established conspiratorial gaze, as well as their deeply rooted antipathy to the over-reaching powers of big government, as discussed in the previous chapter. Echoing some of the central strands of the pro-segregationist position, the Society denounced the malign hand of communism at work behind the civil rights movement, campaigned tirelessly for the impeachment of Earl Warren, and defended the fundamental constitutional principle of states' rights. (Warren, in the view of JBS Founder, Robert Welch, epitomized "the newborn theory that our Constitution means absolutely nothing against the changing sociological views of the Supreme Court Justices of any given decade or generation; that both our Constitution and our laws are simply whatever the Supreme Court says they are.") But the Birch Society did not officially peddle racism; actually welcomed African Americans into its ranks (although black Birchers were certainly few in number), with integrated chapters in the North and segregated ones in the South; and strove to keep racists and anti-Semites out of the organization (which is not to say that such people did not find their way in). This was the position of Reverend Billy James Hargis's Christian Crusade as well. His organization would not tolerate anti-Semitic statements or anti-Negro statements, he told the *Saturday Evening Post* in September 1962. "We are not here to fight Jews . . . or Negroes," he explained. "We are here to fight Communists."

Joseph Mitchell, one of the Citizens' Councils of America's field directors, argued that "our philosophy is the same of the John Birch Society, but the Birch Society refuses to deal with race issues." The mutual anti-statism and conspiratorial inclinations of the two movements is certainly captured in the view of the Association of Citizens' Councils of Louisiana, expressed in the early sixties that "[t]he wheel of federal oppression has many spokes. Beginning with a slow roll in the thirties, it gathered speed and power through the forties and fifties. It now threatens to wipe out the individual will to resist and to grind us as grist for a greedy, socialist-minded dictatorship in Washington." As a result, Councillors and Birchers often found themselves able to cooperate in areas of mutual interest to them. Indeed, as the historian Neil McMillen has noted, many of the CCA's top leaders—including William Simmons; Medford Evans, the managing editor of its official journal; and Louis W. Hollis, its national director—were Birchers, as was Frank Purinton, who headed the New York Citizens' Council, and Kent H. Steffgen, the CCA's first field director for California.

Another person who straddled both these worlds was Major General Edwin A. Walker. A member of the Birch Society since 1959, Walker was also the commander of the Twenty-Fourth Infantry Division, based in Augsburg, Germany. In early 1961, he became embroiled in a high-profile political scandal for allegedly attempting to indoctrinate the troops under his command with JBS material as part of a military education program called "Pro-Blue." Walker was officially "admonished" for his activities and resigned from the army in November. The following February, Walker announced his intention to run for the governorship of Texas, his home state. Campaigning largely on an anti-communist and anti-integration platform—although with an added dose of nationalistic hostility to the United Nations thrown into the mix—he was soundly defeated, finishing dead last in the Democratic primary, with only 134,000 of the 1,400,000 votes cast. Walker resurfaced in Oxford, Mississippi, in September 1962, along with thousands of other protestors, aiming to prevent the admission of African-American student James

Meredith to the University of Mississippi. Two people died and 375 were injured in the ensuing rioting, while Walker was arrested and charged with insurrection and sedition.

The events at Ole Miss played out in an uncanny replication of those at Little Rock five years before. Once again a U.S. president—this time John F. Kennedy—had tried to strike a deal with an obstructionist state governor—this time Ross Barnett. Once again the governor reneged on the deal that had been reached. And once again a state's National Guard had to be federalized—and federal marshals and the U.S. Army dispatched to the area—in order to try to maintain law and order. What's more, in an ironic twist of fate, Walker had actually been the commander of the 101st Airborne Division dispatched by Eisenhower to Arkansas in 1957. ("We are all subject to the laws, whether we approve of them or not," Walker had soberly informed the white students of Central High at the time. "If it were not otherwise, we would not be a strong nation, but a mere unruly mob.") The charges against Walker were eventually dropped, but the former major general emerged from the riot as a heroic figure to the segregationist right. He was given a standing ovation by the Mississippi State House of Representatives in December 1962, for example, and the following year he was invited to address the leadership conference of the CCA that was being held in Jackson, Mississippi. In addition, southern state politicians, the JBS, and the radical right more broadly denounced what was widely portrayed as the "invasion" of Mississippi and the abuses of federal power it was taken to represent.

In 1963 Martin Luther King, working in concert with other civil rights groups, including Fred Shuttlesworth's Alabama Christian Movement for Human Rights, staged a series of massive protests in Birmingham, Alabama, still one of the most segregated cities in the South. In the face of sickening and widespread violence, much of it coordinated by the city's public safety commissioner, Eugene T. "Bull" Connor, and in the full glare of the nation's media, protestors undertook a whole range of sit-ins, boycotts, marches, and mass demonstrations. It was the final spur that was needed to force the Kennedy administration to act. In a nationally televised address on June 11, the president announced that he would be introducing a new civil rights bill to Congress. Among other things, the bill included provisions for desegregating public accommodations such as hotels, restaurants, and shops and empowered the attorney general to initiate school-desegregation lawsuits.

Kennedy would not live to see the legislation enacted, however. Indeed, the bill was effectively stymied in Congress before his assassination on November 22, 1963. Arguing that no "memorial oration or eulogy could more eloquently honor President Kennedy's memory than the earliest possible passage of the Civil Rights Bill for which he fought so long," it was Lyndon Johnson who secured the successful passage of the bill, signing it into law on July 2, 1964. The following year, on August 2, after another series of civil rights protests, including the dramatic and violent confrontations that took place in Selma, Alabama—and despite extensive filibustering in the Senate—a new Voting Rights Act was also signed into law. The act outlawed various devices such as literacy and constitutional interpretation tests, which had been widely used to discriminate against blacks in the South, and also authorized federal officials to register qualified voters directly.

Johnson's Republican opponent in the 1964 presidential election was the Arizona senator Barry Goldwater. Despite being a member of the NAACP, Goldwater was one of only five senators from outside of the South to vote against the Civil Rights Act. He did so, he insisted, not because of racism but because of his fervent belief in the sanctity of states' rights, limited government, and "freedom of association." Not surprisingly, the Arizonian was a firm favorite of the segregationist right, the broader radical right—especially the JBS, with which he was closely identified throughout the 1964 campaign—and the whole nascent conservative movement of the early sixties; he was also fiercely anti-communist and a committed free marketer, opposed to the graduated income tax, for example (the tax was "repugnant" to his "notions of justice," he said). The time had not yet arrived for the ascension of Goldwater's particular brand of conservatism, however—as we shall see in the following chapter, that would come later, during the 1980s, with the election of Ronald Reagan to the White House. In fact, Johnson won the presidency with a record 61 percent of the popular vote (43 million to Goldwater's 27 million) and 90 percent of the Electoral College (486 votes to 52). But among other things, the Goldwater campaign revealed just how much the civil rights struggle, *Brown*, massive resistance, and the "white backlash" was altering the American political landscape.

Goldwater won only six states in 1964. One was his home state of Arizona. The other five were Louisiana, Georgia, Alabama, Mississippi, and

and South Carolina—the very heart of Dixie. For the first time since the end of the Civil War, large numbers of white southerners had abandoned the Democratic Party to vote for a Republican candidate for the presidency, thereby making a significant crack in both the "Solid South" and FDR's New Deal electoral coalition. Seeing the writing on the wall, Goldwater had advised Republican activists back in 1961 that "we're not going to get the Negro vote as a bloc in 1964 and 1968, so we ought to go hunting where the ducks are." This was an early articulation of what would became known as the GOP's "southern strategy," which is to say its attempt to win national elections by focusing on the white vote in the South by mobilizing whites' resentment at the gains being made by African Americans. Crucially, though, and especially after the passage of the Civil Rights and Voting Rights Acts, it was understood that this couldn't be achieved by making an explicit appeal to racism and white supremacy. Instead, a more coded form of appeal—what has been called "dog-whistle" politics—would have to be employed.

Members of the Ku Klux Klan support Barry Goldwater's campaign for the presidential nomination at the Republican National Convention in San Francisco, California, in 1964. Library of Congress Prints & Photographs Division, *U.S. News & World Report* Magazine Photograph Collection, LC-U9-12250M-13A.

Richard Nixon proved adept at this type of politics, and also demonstrated its increasing applicability in the North, during the next presidential campaign in 1968. Running against the liberal Democrat Hubert Humphrey and the former Alabama governor George Wallace, Nixon focused more on the Border States than the Deep South, assuming—correctly—that Wallace would win those. During the election, Nixon never formally renounced his past support for desegregation, but he also made it clear that he would not be rushing to carry out the mandates of the federal courts in the area. He fiercely attacked the "forced busing" of students across segregated neighborhoods, supported "freedom of choice" school plans, and above all else hammered away on "law and order" issues. He was speaking for the "forgotten Americans," he said, the "great silent majority," the "non-shouters, the non-demonstrators . . . those who do not break the law, people who pay their taxes and go to work." To be sure, Nixon was tapping into wider concerns about the Vietnam War, anti-war protestors, the rise of the counter-culture, urban unrest, rioting, and so on, but as the historian Dan T. Carter has written, "Almost every aspect of the 1968 campaign was tightly interwoven with issues of race."

George Wallace's involvement in the election was certainly evidence of this. It also provides a revealing, final illustration of the shifting contours of the American right during this time. Wallace had actually begun his political career as a racial moderate. When he first ran for the governorship of Alabama in 1958, he did so with the endorsement of the NAACP. But after his defeat to John Patterson, who was supported by the Ku Klux Klan, among other pro-segregationist organizations, Wallace vowed that "no other son-of-a-bitch will ever out-nigger me again." It was the same kind of "political awakening" that had overcome Orval Faubus in Arkansas. Wallace was true to his word. After becoming governor in 1962, he promised, during his inaugural address, delivered on the steps of the Alabama State Capitol in Montgomery, on January 14, 1963, "In the name of the greatest people who have ever trod this earth . . . segregation now, segregation tomorrow, and segregation forever!"

Five months later, Wallace attempted—symbolically at least—to prevent the desegregation of the University of Alabama in Tuscaloosa, by blocking its "schoolhouse doors" in a dramatic, televised confrontation with Deputy U.S. Attorney General Nicholas Katzenberg and Alabama's newly federalized National Guard. "I do hereby denounce and forbid this illegal and unwarranted action by the central government," Wallace declared in the seven-minute address he had secretly negotiated with the Kennedy administration as the price to be paid for agreeing to stand aside and allow the two black students, Vivian Malone and Jimmy Hood, to enter the school once he had delivered it. In 1964 Wallace ran against Lyndon Johnson in the Democratic primaries, before being persuaded that it would be better for him and his "long-term interests" to withdraw and leave the field open for Goldwater. According to the historian Dan Carter, among those pressuring Wallace to withdraw was Strom Thurmond, who had now moved to the Republican Party in order to support Goldwater, and the South Carolina textile magnate, Roger Milliken, who was both a member of the JBS and one of the key financial backers of William Buckley's *National Review*.

Governor George Wallace attempts to block integration at the University of Alabama, confronting deputy U.S. attorney general Nicholas Katzenberg at the door of the Foster Auditorium on June 11, 1963. Library of Congress Prints & Photographs Division, *U.S. News & World Report* Magazine Photograph Collection, LC-DIG-ppmsca-04294.

In 1968 Wallace was running on the third-party American Independent Party ticket, with former U.S Air Force general Curtis LeMay his (largely inept) running mate. Wallace did not make any explicit racial claims during the campaign. Indeed, he denied being a racist altogether—"I have never in my public life in Alabama made a speech that would reflect upon anybody because of race, color, creed, religion, or national origin," he would disingenuously drawl during his stump speeches. Instead, like Nixon, he relied on euphemism, coded rhetoric, and subtle—and not so subtle—nods and winks. Many of their targets were the same too: anti-war protestors, hippies, drug takers, troublemakers, agitators, leftists, government bureaucrats, and elitist intellectuals. But Wallace was a very different politician and a very different orator from his Republican opponent. Fiery, angry, sneering, often crude, bare-knuckled, and unashamedly populist—but also humorous, sympathetic, and intuitive—Wallace drew large and enthusiastic crowds wherever he spoke: ten thousand in Memphis and Baton Rouge; twelve thousand in Jackson; fifteen thousand in Dallas. And not just in the South. There were crowds of ten to fifteen thousand in Detroit, Pittsburgh, San Diego, Phoenix, and Minneapolis—and fifty thousand in Boston.

On October 24, 1968, twenty thousand Americans packed into Madison Square Garden in New York City—the largest political rally to take place there since FDR had attacked the powers of "organized money" in 1936—to hear him rail against anarchy in the streets, the breakdown of law and order, forced busing, the destruction of local government, pornography, communism, "a sick Supreme Court . . . sick politicians in Washington," and the whole paternalistic superiority of the liberal, interventionist state:

> The pseudo-intellectuals and the theoreticians and some professors and some newspaper editors and some judges and some preachers have looked down their nose long enough at the average man on the street: the pipe-fitter, the communications worker, the fireman, the policeman, the barber, the white collar worker, and said we must write you a guideline about when you go to bed at night and when you get up in the morning. But there are more of us than there are of them, because the average citizen of New York and of Alabama and of the other states of our union are tired of guidelines being written, telling them when to go to bed at night and when to get up in the morning.

Elsewhere, and more succinctly, Wallace assailed the "intellectual morons who don't know how to park a bicycle straight" and welfare mothers who were "breeding children as a cash crop" and threatened to run over any demonstrator who had the temerity to get in the way of his car.

Wallace was assisted in his campaign by other members of the radical right, including the JBS and the Citizens' Councils. The latter raised $250,000 for him; Bunker Hunt, the son of the Texas oil man H. L. Hunt and a perennial supporter of right-wing causes, contributed a similar amount; and it was reported that the actor John Wayne gave $30,000. But most of the $9 million the American Independent Party generated—its target had been $10 million—came from small donations of $50 or less, much of it from new, direct-mail fund-raising techniques.

Wallace did not seriously expect to win the presidency in 1968. Like the Dixiecrats twenty-years earlier, his hope was to claim enough Electoral College votes to turn the election over to the House of Representatives. In the end, he carried Arkansas, Louisiana, Georgia, Mississippi, and Alabama, gathering forty-six electoral votes. Nixon won the election—just—by 43.4 percent of the popular vote to Humphries's 42.7 percent, and by 301 to 191 in the Electoral College. Still, Wallace's 9,906,473 votes—13.5 percent of the total—were hardly insignificant. Thurmond in 1948 had only managed 1,176,125. And whereas less than 1 percent of northern voters had supported the Dixiecrats in 1948, the figure for the American Independent Party was 8 percent.

Taken together, the Goldwater, Nixon, and Wallace campaigns all pointed toward the increasingly difficult time facing the forces of liberalism and "big government" in the United States, heralding both the rise of the New Right and Ronald Reagan's electoral victory in 1980, to which we turn next. As this chapter has shown, the radical right's vigorous opposition to the Supreme Court's decision in *Brown*, to the attempts of the federal government to equalize American race relations, and to the activities of the civil rights movement is a significant part of this story too. Massive resistance—in all its many and varied forms—may have failed, but it had a profound and lasting impact on American politics and American society both during the 1950s and 1960s and beyond.

4

Out of the Wilderness

Ronald Reagan and the New Right

ON JANUARY 20, 1981, RONALD REAGAN gave his first inaugural address. Aiming to restore public confidence and reinvigorate the
economy in the wake of the soaring unemployment, high inflation, and
low growth rates that had marked the 1970s, he was very clear where he
thought the blame for this situation lay. "In our present crisis, government is not the solution to our problem," he proclaimed; "government
is the problem." It was "no coincidence," he continued, "that our present
troubles parallel and are proportionate to the intervention and intrusion
in our lives that result from unnecessary and excessive growth of government." Accordingly, the new president promised that he would dramatically reduce the role of government in American life, return powers to
the states, curb the size of the federal bureaucracy, cut taxes, and remove
"the roadblocks that have slowed our economy and reduced productiv-
ity." This was all music to the ears of the radical right of this period, the
so-called New Right. Its members had embraced Reagan enthusiastically
and campaigned for him vigorously. They shared his hostility to "big government." They too wanted it "off their backs." Rightly or wrongly, they
generally regarded Reagan as one of their own.

This chapter examines Reagan and the New Right. It focuses especially on the years from the early 1970s through to Reagan's reelection
in 1984, by which point, as we shall see, the relationship between the
two had become increasingly fraught. The New Right was a relatively
broad coalition, both elite and grassroots, of activists, politicians, pressure
groups, campaign organizations, think tanks, lobbyists, religious broadcasters, and businessmen—a veritable "conservative labyrinth" as John

Saloma has described it—one that operated both inside and outside the Republican Party. To some extent the term is a little misleading, however, as there remained a considerable amount of continuity—both in terms of ideas and personnel—between the "New" Right of the seventies and eighties and the older right that had preceded it. Anti-communism, moral traditionalism, and the virtues of the free market remained the central tenets of the New Right's political faith, for example, while many of the movement's most prominent figures, including Richard Viguerie, Paul Weyrich, and Phyllis Schlafly, could trace their political careers back to the Goldwater era, if not before. Indeed, erasing the still-lingering stain that Barry Goldwater's seemingly disastrous 1964 presidential campaign had placed on American conservatism provided the operatives of the New Right with a powerful sense of motivation.

Central to the development of the New Right was the financial and other support provided by American corporations, wealthy business leaders, and their private foundations. Members of the business community in the United States had long had an affinity for right-wing causes and organizations, of course—as we have already seen, in the modern context, it is a relationship that can be traced back to the formation of the American Liberty League in 1934—but beginning in the early 1970s, such corporate activism became both more widespread and more cohesive, with millions of dollars pouring into the political system through direct lobbying, the creation of new political action committees (PACs), and the funding of conservative think tanks, as well as New Right political—and religious—groups.

The newfound assertiveness of the American business class during this period was in large part a direct response to the profound economic problems of the time: declining growth, runaway inflation (12.4 percent in 1974), and rising rates of unemployment (7.5 percent by 1975)—a malign set of ills economists dubbed "stagflation" that, from 1973 to 1975, resulted in the worst American recession since the 1930s. The causes of this economic downturn included the massive military expenditures of the Vietnam War, increased global competition for American companies from Asia and Europe, and, in particular, the "oil price shock" of 1973, when the Organization of Petroleum Exporting Countries (OPEC) placed an oil embargo on the United States in retaliation for its support of Israel during the Yom Kippur War. It then drastically cut oil production, actions that resulted in the quadrupling of oil prices to over $11 a barrel by January 1974. Global events notwithstanding, as far as many prominent business leaders were concerned, however, this sorry situation could only be turned around by launching a full-scale attack on governmental regulation, bureaucracy, excessive taxation, and the entire leftward drift of American society and its unrelenting assault on the "free enterprise" system. It was the supposedly conservative Nixon administration that had created the Environmental Protection Agency (EPA) in 1970 and saddled the economy with wage and price controls in 1971, for example.

Discussing the creation of the new government lobbying organization, the Business Roundtable, established in 1972, James L. Ferguson, the chief executive officer (CEO) of General Foods, explained that "business was getting kicked around compared to labor, consumers, and other groups, and the constant cry within the business community was, 'How come we can't get together and make our voices heard?'" The Business Roundtable was an elite organization; its membership comprised the CEOs of the nation's largest and wealthiest companies, including General Motors, IBM, AT&T, Citibank, General Electric, Alcoa, and DuPont. This was very much intentional. As its executive director John Post noted: "Senators say they won't talk to Washington reps, but they will see a chairman." Business also sought to promote its interests through PACs. After the Nixon Watergate scandal, a series of campaign finance reforms were passed that placed stricter limits on the amount of money individual political candidates could receive as campaign contributions in comparison to PACs. The result was both an explosive growth in the number of these committees and a massive flood of "soft money" into the American political system. In terms of corporate PACs, for example, 89 were in operation in 1974. By 1976 it was 433 and by 1983 the figure was 1,512.

Direct lobbying and enhanced electoral influence were one thing. Altering the broader intellectual climate to make it more favorably inclined to business—and wider conservative—interests was something else, and it was here that right-wing think tanks became important. Infused with generous donations from wealthy conservatives and their private foundations, older think tanks such as the American Enterprise Institute (AEI) and the Hoover Institution joined forces with newly established organizations such as the Heritage Foundation, the Institute for Contemporary Studies, the Lehrman Institute, and the Cato Institute in a concerted effort to alter the "marketplace of ideas" in the United States. The Heritage Foundation especially would play a crucial role in the rise of the New Right.

Using family-run foundations to establish and support these think tanks—as well as rightist organizations more generally—had certain tax benefits for the individuals who controlled them. They also had the additional advantage that donations made by them were not publicly accountable in the way that corporate donations largely were. As a result, it is not possible to say for certain just how much money was being funneled to conservative causes in this way, although estimates suggest that it was close to $20 million a year by 1980. Among the most significant donors were: the Scaife Family Foundations, headed by Richard Mellon Scaife, heir to the Carnegie-Mellon fortune; the Adolph Coors Foundation, run by the brewing magnate Joseph Coors; the Bechtel Foundation, funded by the largest privately owned construction and civil engineering company in the United States; the Smith Richardson Foundation based on the Vicks VapoRub company; the Koch Family Foundations, founded by Charles and David Koch, who would go on to be key benefactors of the Tea Party movement in the twenty-first century and whose father had been a key supporter of the John Birch Society during the 1960s; and the John M. Olin Foundation, which was supported by the family's agricultural, chemical, and munitions businesses.

Financial support for the New Right did not just come from above, however; it also came from below. Here too the post-Watergate reforms were important, particularly the Federal Campaign Act of 1974, which introduced a limit of $1,000 on individual campaign contributions, thereby stimulating the growth of direct-mail appeals to potential contributors to political campaigns. The undisputed king of direct-mail fund-raising was the New Right organizer Richard Viguerie. Born in Texas in 1933, Viguerie first began working in this area as executive secretary of the conservative student group Young Americans for Freedom, but it was his experience with the Goldwater and George Wallace campaigns that was really critical. His company, the Richard A. Viguerie Company (RAVCO), was established in 1965 with the names of 12,500 people who had contributed $50 or more to Goldwater in 1964. By the early 1980s, having amassed a computerized database of twenty million people, it was raising millions of dollars annually for right-wing political candidates, PACs, think tanks, lobbyists, and pressure groups.

RAVCO functioned as both a crucial fund-raiser and an organizational hub for the New Right, as a vital communications outlet, as well as a critical training ground for its activists. Among its publications were *New Right Report* and *Conservative Digest*, for example. Viguerie also wanted to broaden the traditional reach of the Republican Party, to make it, as he put it in his 1981 book, *The New Right: We're Ready to Lead*, the party of "Main Street, not Wall Street." It was an ambitious and far-reaching vision, one that fused conservatism with populism in an attempt to shift the entire American political landscape to the right.

Viguerie was assisted in these efforts by another key New Right organizer, Paul M. Weyrich. "We are different from previous generations of conservatives," Weyrich asserted. "We are no longer working to preserve the status quo. We are radicals, working to overturn the present power structure of this country." Born in Racine, Wisconsin, in 1942, Weyrich, like Viguerie, was a Catholic with strong anti-abortion views, who had become active in conservative causes as a university student and campaigned for Goldwater in 1964. He was also an admirer of his late home state senator Joe McCarthy. It was Weyrich, along with his colleague Edwin J. Feulner Jr., who persuaded Joseph Coors and Richard Scaife to provide the initial funding to set up the Heritage Foundation in 1973: Coors's donation was $250,000; Scaife's $900,000. Toward the end of the seventies, under threat of losing its tax-exempt status, the Foundation turned increasingly to small-dollar contributions solicited through Viguerie's direct-mail methods to finance its operations. Weyrich was also responsible for the creation of the New Right PAC, the Committee for the Survival of a Free Congress (CSFC); its off-shoot, the Free Congress Research and Education Foundation; and a host of other influential single-issue organizations and groups. The two other key New Right organizers of the period were John "Terry" Dolan, founder and head of the National Conservative Political Action Committee (NCPAC), and Howard Phillips, a disillusioned member of the Nixon administration, who established the right-wing lobbying group the Conservative Caucus in 1974.

Significantly, these New Right political operatives also saw an opportunity to align themselves with—and to encourage the development of—the rapidly growing evangelical movement in the United States, a grouping that, in turn, became known as the New Christian Right. These evangelical Christians stressed their "born again" religious experiences, the inerrancy of the Bible, and the importance of personal salvation. Although certainly not monolithic in their theology nor their politics— there can be a strong progressive or social justice strand to evangelicalism, for example—white evangelical Christians in particular have tended to be much more sympathetic to conservative causes than liberal ones. Yet, for much of the twentieth century, with the notable exceptions of Billy James Hargis's Christian Crusade, Fred Schwartz's Christian Anti-Communism Crusade, and Carl McIntire's American Council of Christian Churches (see chapter 3), they had also mostly kept their distance from worldly matters and electoral politics. So what changed in the 1970s? What prompted evangelicals' shift toward political activism at this time?

It was a combination of factors. They were reacting to the perceived permissiveness and licentiousness of the cultural and social changes wrought during "the sixties" as these came to fruition in the following decade. They were deeply concerned that their faith and their core beliefs were being attacked by the increasingly intrusive activities of the interventionist state. And they feared that the nation overall was turning away from God's chosen path. On a range of issues, including school prayer, abortion, pornography, gay rights, women's rights, sex education, school textbooks, drugs, divorce, promiscuity, and the teaching of evolution, evangelicals and their leaders felt under significant threat and they were determined to respond. It was no coincidence that many of these issues related to education and the family. It was precisely because the threats hit so close to home that they needed to be resisted so strongly. The frightening advance of "secular humanism"—as these broad trends in American life were often termed—needed to be halted as soon as possible.

As with the backlash against the rise of the civil rights movement discussed in the previous chapter, decisions of the Supreme Court played an important role in the political awakening of the religious right. In *Engel v. Vitale* (1962) and *Abington School District v. Schempp* (1963), the Court banned both prayer and Bible readings in public schools. In *Jacobellis v. Ohio* (1964), it significantly loosened prohibitions on obscenity. (Overturning the conviction of an Ohio theater owner who had shown Louis Malle's 1958 film *The Lovers*, the Court determined that to be "obscene," films—and other artistic works—had to be "utterly without social importance.") And in 1973, in *Roe v. Wade*, it established a woman's constitutional right to abortion. Striking down state laws that had criminalized women for terminating their pregnancies, the Court's majority decision—seven to two—was based on women's "right to privacy" under the Fourteenth Amendment. Catholics initially took the lead in the attempt to overturn *Roe v. Wade*, but the case also had a galvanizing effect on the evangelical community. "This decision runs counter not merely to the moral teachings of Christianity through the ages but also the moral sense of the American people," argued an editorial in the leading evangelical magazine *Christianity Today*, in February 1973. It was a decision "for paganism and against Christianity," the editorial went on, warning that "Christians should accustom themselves to the thought that the American state no longer supports, in any meaningful sense, the laws of God, and prepare themselves spiritually for the prospect that it may one day formally repudiate them and turn against those who seek to live by them."

The broader expansion of women's rights and the demands of the feminist movement were also a major cause of concern at this time, and not just for evangelicals. The most pressing issue in this respect was the potential addition to the Constitution of a new Equal Rights Amendment (ERA). This stated: "Equality of rights under the law shall not be denied or abridged by the United States, or by any state, on account of sex." Having successfully emerged from Congress in March 1972—a mere forty-nine years after first being introduced in 1923—in order to become law, the ERA needed to be ratified by thirty-eight of the states (three-fourths of the total of fifty, in accordance with Article 5 of the Constitution). By early 1973 it had received the approval of thirty states, but this quick progress was soon brought to a crashing halt, in no small part due to the efforts of the Stop ERA campaign organized by the longtime right-wing activist Phyllis Schlafly.

Schlafly was born in St. Louis, Missouri, in 1924. A devout Catholic and mother of six, she attended Maryville College of the Sacred Heart in her hometown before transferring to Washington University. She received an MA in political science from Radcliffe College in Cambridge, Massachusetts, in 1945 and worked for the forerunner of the AEI, the American Enterprise Association, in Washington, and as a researcher for several congressmen before running for Congress herself in 1952. With her husband, Fred, she established the anti-communist Cardinal Mindszenty Foundation in 1958 and was closely associated with the radical right, the John Birch Society in particular, throughout the 1960s. She was president of the Illinois Federation of Republican Women from 1960 to 1964 and vice president of the National Federation of Republican Women from 1964 to 1967. In 1964 her self-published first book, *A Choice Not an Echo*, in support of Barry Goldwater's campaign to be the GOP nominee, sold more than three million copies. She followed this with a series of books on national defense, which she wrote with the retired U.S. Navy rear admiral Chester Ward, including *Strike from Space* in 1965 and *The Betrayers* in 1968. And in 1970 she ran again for Congress (again unsuccessfully). All of which is to say that, as her biographer Donald Critchlow has pointed out, Schlafly already had a national reputation and a significant following when she became involved with the New Right, the New Christian Right, and the anti-ERA campaign.

Schlafly established Stop ERA in 1972 with the help of Senator Sam Ervin (R-NC). She was its national chairwoman, official spokesperson, and chief organizer. (The group's name was actually an acronym. It stood for: Stop Taking Our Privileges with this Extra Responsibility Amendment.) With indefatigable energy and immense skill, she coordinated a range of people, groups, and churches of various denominations, including Methodists, Baptists, Mormons, and the Church of Christ, in a broad-based, large-scale, mostly grassroots lobbying effort to prevent the passage of the ERA. Raising funds and awareness through Richard Viguerie's direct-mail company, Schlafly and her allies produced newsletters, distributed buttons and pamphlets, initiated letter-writing campaigns, created workshops, held state conferences, organized demonstrations, and picketed legislators in opposition to the amendment. The principal arguments used against the ERA were that it was unnecessary; that it was "a takeaway of women's rights," including the right to child support and alimony; that it was an attack on the traditional family unit; that it would require the conscription of women into the armed forces and "identical treatment in combat"; that it would lead to the establishment of unisex public restrooms; and that it was all a gigantic "power grab" by the government that would undermine the states while increasing the size of the federal bureaucracy.

New Right activist Phyllis Schlafly demonstrates with other women against the Equal Rights Amendment in front of the White House in Washington, D.C., in February 1977. Library of Congress Prints & Photographs Division, *U.S. News & World Report* Magazine Photograph Collection, LC-DIG-33891-33.

The campaign was successful. The organization forced the Republican Party to remove the amendment from its official platform during its 1980 convention, and it was still three states short of the required thirty-eight when the ten-year deadline imposed by Congress for ratification was reached on June 30, 1982. (The deadline had originally been seven years, but Congress extended it in October 1978, after intense lobbying from the National Organization of Women and other women's rights groups, which had generally been caught off-guard by the strength and effectiveness of the Stop ERA movement.) Defeat of the ERA was significant not just for Schlafly but for the entire New Right coalition. The campaign had drawn thousands of right-wing women, especially evangelical women, into politics for the first time; membership of the organization reached fifty thousand by 1975, at which point Schlafly changed its name to the Eagle Forum, and was largely white and middle class, with 98 percent of members belonging to a church of one kind or another. And it had achieved its victory despite the amendment having overwhelming public and political support, as opinion polls of the time clearly demonstrated—and as votes of over 90 percent in both houses of Congress and the support of thirty-five state legislatures further testified.

Another compelling issue was the Internal Revenue Service's (IRS) "assault" on evangelical and fundamentalist Christian schools. During the Nixon administration, the IRS began denying tax exemptions to private schools that remained racially segregated, including religious institutions such as Bob Jones University in Greenville, South Carolina. This policy was upheld by the courts in the case of *Green v. Connally* (1971). In 1978 the IRS went further, proposing a new set of regulations that would require these schools to either have a certain quota of minority students or to officially certify that they operated "in good faith on a racially non-discriminatory basis." Both the proposed new regulations and the ongoing dispute over tax exemptions caused a storm of protest within the evangelical community. They were seen as a clear attack on religious freedom and on the rights of parents to educate their own children according to their own values and beliefs and yet further evidence of unwanted—and unwarranted—governmental intrusion into people's private lives. Framing the dispute in this way both downplayed the importance of the issue of racial discrimination and ignored the fact that tax exemptions are themselves a form of public subsidy.

With the support of the New Right's Paul Weyrich and Richard Viguerie, an extensive campaign was launched to force the IRS to back down. The White House, Congress, and the IRS itself were flooded with letters of protest. The Heritage Foundation weighed in, as did evangelical leaders such as Jerry Falwell and Pat Robertson (discussed further below), while new organizations like Christian School Action—later to become the National Christian Action Coalition and headed by Robert Billings—were established. It was a pivotal moment, one absolutely central to the rise of the New Christian Right in American politics. The "federal government's move against Christian schools . . . absolutely shattered the Christian community's notions that Christians could isolate themselves inside their own institutions," Weyrich explained. Religious groups now understood that "Big Government was coming after them as well. There was overnight conversion. It was electrifying," he said. Referencing one of the defining events of the American Revolution, *Christianity Today* portrayed the government's "interference" with the

Christian school movement as "the Stamp Act of the Religious Right." Within a year the IRS had relented, the new regulations were shelved, and a powerful new political constituency had been awakened.

For the strategists of the New Right, the evangelical community was obviously both a natural ally and a rich source of potential new recruits. Here was a previously untapped conservative grouping in the tens of millions that was now willing, it seemed, to devote time, money—and hopefully votes—to help defeat the forces that were believed to be threatening the nation: communists, intrusive government, and moral decay foremost among them. Adding considerably to the allure of this relationship, from the point of view of Weyrich and his colleagues, was that it also gave them access to the vast communications network known as the "electronic church" and to the highly influential evangelical preachers who presided over it. Foremost among these "televangelists," as they were generally called—although some preferred the more neutral term "religious broadcaster" to describe themselves, which, in truth, better reflected the mix of radio and television stations that made up this network—were Pat Robertson, Jim Bakker, Jimmy Swaggart, and Jerry Falwell.

Robertson was the pioneer. Born in Lexington, Virginia, in 1930, he was the son of the conservative Democrat, anti–New Deal—and future Dixiecrat and signer of the Southern Manifesto—congressman and senator A. Willis Robertson. After his initial schooling, Pat—his given name was actually Marion, but he rejected it for being too effeminate—served as a marine captain in Korea and received a law degree from Yale. Having failed the New York bar exam and half-heartedly tried his hand at business, in 1956 he was introduced by his mother, Gladys, to a traveling evangelist called Cornelius Vanderbreggen. Robertson was "born again," and in the fall of 1957, he enrolled at the Biblical Seminary of New York. Two years later, married, with a new family, he bought a run-down television station in Portsmouth, Virginia. "The Lord told me to buy a station. I didn't own a TV set," Robertson explained. "My kids were excited; they thought I was buying a TV. They were disappointed that it was only a station." It took two years for Robertson to even get his newly named Christian Broadcasting Network (CBN) on the air—its first broadcast took place in October 1961—but by 1972 it was bringing in $2 million annually. The network continued to grow during the 1970s, as radio stations and additional TV stations were added to it, and by the early 1980s, it had amassed thirty million subscribers and an annual budget of $230 million.

The *700 Club*, named for the seven hundred contributors who had donated $10 a month to keep the fledging station going during its most difficult years, was CBN's flagship show. Hosted by Robertson, it eschewed a traditional church meeting or revivalist approach, adopting a polished and sophisticated talk show or news magazine format instead. National and international issues were addressed from a "Biblical perspective." There were in-studio and live-by-satellite interviews with prominent newsmakers, religious figures, politicians, and celebrities. But there were also "human interest" stories, musical guests, and advice on child-rearing, financial matters, and "phone-in counseling." Before a studio audience, on a set designed to look like someone's living room, Robertson was cool and relaxed, informed and authoritative, pleasant and persuasive. He was also ambitious and politically calculating. "We have enough votes to run this country," he said, with respect to the rise of the New Christian Right. "And when the people say, 'We've had enough,' we are going to take over."

Bakker and Swaggart more closely fit the stereotype of the "typical" televangelist preacher: flamboyant, theatrical, and charismatic; weeping uncontrollably one moment, delivering fire-and-brimstone jeremiads the next, as they solicited donations from their audiences in highly emotive—and often hugely entertaining—public appeals. Bakker had actually gotten his start alongside Robertson on the *700 Club* but left in 1972, after a series of disputes with his onetime mentor. He moved first to the California-based Trinity Broadcasting Network, founded in 1973 by Paul and Jan Crouch, before establishing his own PTL network with his wife, Tammy, in North Carolina the following year. (PTL stood for "Praise the Lord" and then "People that Love," but after a series of financial and sexual scandals in the late 1980s, it was widely ridiculed as the "Pass the Loot" network.) Swaggart's World Ministry Center was based in Baton Rouge, Louisiana, but as with Bakker and Robertson— and Jerry Falwell—his weekly shows were syndicated across the country on hundreds of stations and, indeed, around the world. (As the eighties drew to a close, Swaggart too became embroiled in scandal, when it was discovered that he had been soliciting prostitutes on a regular basis.)

Falwell's *Old Time Gospel Hour* ran on more than 300 television stations and 375 radio stations, reaching millions of viewers and listeners every week. He also had his own broadcasting network, the National Christian Network (NCN), drawing in $115 million a year by 1985, and his own church, the Thomas Road Baptist Church, located in his hometown of Lynchburg, Virginia, where he was born in 1933. The church had begun in an old factory building in 1956 with thirty-five congregants; by the early eighties its membership was close to twenty thousand. It was his weekly eleven o'clock Sunday morning sermon at Lynchburg that was broadcast as the *Old Time Gospel Hour*. A gifted marketer, technologically literate, and media-savvy, Falwell also created a Christian Academy school, a correspondence school, a bible institute, a seminary, an international bible center, and the fully accredited Liberty Baptist College (which became Liberty University in 1984).

Opposed to desegregation and the civil rights movement, which he regarded as "communist-inspired," Falwell had fiercely criticized Martin Luther King Jr. and other religious leaders for "meddling" in political affairs during the 1960s, but like other evangelicals, he had been politicized by the developments in American society since that time, including the fear that his private—segregated—Christian Academy would lose its tax-exempt status. "If you would like to know where I am politically, I am to the right of whatever you are. I thought Goldwater was too liberal," he explained. Not surprisingly, then, he was more than amenable when the leaders of the New Right came calling with the idea to create yet another new political organization, this one to be called Moral Majority (MM).

It was in the spring of 1979 that Weyrich, Viguerie, and Howard Phillips—who was the person who had come up with the name—traveled to Lynchburg to meet with Falwell to sell him on the idea. The meeting had been facilitated by Robert Billings and Edward McAtter, the head of the Christian Freedom Foundation, which was funded by J. Howard Pew's Sun Oil Company in the hope of getting more "real Christians" into public office. The organization was formally incorporated as Moral Majority Inc. that June. Falwell led it and Billings was its first national director. Among its board members were Charles Stanley of the First Baptist Church of Atlanta, Greg Dixon of the Indianapolis Baptist Temple, James Kennedy of the Coral Ridge

Presbyterian Church in Florida, and Tim LeHaye, who along with his wife, Beverly, directed the D.C.-based lobbying group Family America. Tim LeHaye was also the author of the influential conspiratorial tome *The Battle for the Mind* (1980), which warned that the secular humanists were planning "a complete world takeover by the year 2000," as well, later, of the extraordinarily successful *Left Behind* series of premillennial apocalyptic novels (more than seventy million sold).

Moral Majority aimed to mobilize "the vast majority of Americans against 'humanism.'" "We are fighting a Holy War and this time we are going to win!" declared Falwell. It would vigorously "defend the free enterprise system, the family and Bible morality," while being strong on national defense and stridently anti-communist in foreign affairs. It would also be ecumenical. Adopting the principle of cobelligerence— the idea that common enemies and common morals could overcome any doctrinal differences that existed between people of different faiths—not just evangelicals, but fundamentalists, mainline Protestants, Catholics, Mormons, and Jews were all welcome within the organization. In practice, however, as was reflected in the composition of its board of directors, it tended to attract evangelicals in much greater numbers than members of other denominations. Fully 90 percent of MM's state leaders were Baptist ministers, for example.

Any lingering doubts that might have existed about the appropriateness of mixing the spiritual with the political were also overcome. "What can you do from the pulpit?" Falwell asked his fellow ministers. "You can register people to vote. You can explain issues to them. And you can endorse candidates, right there in the church on Sunday morning." The organization's impact was immediate. Within a few months it claimed to have attracted four hundred thousand members, raised $1.5 million, and registered close to three million new voters. The overall pool of white evangelical voters alone was believed to be around forty-five million, or about 25 percent of the entire electorate—hence their potential power. MM published a monthly *Moral Majority Report*, issued "moral report cards" on political candidates so that voters would be "well informed" come polling day, held "Clean-Up America" rallies, and sponsored TV shows with provocative titles like *America, You're Too Young to Die*. Later in the eighties, it would establish its own Moral Majority PAC, organize a National Conference on Pornography, push new Human Life anti-abortion legislation, campaign against homosexuality, and help support the Coalition for Better Television, among other activities.

Moral Majority's stress on "the family" and "family values" was no accident. It was a very conscious—and very effective—strategy. "The family will be to the decade of the 1980s what environmentalism and consumerism have been to the 1970s and what the Vietnam war was to the 1960s," explained Paul Weyrich, one of the strategy's principal architects, in the August 1979 issue of *Conservative Digest*. "The threat to the family has caused leaders of various denominations to put aside their sectarian differences and, for the first time in decades, to agree on basic principles worth fighting for." "Each part of the coalition brings something useful," he went on:

> The fundamentalist/evangelical Protestants bring a knowledge of and devotion to the Bible which no politician can shake. In addition, they have mastered the use of television and radio for their efforts, and this will make communications easier. The Catholics . . . bring philosophical underpinnings which can help make the coalition impervious to attack, so that this alliance will not be swept away as happened earlier in the century. . . . The Mormons bring a superb knowledge of organization and outreach, and the Orthodox Jews bring not only family tradition but the ability to be productively aggressive.

Other members of this "pro-family coalition" included James Dobson's Focus on the Family group; Beverly LeHaye's Concerned Women for America; Schlafly's Eagle Forum; Christian Voice, which had developed out of the anti-gay movement in California and Florida and which originated the idea of issuing moral report cards for political candidates; and Religious Roundtable, one of the principal coordinating groups of the religious right, headed by Ed McAteer, which was modeled explicitly on the Business Roundtable. Illustrative of the increasing political activism of the New Christian Right, in April 1980 the first of a series of Washington for Jesus prayer meetings—with anywhere between two hundred thousand and five hundred thousand Christian conservatives taking part—was convened in the nation's capital.

Weyrich, together with his colleagues and allies, had fired the opening shots of the "culture wars" that would roil American society into the 1990s and beyond. More immediately, though, the stage was set for the upcoming 1980 elections, and in Ronald Reagan both the New Right and the New Christian Right had a presidential candidate in which they had high hopes.

By any measure, Reagan's journey to become the standard-bearer of the American right was a remarkable one. He was born in Tampico, Illinois, on February 6, 1911, the second son of his lapsed Catholic, alcoholic father, Jack, and his fervently religious mother, Nelle, a devoted member of the Protestant Disciples of Christ Church. Having moved six times in the previous six years, in 1920 the family settled in Dixon, Illinois, where Ronald—or "Dutch" as he was known—attended high school and gained his first taste of celebrity as a local lifeguard. (The nickname was the result of his father's habit of referring to his son as his "fat little Dutchman" when he was an infant.) Reagan was studying at Eureka College, run by the Disciples of Christ, when the Great Depression struck. His father, a lifelong Democrat, lost his job as a traveling salesman and was unemployed for six months before securing a position with the Illinois Emergency Relief Commission. This was followed by work with two federal New Deal agencies, the Civil Works Authority and the Works Progress Administration. Having prominently displayed an FDR button on his lifeguard's bathing suit throughout the summer of 1932, Ronald was further able to show his appreciation for Roosevelt and his politics by casting his first-ever presidential ballot for FDR in the November elections. It was a political identification that would last until the mid-1950s.

Following his graduation from Eureka College in June 1932, Reagan became a radio sports announcer, one of the best in the Midwest, renowned for his vivid "re-creations" of baseball games. As was common practice at the time, smaller radio stations like WOC in Des Moines, Iowa, where first Reagan worked, didn't actually send announcers to the games. They remained in the studio, reliant on ticker tape reports that they transformed into simulated—and hopefully stimulating—"play-by-play" accounts. In 1937, while traveling with the Chicago Cubs for spring training, Reagan took and passed a screen test for the Warner Bros. film studio. On May 20 that year he left Des Moines for Hollywood. He was going to be a movie star.

Reagan's film career began in B-movies, but he gradually became an A-lister, one of the highest-paid actors in Hollywood. His films included the uplifting *Knute Rockne: All-American* (1940), in which he plays the dying football star, George Gipp, who inspires his Notre Dame team to victory with his exhortation to "Win one for the Gipper!"; the dark melo-drama *Kings Row* (1942) about the hypocrisies of small-town life, where he plays the hero Drake McHugh, whose legs are unnecessarily ampu-tated by a sadistic doctor, leading him to cry out in horror, "Where's the rest of me?" (which became the title of Reagan's first autobiogra-phy, published in 1965); and the lighthearted comedy *Bedtime for Bonzo* (1951), in which, as Professor Peter Boyd, Reagan endeavors—with mixed results—to "educate" his chimpanzee co-star, the aforementioned Bonzo; as well as a raft of westerns, war films, and crime dramas. His last feature film was the only one in which he played a "bad guy": 1964's *The Killers*, based on an Ernest Hemmingway short story and directed by Don Siegel.

Ineligible for combat during the Second World War because of his terrible eyesight, Reagan spent the war years in Los Angeles making training films and documentaries for the First Motion Picture Unit of the U.S. Air Force, aka the "Celluloid Commandoes." His return to the film industry at the war's end saw him getting increasingly involved in poli-tics. He was still a passionate New Dealer—a "hemophiliac liberal," as he would later describe himself—a member of the decidedly left-leaning Hollywood Independent Citizens Committees of the Arts, Sciences and Professions (HICCASP), and the American Veterans Committee (AVC), who stumped enthusiastically for Harry Truman in 1948. However, his involvement with HICCASP and AVC, and especially his presidency of the Screen Actors Guild (1947–1952), exposed him to the secretive mach-inations and anti-democratic practices of Hollywood's communists and their sympathizers as they battled it out with the industry's liberals for control of these organizations. The experience had a profound effect on Reagan, stimulating an unwavering anti-communism that would inform his thinking—and his politics—for the rest of his life. It also led him to become a secret informer for the FBI.

Reagan's shift to the right was gradual. It was facilitated by several fac-tors, including his 1953 marriage to the actress Nancy Davis, whose fam-ily was staunchly conservative, particularly her stepfather, the wealthy Chicago neurosurgeon Loyal Davis. (Reagan's eight-year marriage to Jane Wyman, another actress, had ended in 1948.) The high rates of taxation he was paying also played a part. "True, I'd been making handsome money ever since World War II, but that handsome money lost a lot of its beauty and substance going through the 91 percent tax bracket," as he put it. He also claimed that a five-month stint filming *The Hasty Heart* in the United Kingdom in 1948–1949, during the early years of the establishment of the British welfare state, had shed him of "the last ideas I ever had about government ownership of anything." It had been his first trip outside the United States. But the most important factor by far was his recruitment by General Electric, in the summer of 1954, to be one of the company's official spokesmen and the host of its new weekly, primetime television program, *General Electric Theater*.

The job required him to spend sixteen weeks a year touring GE's production plants around the nation, speaking to its workers and managers—as well as to other businesses, charities, civic groups, and fraternal organizations—about the company's anti-labor, anti-regulation philosophy and the overriding virtues of American free enterprise. Tutored by GE's "communication's man," Earl B. Dunckel, but writing his speeches himself—Reagan had always been a voracious accumulator of facts, statistics, stories, anecdotes, and jokes (some more reliable than others)—his presentations became increasingly political and increasingly conservative, his delivery more polished and effective. At the same time, hosting *General Electric Theater* gave Reagan financial security just when his movie career was faltering, its audience of millions helping to keep him in the public eye.

Reagan supported Richard Nixon in the 1960 presidential election, making more than two hundred speeches on his behalf. He had wanted to register as a Republican for the campaign, but Nixon persuaded him that his efforts would be more potent if he was a member of the "Democrats for Nixon" group. His formal switch in party registrations took place in 1962. Overall, during the early sixties, Reagan was closely identified with the radical right in the United States. He appeared at Christian Anti-Communism Crusade rallies with Fred Schwarz; spoke at a fundraising dinner for Congressmen John Rousselot (R-CA), a high-profile member of the John Birch Society; and accepted public service awards from segregationist governors Ross Barnett of Mississippi and Orville Faubus of Arkansas. According to journalist Seth Rosenfeld, in his book *Subversives*, a "reliable" informer had told the FBI in June 1960 that Reagan secretly belonged to the Beverly Hills chapter of the Birch Society, although it is not clear whether the agency actually investigated the allegation. Indeed, his association with right-wing extremism was so strong that members of Barry Goldwater's team had severe doubts about the wisdom of asking Reagan to deliver a televised address on their candidate's behalf in 1964.

Goldwater gave the go-ahead, however, and on October 27, 1964, Reagan appeared on NBC to deliver a pre-recorded version of what was essentially the same talk he had been giving around the country for the past several years as a spokesman for GE. Titled "A Time for Choosing"—but more often referred to by conservatives simply as "The Speech"—the address didn't have much impact on Goldwater's fortunes, but it did have a profound impact on Reagan's own career. It set out Reagan's—and the emergent right's—case for smaller government, fewer regulations, a stronger national defense, and traditional American values, with grace, confidence, and authority. The "issue of this election," he said, was "whether we believe in our capacity for self-government or whether we abandon the American Revolution and confess that a little intellectual elite in a far distant capitol can plan our lives for us better than we can plan them ourselves." Thirty years of "government planning and welfare" had not been a success, he argued. Taxes were too high, businessmen faced harassment wherever they operated, and the state had detrimentally "laid its hand on health, housing, farming, industry, commerce, [and] education." Freedom itself was under threat. Borrowing shamelessly from FDR—although no longer a New Deal Democrat, his admiration for Roosevelt as a leader had not faltered—Reagan concluded grandiosely, arguing: "You and I have a rendezvous with destiny. We'll preserve for our children this, the last best hope of man on earth, or we'll sentence them to take the last step into a thousand years of darkness."

Impressed by Reagan's politics but more especially by his performance, a group of wealthy, self-made businessmen, led by nursing home magnate Charles Z. Wick, drugstore millionaire Justin Dart, auto dealer Holmes Tuttle, and oilmen A. Y. Rubel and Henry Salvatori, pushed him to run for the governorship of California in 1966. "We recognized that he had a certain magic quality—he didn't lose the audience," as Wick put it. Reagan campaigned as an outsider. "I am not a politician. I am an ordinary citizen with a deep-seated belief that much of what troubles us has been brought on by politicians," he declared. He defeated the two-term liberal incumbent, Edmund G. "Pat" Brown, by close to a million votes and was elected again in 1970.

During his time as governor of California, Reagan continued his rhetorical assault on big government and took a hard-line on war pro- testors, the black power movement, student radicals, and the whole counter-culture—"Their signs say make love not war. But they don't look like they could do much of either," he said, in a characteristic quip. Yet he also displayed a pragmatic and compromising side, a will- ingness to work with Democratic legislators and to back down when needed. Indeed, from a conservative perspective, his overall record left much to be desired: in order to solve the state's budget deficit—which he had inherited from Brown—he agreed to the largest tax increase in California's history; signed an abortion law that allowed for the termi- nation of pregnancies that had occurred as a result of rape or incest or if a mother's health was in danger; and, despite passing more than forty "law and order" bills, presided over a considerable rise in the state's crime rates. He did successfully reduce property taxes (by $4 billion) and slow the growth of the state bureaucracy; and he also introduced major "welfare reform," removing more than three hundred thou- sand people from the state's rolls by 1974. Yet perhaps Reagan's great- est achievement was that he had demonstrated the electability of his particular brand of conservatism, transforming his own image in the process. No longer was he widely considered to be a right-wing zealot. Now he was a potential president.

Reagan challenged Gerald Ford in the Republican primaries in 1976, losing narrowly to Nixon's former vice president, who then himself lost—even more narrowly—to the Democratic Party candidate, Jimmy Carter (by 50.1 percent to 48 percent of the popular vote). In retrospect, this was probably to Reagan's advantage. Conditions were much more favorable to him in 1980. Indeed, economically and in terms of its stand- ing in the world, the United States seemed to be at an almost catastrophi- cally low ebb. Following another oil price shock in 1979, stagflation had returned with a vengeance, long lines snaked around the nation's gas stations, and the so-called misery index—the combined rates of unem- ployment and inflation—climbed to 20.1 percent. American hostages had been taken captive by Iranian revolutionaries in the U.S. embassy in

Tehran—fifty-two of them would be held for more than 444 days—left-wing insurgents were running amok in Latin America, and a seemingly emboldened Soviet Union had invaded Afghanistan.

On July 15, 1979, Carter delivered an address to the nation on its "crisis of confidence." (Although it is often referred to as "the malaise speech," the president never actually used that term.) Too many Americans worshipped "self-indulgence and consumption," he said; they possessed "a mistaken idea of freedom," which would lead only to "fragmentation and self-interest." Setting out his specific proposals for solving the country's ongoing energy crisis, he urged his fellow citizens "for your good and for your nation's security, to take no unnecessary trips, to use carpools or public transportation whenever you can, to park your car one extra day per week, to obey the speed limit, and to set your thermostats to save fuel." Many Americans felt that Carter was just blaming them while offering no real solutions. This was not Reagan's approach. In his final campaign address of 1980, he countered by asking: "Does history still have a place for America, for her people, for her great ideals? There are some who answer 'no,' that our energy is spent, our days of greatness at an end, that a great national malaise is upon us. They say we must cut our expectations, conserve and withdraw, that we must tell our children not to dream as we once dreamed." During the past year, he had traveled to "every corner of the United States," he continued, and he found "no national malaise . . . nothing wrong with the American people." They were "frustrated, even angry at what has been done to this blessed land," but they remained as "sturdy and robust as they have always been."

Reagan was aided in his bid for the White House not just by emergence of the New Right and the New Christian Right, but by other developments on the American right as well. Libertarians like those at the Cato Institute, funded by the Koch family, pushed for business deregulation, smaller government, and greater personal freedom. Neo-conservatives such as Irving Kristol and Norman Podhoretz attacked liberal social welfare policies and agitated for a more robust attempt to "win" the Cold War. (The neocons, as they become known, were initially composed mostly of disgruntled former Democrats; liberals who had been "mugged by reality," as Kristol famously termed them.) A national "tax revolt," launched in California as Proposition 13 in 1978 by the seventy-five-year-old businessman Howard Jarvis and his activist ally Paul Gann, was also taking place. "You are the people, and you will have to take control of the government again, or else it is going to control you," Jarvis warned. Meanwhile, many white working-class voters in the North, opposed to the "reverse discrimination" of affirmative action, "forced" busing, and rising crime rates, were joining with their southern counterparts in shifting their allegiances from the Democrats to the Republican Party—"Reagan Democrats," as these voters would come to be called.

Reagan's 1980 campaign offered something for all these groups. He demonstrated a mastery of the "dog-whistle politics" pioneered by George Wallace and Richard Nixon when he spoke in favor of states' rights at the Neshoba County fair in Mississippi, not far from where civil rights workers Michael Schwerner, Andrew Goodman, and James Chaney had been murdered in 1964. He promised to restore America's might, cut government spending, lower taxes, and unleash the nation's entrepreneurial spirit. He told a gathering of fifteen thousand evangelical Christians in Dallas that he understood that "you can't endorse me. But I want you to know that I endorse you." And despite some missteps along the way—suggesting that trees caused more pollution than cars, being unable to recall who the French president was—above all, he projected confidence and optimism, the sense that America's best days still lay ahead of it. "In aiming to undo the actual New Deal, Reaganism represented a New Deal in American conservatism, aligning, as never before in the nation's history, pro-business economics and regression on civil rights with democratic, even populist, forward-looking political appeals," as the historian Sean Wilentz has written.

Reagan won the 1980 election with 43.9 million votes (51 percent of the total) to Carter's 35 million (41 percent), and by 489 electoral votes to 49. (Independent John Anderson received almost 6 million votes.) The Democrats held on to the House of Representatives, albeit with a reduced majority, but they lost control of the Senate for the first time since 1954. The right rejoiced. Reagan had delivered them to the promised land at last.

Yet, just as had happened in California when he was governor, Reagan the president proved to be less rigidly conservative in practice than he seemed as a candidate.

Things began well enough. Embracing "supply-side economics," in early 1981, the president proposed cuts in federal income and business taxes of 30 percent to help revive the economy. The theory, which had been incubated in right-wing think tanks and extensively funded by New Right supporting foundations such as the Smith Richardson Foundation, maintained that large tax cuts of this kind would dramatically stimulate investment, create more jobs, and actually raise tax revenues, benefiting not just the rich and corporations but those on lower incomes as well, as the economy as a whole grew. Critics dismissed the idea as a polished-up version of the discredited "trickle-down" theories of the 1920s; Vice President George H. W. Bush had ridiculed the plan as "voodoo economics" when running against Reagan during the Republican primaries. But following extensive lobbying by business groups, the New Right, and the administration itself—and on the back of a public wave of sympathy for the president after his attempted assassination by John Hinckley in March 1981—Congress passed Reagan's bill as the Economic Tax Recovery Act in July. The final legislation altered the proposed tax cut to 25 percent—still the largest single tax cut in U.S. history—reduced the top tax rates from 70 percent to 50 percent; cut capital gains, estate, and gift taxes; eliminated bracket creep; and increased depreciation allowances for businesses. Reagan signed it into law on August 13, along with the Omnibus Reconciliation Act, which cut government spending by some $35 billion, mostly in areas such as low-income housing, food stamps, school lunches, and aid to families with dependent children: anti-poverty programs that had been largely created during the 1960s under Lyndon Johnson's Great Society reforms.

Government regulations were cut back in the banking sector, in the communications industry, in the workplace, and with respect to the environment, and New Right figures such as James G. Watt and Rob Billings were brought into the administration. Billings joined the Department of Education; Watt became secretary of the interior. Watt, the founder of an anti-environmental advocacy group, the Mountain States Legal Foundation, funded by the Coors family, rejected the entire regulatory mission of the agency he headed. He imposed a moratorium on the creation of new national parks; closed down the Office of Surface Mining, which was supposed to watch over the strip-mining industry; and opened up previously sequestered land to logging, mining, and oil companies. "I don't believe the government should stand in the way of the free market, and I'm here to do what I can to make sure it doesn't," he stated. Anne Gorsuch Burford—mother of the future Supreme Court Justice Neil Gorsuch—provided another example of this approach as Reagan's head of the EPA.

Reagan demonstrated his bona fides with respect to labor issues, as well as burnishing his reputation as a "strong" leader more generally, when, on August 5, 1981, he fired more than eleven thousand members of the Professional Air Traffic Controllers Organization (PATCO), who had ignored his forty-eight-hour deadline to return to work. The workers had gone on strike to obtain better pay and conditions in violation of a ban on such action by federal employees working in critical industries. That PATCO had been one of the few unions to support Reagan in 1980, or that he himself was a former union leader did not deter the president in the slightest. Air traffic controllers from the military were brought in to keep the nation's skyways open until new civilian personnel could be trained.

Reagan also projected strength, his and the nation's, by authorizing a massive increase in military expenditure—"Defense is not a budget item," he told his staff, including Defense Secretary Caspar Weinberger. "You spend what you need"—including on a new Strategic Defense Initiative (better known, more colloquially, as the "Star Wars" program) that was intended to create a space-based laser system that would shoot down nuclear missiles before they could reach American soil. The right's deeply rooted anti-communism was also given clear support, nowhere more so than at a meeting of the National Association of Evangelicals, on March 8, 1983, in Orlando, Florida, when the president denounced the Soviet Union as an "evil empire" and the "focus of evil in the modern world."

Yet, despite all this, many in the New Right remained dissatisfied. In November 1980, during the Reagan transition, the Heritage Foundation had produced an enormous twenty-volume, three-thousand-page report entitled *Mandate for Leadership: Policy Management in a Conservative Administration*. Among other things, it called for the complete elimination of the Department of Education, the Department of Energy, and the EPA; an end to affirmative action programs; reduced rights for accused criminals; the abolition of restrictions on domestic intelligence work; the return of congressional panels on un-American "subversion"; and a general strengthening of the national security state. "It is axiomatic that individual liberties are secondary to the requirement of national security and internal civil order," the report stated. When little of this had been put into effect by the end of 1981, Heritage issued the administration a "pass but try harder" grade in its end-of-year assessment. In addition, while the tax cuts and the attempt to reduce government spending were certainly welcome, Reagan was doing nothing to tackle the really big-ticket entitlement programs like Social Security and Medicare, which together accounted for 48 percent of the government's budget—not least because, as Reagan well understood, they remained extremely popular with voters despite their immense cost. Rather, in 1983, he accepted the recommendations of a bipartisan committee led by the economist Alan Greenspan that Congress "should not alter the fundamental structure of the Social Security program or undermine its fundamental principles." In order to keep the program solvent, the president agreed to increase payroll taxes as well.

Reagan also demonstrated his "pragmatism" in the face of the recession that struck the country in 1982. It was even worse than the economic downturn of 1973–1975. Unemployment climbed to more than eleven million, thousands of businesses failed, the housing market crashed, and the federal deficit ballooned to $200 billion a year. (The deficit when Carter left office had been $80 billion.) In response Reagan signed the Tax Equity and Fiscal Responsibility Act into law, which raised taxes on business and created new excise taxes on goods like tobacco and alcohol. In total, Reagan raised taxes three times while in office—although he would euphemistically refer to these actions as "revenue enhancers" rather than tax increases—and the overall tax burden remained much the same at the end of his two terms as it had been at the beginning. Howard Phillips's Conservative Caucus and Terry Dolan's NCPAC's preferred response to the recession was the implementation of what Allan Lichtman calls an "austerity budget," one that would have cut domestic spending by 30 percent, increased military spending by 20 percent, introduced further tax cuts, and continued with more government deregulation.

If the leaders of the nominally secular New Right had ample reason to feel disillusioned, this was even more the case for those in the New Christian Right. Other than continuing to offer extensive rhetorical and symbolic support, Reagan, both in his first term and during his second, failed to deliver on any of the major social or moral issues that were so

important to the religious right. There was no constitutional amendment
on abortion; no return to school prayer; no clamp down on pornography, promiscuity, or gay rights. There wasn't even a restoration of the tax
exemptions private church schools had lost. There was, though, a highly
controversial, ineffective, and costly "war on drugs." And although Reagan successfully appointed Antonin Scalia, Sandra Day O'Connor, and
Anthony Kennedy—but not Robert Bork—to the Supreme Court, only
Scalia would prove to be reliably conservative in his judgments.

By 1983 Richard Viguerie was accusing Reagan of simply paying "lip
service" to the New Right and its philosophy, complaining that behind the
façade of the much-lauded "Reagan Revolution," conventional politics was
going on very much as usual. Viguerie even toyed with the idea of running a new third-party "populist" candidate against the president in 1984.
Viguerie's thinking on this matter was set out in his book *The Establishment
vs The People: Is a New Populist Revolt on the Way?*, in which he assailed
"Big Business, Big Banks, Big Media, Big Unions, Big Government, and
their allies" and offered "100 Ways to Make America Great Again."

By the time the election came around, however, the economy had
recovered dramatically. Whether this was because of "Reaganomics,"
changes in the global market, or the federal government's (classically
Keynesian) increased deficit financing and massive military spending
spending—$800 billion during its first four years in office—remains a
matter of much debate. In any event, no one, certainly not the Democratic candidate Walter Mondale, was in any position to seriously challenge the incumbent in 1984. It was "morning again in America," as Reagan's campaign slogan had it. Optimism surged, patriotism flourished,
and unabashed consumerism quickly became the order of the day. (It
was during this period that future president Donald J. Trump first came
to widespread public attention. His ghostwritten first book, *The Art of the
Deal*, was published in 1987, for example.) Reagan defeated Mondale eas-
ily, by 54.5 million votes to 37.6 million, and by 525 electoral votes to 13.

Reagan's second term was marked by the "gridlock" of divided government, especially after the Democrats added control of the Senate to
that of the House in the 1986 midterm elections; by a major scandal over
a secret CIA program to sell weapons to Iran in order to secure the release
of American hostages in the Middle East and the subsequent diversion
of the profits on these weapons sales to the Nicaraguan contras who

were trying to overthrow the left-wing Sandinista government of Daniel Oretga; and by a series of ground-breaking summits with the Soviet Premier Mikhail Gorbachev—in Reykjavik, Washington, and Moscow, between 1986 and 1988—that led to the passage of one major arms control agreement (the Intermediate-Range Nuclear Forces Treaty of 1987) and, more importantly, significantly lowered Cold War tensions overall. (Despite his long history of anti-communism, and although much celebrated later as the person who had "won the Cold War," at the time Reagan was criticized by many on the right for his willingness to "sell out" the United States in this way.) In the end, Reagan left office with an approval rating of 63 percent, the first president to complete two terms in office since Dwight Eisenhower in 1961.

President Ronald Reagan in the Oval Office, Washington, D.C., in 1986. Despite its practical limitations, Reagan's rhetorical assault on "big government" made him a hero to the radical right, as well as to conservatives more broadly. Library of Congress Prints & Photographs Division, Carol M. Highsmith Archive, LC-DIG-highsm-14732.

Assessing Reagan's overall legacy, especially from the perspective of the radical right and its goals during this period, is difficult. On the one hand, the misery index was down to 9.6 percent by 1989. The country's gross domestic product (GDP) had doubled, close to eighteen million new jobs had been created, and billions of dollars of new wealth generated (although not very evenly distributed). Indeed, under Reagan's stewardship, the nation had witnessed the longest period of peacetime growth in its history. But he had not ushered in an era of small government or successfully reined in the social welfare spending of the New Deal state. Far from it. Federal taxes accounted for 19.4 percent of the national income in 1981; in 1989, the figure was 19.3 percent. The federal government actually employed more people in 1989 than it had in 1981 (3.1 million compared to 2.9 million). Federal spending as a percentage of GDP was also higher—at 21.2 percent—than it had been when the president took office. Meanwhile, the national debt had metastasized to $2.7 trillion dollars (53 percent of GDP, compared to 33 percent in 1981)—Reagan's "greatest failure," according to his biographer Lou Cannon.

On the other hand, Reagan had not just demonstrated the broad appeal and electoral viability of a more radical right-wing conservatism; he had helped to fundamentally transform American political life. "What Reagan ushered in was a skepticism toward government solutions to every problem, a suspicion of command-and-control, top-down social engineering. . . . That's a lasting legacy of the Reagan era and the conservative movement, starting with Goldwater," noted Barack Obama, when asked about his predecessor in 2009. After Reagan, questions about taxation, government spending, welfare, and the appropriate size of the state became central to U.S. politics, with "big government" liberals pushed increasingly onto the defensive. He had also successfully continued the "southern strategy" initiated by Goldwater, Wallace, and Nixon, drawing millions of former Democrats into the Republican Party, hastening the breakup of FDR's New Deal coalition, and pushing the GOP itself further to the right.

As for the New Right and the New Christian Right, the second half of the 1980s were not good years. Not just their influence but their energies waned. Having bound themselves firmly to the Reagan presidency, they found it very difficult to pull away when the administration started to disappoint them. The movement itself also suffered setbacks. Terry

Dolan died in 1986. Both Viguerie's RAVCO company and Falwell's Moral Majority were beset with financial problems, and leading televangelists Jim Bakker and Jimmy Swaggart were underdone by scandals in their respective ministries. Pat Robertson made an abortive bid for the presidency by entering the Republican primaries in 1988, but having finished second in Iowa's caucus and third in South Carolina, he was soon forced to drop out of the race. He won only 9 percent of the Republican vote, as George H. W. Bush went on to secure both the nomination and the presidency.

Nonetheless, as this chapter has shown, the impact of the New Right coalition had still been considerable. Its members had pioneered new ways of fund-raising, created a plethora of new political organizations, and drawn thousands of grassroots activists into the political process for the first time. They had established influential think tanks, fought numerous campaigns, and helped propel moral and social issues onto the nation's political agenda. They had forged powerful links between the business community, the religious right, and the Republican Party, and whatever their sense of disappointment at its final record of achievement, they had helped to usher in the Reagan presidency, the crowning moment of American conservatism to date.

The New Right had also laid the groundwork for many political and cultural conflicts to come. In particular, as we shall see in the chapters that follow, a profound suspicion and deep distrust of government would remain central to the radical right as it continued to develop in the 1990s and beyond.

5

Radicalism Rising

Conspiracies and Anti-Statism at Century's End

AT 9:02 A.M. ON APRIL 19, 1995, a massive truck-bomb exploded outside the Alfred P. Murrah Federal Building in Oklahoma City, killing 168 people and injuring more than 500, the worst act of domestic terrorism in American history. It was carried out by an anti-government extremist called Timothy McVeigh with the aid of his friend Terry Nichols. McVeigh was a veteran of the Gulf War of 1990–1991, who had been radicalized by his experiences in the nation's white supremacist and gun cultures and especially by his conspiratorial understanding of the federal government's "attack" on the Branch Davidian complex at Waco, Texas, in April 1993, although the particular inspiration for the bombing seemed to have been provided by a racist novel called *The Turner Diaries* written by William Pierce under the pseudonym Andrew MacDonald. One of the consequences of the bombing was to cast a spotlight onto an entirely new radical right-wing political movement in the United States, the militia movement, whose members were both heavily armed and prone to comparing themselves to the nation's Revolutionary-era founding fathers— "We're the George Washingtons of today," as Bob Fletcher, a member of the Militia of Montana, put it.

As it turned out, neither McVeigh nor Nichols formally belonged to a militia group, but there was little doubting that they shared many of the same views. On May 5, 1995, during a commencement address at Michigan State University, President Bill Clinton forcefully condemned "the militias and all others who believe that the greatest threat to freedom comes from the government instead of from those who would take away our freedom." "How dare you suggest that we in the freest nation on earth live in tyranny! How dare you call yourselves patriots and heroes!" he went on. He added that in his view there was "nothing patriotic about . . . pretending that you can love your country, but despise your government."

This chapter examines the rise of the militia movement, but it also continues the story of the last chapter by addressing the increasingly rightward shift of the Republican Party throughout the 1990s, focusing especially on House Speaker Newt Gingrich (GA) and his "Contract with America." Indeed, as we shall see, Gingrich and his allies were some of the "others" Clinton was taking aim at in his speech at Michigan State, and their hostility toward the president would ultimately lead to his impeachment in 1998. Additionally, the chapter explores how the New Christian Right—now largely referred to simply as the Christian Right—continued to develop, particularly in the form of Pat Robertson's new organization, the Christian Coalition, led initially by Ralph Reed. Finally, the conspiracy theories and anti-government rhetoric coursing through the nation more broadly—especially on its airwaves—are considered. We begin, though, with the 1992 presidential election, and the right-wing and populist challenges George H. W. Bush faced from within his own party.

Despite gamely presenting himself as a "genuine" conservative, Bush's four years in office had revealed him to be exactly what he always was: a Republican moderate. He had successes overseas—deposing the Panamanian dictator and drug trafficker Manuel Noriega in 1990; winning the first Gulf War in 1991; presiding calmly over the ending of the Cold War and the formal dissolution of the Soviet Union on December 25, 1991—but domestically he infuriated the right by raising taxes in an attempt to deal with massive budget deficits bequeathed to him by his predecessor. In doing so, not only did he supposedly betray Reagan's legacy, he also broke a central campaign promise—"Read my lips: No new taxes," he had famously pledged in 1988. Worse still, the economy had slid back into recession, with unemployment rising to 7.8 percent by mid-1991. As a result, Bush faced not one but two radical challengers in 1992, first in the Republican primaries with Pat Buchanan and then in the general election itself from Ross Perot. Both provided early heralds of some of the language and some of the ideas that would come increasingly to the fore in American politics in the years to come.

Patrick "Pat" Buchanan was a former special assistant and speech-writer to Richard Nixon, a newspaper columnist, and a director of communications for Ronald Reagan. After leaving the Reagan White House in 1987, he became the co-host of cable station CNN's combative new nightly talk show, *Crossfire*. A self-styled "pit bull of the right," Buchanan wanted to outlaw abortion, end affirmative action programs, cut taxes, and freeze all government spending. A committed nationalist and isolationist, he also wanted to dramatically reduce immigration and eradicate "unfair" free trade agreements that he believed undermined the American economy. To this end, he proposed the creation of a two-hundred-mile long "Buchanan fence" across the Mexican border and promised to put "America first." Amazingly, despite limited finances and almost no campaign organization, Buchanan won 34 percent of the vote in the opening New Hampshire primary (to Bush's 53 percent). In March he drew almost 28 percent of the vote in Bush's home state of Texas, and overall he took 22.5 percent of the votes cast in the primaries.

As far as "protest" campaigns go, it was highly effective, and one of its consequences was to push Bush further to the right. This was evident in the official Republican platform, which, among other things, called for a complete ban on abortion, opposed gay rights, denounced the public funding of "obscene" art, and endorsed school prayer, home schooling, and the "traditional American family," while promising to lower taxes, cut government regulations, and defend "the individual against the domineering state." But it was made even clearer during the Republican convention, held in Houston in August 1992. Featuring prominent speeches from many right-wing conservatives, including a reenergized Pat Robertson, discussed below, and Marilyn Quayle, the wife of Bush's vice president Dan Quayle, it was Buchanan who stole the show on the convention's opening night with his ominous primetime declaration that there was "a religious war going on in our country for the soul of America." It was a "cultural war," he proclaimed, "as critical to the kind of nation we will one day be as was the cold war itself."

H. Ross Perot shared some of Buchanan's concerns and stressed some of the same issues—although not the cultural or social ones—but overall his attacks on Bush had a more populist, less ideological edge to them. Perot was a billionaire businessman from Texarkana, Texas, who had made his fortune through his Electronic Data Services company, which

he founded in Dallas in 1962. The company was the beneficiary of lucrative federal government contracts during the 1960s, including for the
computerization of Medicare and Medicaid records. A fervent supporter
of the Vietnam War, he fell out with the Nixon administration over what
he regarded as its inadequate handling of the issue of American prisoners
of war and those missing in action. He continued his POW-MIA campaign under Reagan and was even given access to classified documents,
until his security clearance was revoked. That Bush, then Reagan's vice
president, was tasked with informing Perot of this provided Perot with
an added level of personal animus toward his fellow Texan.

Perot announced his intention to run as an independent candidate
against Bush on CNN's *Larry King Live* show on February 20, 1992; he
had been hinting at the possibility for some time before this and insisted
that he was only now entering the race because of the groundswell of
support for his (nominally) grassroots United We Stand organization. It
was a campaign that was conducted mostly in the media—especially on
television—and which emphasized his business competence alongside
his folksy, down-to-earth common sense. Throughout, Perot assailed
the Bush administration—and the federal government more broadly—
for its incompetence, ineffectiveness, and irresponsibility. The budget
deficit "was like a crazy aunt we keep down in the basement," he said.
"All the neighbors know she's there but nobody wants to talk about her."
He warned that the North American Free Trade Agreement between
Canada, Mexico, and the United States would swiftly lead to the "giant
sucking sound" of jobs being drawn out of the country. In fact, the whole
"federal jalopy" was broke, Perot contended, and it needed someone like
him to "get under the hood" of gridlocked government and fix it.

By June, according to opinion polls, Perot was actually the front-runner in the entire race—with 39 percent of support, compared to 31 percent for Bush and 25 percent for Clinton—but a month later, on July
16, he mysteriously dropped out. At the time, he said it was because
"the Democratic Party had revitalized itself," and he had concluded
that he could no longer win. When he reentered the campaign in October, he explained that his initial withdrawal had actually been because
the Republican Party had been secretly plotting to smear his daughter's
good name with an altered photograph depicting her as a lesbian and also
intended to disrupt her wedding. "I can't prove any of it today," he told

Businessman Ross Perot with Republican freshmen Congress members speaking at a press conference in the U.S. Capitol in May 1993. Library of Congress Prints & Photographs Division. Photographed by Maureen Keating. LC-DIG-ppmsca-38866.

CBS's *60 Minutes*. "But it was a risk I did not have to take, and a risk I would not take where my daughter is concerned." White House spokesman Marlin Fitzwater countered that the "fantastic" allegations were "all loony," while the *New York Times* pointed out that Perot had a well-established reputation for embracing "conspiracy theorists from both the far left and the far right wings of politics."

As already noted, Bush's Democratic opponent in 1992 was the five-time governor of Arkansas, William Jefferson Clinton. Although a professed admirer of both FDR and JFK, his campaign reflected just how much of an impact the Reagan years had had on the political culture overall. Clinton was a "New Democrat," he said, one seeking a "third way" beyond the traditional enmities of left and right. He would work with business, was in favor of "opportunity," wanted to tackle the deficit, and intended to cut taxes for the middle class. He would reduce crime, uphold the death penalty, build a strong military, and "end welfare as we know it." But he would also extend health care, invest heavily in education and infrastructure, and create a greater sense of "community." As he explained to the Democratic Leadership Council's national convention in early 1991: "Too many of the people who vote for us . . . have not trusted us in national elections to defend our national interests abroad, to put their values into our social policy at home, or to take their tax money and spend it with discipline. We have got to turn these perceptions around or we cannot continue as a national party."

Having initially underestimated Clinton, as the campaign reached its final weeks, Bush tried to impugn his character and his patriotism, including by suggesting that he had secretly visited Moscow for nefarious purposes when he was a Rhodes scholar at Oxford University and that he had tried to renounce his citizenship in order to dodge the draft during the Vietnam War. It was to no avail. Sticking to his campaign mantra of "It's the economy, stupid!"—the message was affixed to the wall of his national headquarters in Little Rock, Arkansas—Clinton won by 44.9 million votes (43 percent of the total) to Bush's 39.1 million (37.4 percent) and Perot's 19.7 million (19 percent). In the Electoral College the vote was 370 to 168. The Democrats also maintained control of both houses of Congress, losing nine seats in the House but gaining one in the Senate.

Setting a precedent that would be followed during the presidency of Barack Obama, the Republican right determined to oppose Clinton from the outset, refusing to cooperate in any way with his legislative agenda and seeking to undermine him at every turn. To a considerable extent, the right regarded Clinton as an "illegitimate" president. After all, he had "won" with less than 50 percent of the vote, and only then—they reassured themselves—because Perot's quixotic candidacy had split the Republican vote. (Subsequent analysis showed this not to be the case. Perot's support came equally from both parties. As E. J. Dionne, among others, has pointed out, Clinton would still have won an outright majority even "if Perot had not rejoined the contest.") The legislative opposition manifested itself in the Republicans' refusal to cast even a single vote in favor of Clinton's initial budget, but it was most evident in the party's determination to resist the administration's signature first-term initiative: health care reform.

Creating a health care system that would guarantee insurance for every American citizen had been a goal of the Democratic Party ever since the days of Harry Truman. Bypassing Congress, Clinton entrusted the drafting of his proposal—which he promised to deliver within his first one hundred days in office—to a health care task force led by his wife, Hillary Rodham Clinton, and his longtime policy advisor Ira Magaziner. That Hillary Clinton was unelected and that much of the task force's work was completed in secrecy did not help endear the resultant 1,300-page proposal to its opponents, but then again whatever had emerged from the task force was always going to be resisted by those on the American right. William Kristol—Dan Quayle's former chief of staff and the son of prominent neoconservative Irving Kristol—had made this very clear in a memo he sent to Republican leaders in December 1993.

Irrespective of the practical objections one could make about the specifics of the Clinton plan—and there were many—Kristol was candid about the ideological and political necessity of killing the proposed legislation. Not for nothing was the memo titled "A Serious Threat to the Republican Party." "Passage of the Clinton health care plan, *in any form*," he argued,

> would guarantee and likely make permanent an unprecedented federal intrusion into and disruption of the American economy—and the establishment of the largest federal entitlement program since Social Security. Its success would signal a rebirth of centralized welfare-state policy at the very moment we have begun rolling back that idea in other areas.

In addition, implementation of the bill would "revive the reputation" of the Democrats as "the generous protector of middle-class interests," while damaging the GOP's own reputation in that area. It would also encourage the introduction of more "progressive" legislation in the future. For all these reasons—and many others—Kristol advised that delivering an "unqualified political defeat of the Clinton health care proposal" was essential. "Its rejection by Congress and the public would be a monumental setback for the president, and an incontestable piece of evidence that Democratic welfare-state liberalism remains firmly in retreat," he explained.

Both within Congress and without, right-wing opponents of the bill went to work. Dick Armey (TX), chair of the House Republican Conference, rallied the faithful by calling the health care proposal "the most important domestic policy debate of the past half-century"—the "Battle of the Bulge of big-government liberalism." The rising star of the radical congressional right, House minority whip Newt Gingrich (GA), argued that the Clintons "were going against the entire tide of Western history" with their planned reforms. "I mean centralized, command bureaucracies are dying," he explained. "This is the end of that era, not the beginning of it." The Business Roundtable, the National Association of Manufacturers, the U.S. Chamber of Commerce, and the American Medical Association all opposed the bill, as did the Heritage Foundation and other members of the New Right and the New Christian Right. Insurers large and small joined with Pat Robertson's Christian Coalition (see below), the American Conservative Union, and other groups to create the Coalition for Health Insurance Choices and Citizens Against Rationing Health Care. In total more than $50 million was spent on political advertising opposing the Clinton plan, including a widely broadcast series of television commercials produced by the Health Insurance Association of America, in which an attractive, fictional, middle-class couple called "Harry and Louise" expressed their deep concerns about the plan's costs, its restrictive choices, and the expected expansion of government control over their lives.

In the end, Clinton wasn't even able to get his proposals onto the floor of Congress for a vote. The whole idea of health care reform was abandoned for good in August 1994. It was a humiliating failure—although battle would resume again during the Obama and Trump administrations.

With Clinton weakened and the 1994 midterm elections fast approaching, the radical Republican right sensed its opportunity. Led by Gingrich and Armey but aided by the Republican National Committee and the "public opinion guru" Frank Luntz, a wide-ranging and intensely conservative manifesto called "Contract with America" was drafted. In September, on the steps of the U.S. capitol, 367 Republican congressmen officially signed themselves up to it. ("If we break this contract, throw us out," they all pledged.) In an "era of official evasion and posturing," the Contract promised to "restore the bonds of trust between the people and their elected representatives" and to bring an end to government that was "too big, too intrusive, and too easy with the public's money." More concretely, the Contract set out ten specific bills the House Republicans said would be swiftly introduced if they were successful in the forthcoming election. Included among them were proposals for: a "balanced budget/ tax limitation amendment," tougher punishments for criminals, significant reductions in welfare, tort reform to limit costly lawsuits against business owners, cuts in capital gains tax, a "first ever vote on term limits to replace career politicians with citizen legislators," and a ban on U.S. troops serving under the command of the United Nations. To sweeten their appeal even further, each of the legislative proposals were given a suggestive sounding name such as the American Dream Restoration Act, the National Security Restoration Act, the Parental Responsibility Act, and the Taking Back Our Streets Act.

Whether or not the Contract with America was decisive in the midterms—and post-election surveys suggested that it wasn't—the results were nonetheless devastating for Clinton and the Democratic Party. The Republicans gained fifty-four seats in the House, giving them a majority for the first time since 1954 (by 230 to 204), and they also took control of the Senate (with a 52 to 48 majority). Even more significantly, the 1994 election completed the southern realignment of the Republican Party. For the first time in American history, a majority of white southern Protestants had voted for Republican candidates. The GOP gained control of the House precisely because it had won the South. What's more, many of these incoming southern congressmen—there were seventy-three freshman Republicans in total—were even more right-wing than Gingrich and his established congressional colleagues. It wasn't just an "anti-Clinton vote," explained Senator Phil Gramm (R-TX) triumphantly; it was an "anti-government vote."

Indeed, overall, it is important to recognize just how consequential the 1994 midterm elections were. As Allan Lichtman has written, only "America's increasing diversity kept the GOP from becoming the nation's majority party after 1994." Because of these demographic changes—declining numbers of whites compared to increasing numbers of blacks, Hispanics, and Asians on the electoral roll—although the Republican victory did not finally reverse the old "New Deal realignment" of FDR, it did bring the GOP "into near parity with Democrats." The consequence would be an increasingly close-fought and an increasingly polarized—and bitterly partisan—politics in the United States from 1994 onward.

The Republicans were aided considerably in the midterms by the revived efforts of the Christian Right, especially Pat Robertson's new political organization, the Christian Coalition. Although he had been soundly defeated in his 1988 presidential bid (see chapter 4), Robertson had not given up on his ambitions to make America a "Christian nation." In January 1989 he asked a fresh-faced, twenty-seven-year-old called Ralph Reed to head up what would become the Coalition (at the time the proposed organization was still without a name). Reed officially became its executive director the following year. Born in Virginia, Reed had a PhD in history from Emory University, in Atlanta, Georgia; was a director of the National College Republicans; and had worked for the congressional campaigns of both Newt Gingrich and Jack Kemp (R-NY). Reed was energetic, articulate, and politically sophisticated; Robertson had made an inspired choice. Under Reed's leadership, within five years the Coalition had 1,600 chapters around the country, 1.6 million members, and an annual budget of $25 million—or so, it claimed; the exact numbers are difficult to verify.

Mirroring Robertson's own behind-the-scenes influence on the organization—a result, in part, of the widespread public suspicion of televangelists that had resulted from the scandals that engulfed the electronic ministry at the end of the 1980s—Reed initially adopted a stealth-based approach to achieving the Coalition's aims. "I want to be invisible," he informed the *Virginia Post* in 1991. "I do guerilla warfare. I paint my face and travel at night. You don't know it's over until you're in a body bag. You don't know until election night." Accordingly, Coalition activists were advised to moderate their language—to avoid talking about "religious war" or the perils of "secular humanism," for example—not even to "mention the name Christian Coalition in Republican circles," to "emphasize inclusion, not exclusion," and to "be tolerant of diverse views." The organization also first focused its efforts on the local and state level—on school boards, city councils, county commissions, state legislatures, and the like—in order to build up its power and influence, before moving on to Washington. In addition, like its predecessor, Jerry Falwell's Moral Majority, the Coalition was ecumenical in its political endeavors. Its overriding aim, it said, was to make "government more responsive to the concerns of Evangelical Christians and pro-family Catholics." In order to maintain its tax-exempt status, it was also officially—although not very convincingly—nonpartisan.

The stunning growth and success of the Coalition was such that it wasn't able to operate "under the radar" for very long. Having vocally opposed Clinton's "Don't Ask, Don't Tell" policy on gays in the military and spent more than $1 million helping to defeat his health care proposals, in 1994 it turned its attention to the upcoming midterm elections. The results were spectacular. Reed, along with his allies on the religious right, succeeded in mobilizing white evangelicals in record numbers—somewhere in the region of four million. Fully 70 percent of the votes they cast went to Republican candidates as they became the GOP's largest single voting bloc. It was true that the Christian Right's influence was amplified by the relatively low overall turnout of 38 percent, but that was part of the point: Christian conservatives cared enough to take part; they were ready and willing to mobilize. Furthermore, as Frances Fitzgerald has noted, the Coalition's initial localized emphasis had also paid dividends, as it came "to dominate the Republican Party apparatus in a dozen states, including Texas and Florida."

Leveraging its now undeniable importance, in May of 1995 the Coalition drafted its own "Contract with the American Family," a set of "pro-family" legislative proposals intended to both support and extend the Republican's "Contract with America." (Gingrich had intentionally avoided mentioning potentially divisive cultural and social issues in his document in order to give it the broadest possible appeal. After the election results, this no longer seemed a necessary concern.) Included among them—in mirroring ten-point form—were calls for guaranteed school prayer, the abolition of the Department of Education, the elimination of public funding for the National Endowment of the Arts, limits on abortion and pornography, and a voucher system that would allow religious parents to send their children to schools of their choosing. Few of these goals would be achieved while Clinton was president—or indeed, thereafter—but the Christian Right had nonetheless become a central—some would say indispensable—part of the Republican Party. Its influence would outlast both Ralph Reed (with Robertson's blessing, he resigned from the organization in 1997 to start his own political consultancy business) and the Christian Coalition itself.

As the victorious new Speaker of the House, Gingrich wasted no time attempting to consolidate his power and to put the Contract with America into effect. Ignoring long-established seniority rules, he appointed committee chairmen who would be personally loyal to him, and by April 7, 1994—just as he had promised—the House had voted on all of the

Contract's main provisions. However, although nine were approved, with the exception of some relatively minor tax cuts, the successful deregulation of the telephone and cable television industry, and the restructuring of the Aid to Families with Dependent Children Act, which provided financial aid to children in low-income families, none of the Contract's really major reforms were ultimately able to find their way through the opposition they encountered in the more centrist Senate or beyond Clinton's presidential veto. Nor was Clinton as finished as he seemed. Drawing on the advice of the political strategist Dick Morris, he began to practice the politics of "triangulation," which meant, he said, "bridging the divide between Republicans and Democrats and taking the best ideas of both." More critical observers saw it as a shift from a governing approach based on principle to one based on simple popularity.

The president was aided in his fight back by the events surrounding the bombing of the Murrah Federal Building in Oklahoma City on April 19, 1995. Not only did he display an extraordinary empathy for those who had been killed and injured in the attack, as well as their families, as he led the nation through its period of mourning with moving eloquence, but from a political perspective he also found an effective way to connect the bombing with the right-wing assault on government that was taking place both in Congress and the wider political culture. In order to understand this more fully, though, we first need to examine the bombing, the militia movement, and this broader political culture, including its conspiracy theories, more fully.

Extensively armed, driven by a deep distrust of the federal government, and often given to incendiary rhetorical outbursts, militias first began to appear on the American political landscape in early 1994. The two foundational groups were the Militia of Montana, formed in February, and the Michigan Militia, established in April. The movement spread extremely rapidly. By 1996, according to monitoring agencies such as the Southern Poverty Law Center's (SPLC) "Militia Task Force," there were close to 450 militia groups operating in all fifty states. Estimates of the total size of the movement in the mid-nineties ranged widely from seven thousand to three hundred thousand, but when militia sympathizers and "militia support groups" were added in, the figure rose to anywhere between five and twelve million. Part of the problem in obtaining reliable information on the movement was that it was both highly localized and extremely decentralized. There was no national organization to which all militia members belonged and no overall leader directing its affairs. Instead, what developed was a loosely related collection of individuals and groups with certain shared concerns, a spontaneous and genuinely grassroots new political movement.

Three events in particular spurred the formation of the movement. First was the siege of Randy Weaver and his family at Ruby Ridge, Idaho, in August 1992. Weaver was a white supremacist who had been arrested in January 1991 for selling two sawed-off shotguns to an undercover informant of the federal Bureau of Alcohol, Tobacco, and Firearms (ATF). On August 21 the following year, six camouflaged and heavily armed members of the U.S. Marshals service were conducting surveillance of Weaver's property when they were disturbed. A firefight ensued in which one of the Marshals, William Degan, and Weaver's fourteen-year-old son were killed. During the resultant eleven-day stand-off, Weaver's wife was also shot and killed by an FBI sniper. In April 1993 Weaver stood trial for the murder of Degan and other charges, but he was found guilty only of having failed to appear in court to answer the charge concerning the shotguns and of committing an offense while on release from a federal magistrate. In August 1995, he was awarded $3.1 million in settlement of a civil suit he had brought against the federal government.

The events at Ruby Ridge were followed by the disastrous assault on the Branch Davidian compound of David Koresh at Waco, Texas, in April 1993. The ATF suspected that Koresh and his followers—about 130 Davidians and their families lived at the Mount Carmel site—were involved in the manufacture and sale of illegal weapons and explosives, and there were additional concerns about the possibility of child abuse and a potential drug-making laboratory. On February 28, 1993, the ATF attempted to serve a search and arrest warrant on Koresh, but a gun battle erupted in which four federal agents were killed and another twenty wounded. Five Davidians also lost their lives. The FBI's elite Hostage Rescue Team was called in to take command, but negotiations failed. On April 19, armored tanks equipped with battering rams began inserting canisters of CS gas into the compound in the hope of finally "flushing" the Davidians out. After four hours, a fire broke out inside the complex—subsequent investigations determined that it had been deliberately started by the Davidians themselves—killing at least seventy-four men, women, and children, as the whole event was broadcast live on television. In 1994 eleven survivors from the fire stood trial for conspiracy to murder federal agents and other lesser offenses. Four were acquitted, five were convicted of voluntary manslaughter, and two were found guilty on weapons charges.

Neither Ruby Ridge nor Waco reflected well on the government. In both cases the scale of the operations seemed out of all proportion to the crimes that had supposedly been committed. In addition, not only did the jury in Randy Weaver's trial conclude that he had been deliberately entrapped by the ATF on the original shotgun charges against him, but it also soon became apparent that instead of "stockpiling" weapons to prepare for some kind of showdown with the state, Koresh had actually been trading them as part of a legitimate business venture to generate funds to support his church. The allegations of child abuse that had reportedly swayed Attorney General Janet Reno to approve the use of tear gas also proved to be false. Nor were the Davidians illegally manufacturing drugs. In fact, although it was firmly denied by the ATF, at least part of the motivation for the large-scale, high-profile nature of the initial raid on the compound—referred to as "Operation Showtime"—seemed to have been congressional budget hearings scheduled for March 10, 1993. The agency had been under threat since the Reagan administration had threatened its disbandment in the 1980s, and so, critics suggested, needed a big "success" in order to improve its prospects in those hearings.

For those on the American far right, however, what took place at Ruby Ridge and Waco seemed much more sinister. Both events were taken as providing clear evidence not just of oppressive government agencies at work but of the state intentionally targeting groups with "unconventional" views. The implications were disturbing. Who would be next? As Bob Clark, a member of the Michigan Militia, explained to the journalist Mack Tanner in early 1995:

> First the feds put that Reverend Moon character in jail for tax evasion. I thought that was a great idea. Then they went after that guy from India with all those limousines in Oregon, which was okay with me too. But I started getting worried when I learned about what happened to

> Randy Weaver. When the FBI killed all those people in Waco, I asked
> myself who they were going to come for next, the Baptists?

Waco in particular, by appearing to establish a pattern of governmental
misdeeds, had a major impact on the development of the militia movement, seeming to offer "proof," in the words of scholar Jeffrey Kaplan,
"that the U.S. government had declared open season on its citizens."
Both the Militia of Montana and the Michigan Militia described it as
their "wake-up call," for example.

It also had a profound effect on the Oklahoma City bomber, Timothy McVeigh. He traveled down to Mount Carmel during the fifty-one-
day "siege," where he sold anti-government pamphlets out of his car. As
his biographers Dan Herbeck and Lou Michael have shown, McVeigh's
understanding of what had happened to Koresh and his followers was
based, to a considerable extent, on the "evidence" presented in future
militia leader Linda Thompson's conspiratorial videos *Waco: The Big Lie*
and *Waco II: The Big Lie Continues*. His conclusion was that the "government's sole intention" had been "to destroy the Davidians." It was no
coincidence, therefore, that the bombing of the Murrah Building took
place on the second anniversary of the ending of the "Waco massacre."

One final matter connected Ruby Ridge and Waco, and that was the
issue of guns and gun rights. Hence when the Brady Handgun Violence
Prevention Act became law in November 1993, the response was dramatic. This was the third event central to the militia movement's rise.
Named for James Brady, Reagan's press secretary, who had been shot
during John Hinckley's attempted assassination of the president in 1981,
the Act was the first major piece of federal gun control legislation since
the Gun Control Act of 1968. Its principal effect was to institute a five-
day waiting period for the purchase of handguns. To militia members
and many in the wider gun lobby, however, the law was both an unwarranted attack on Americans' constitutional right "to keep and bear arms"
and the baleful harbinger of even more restrictive measures to come—as
was seemingly confirmed by provisions in the following year's Violent
Crime Control Act that banned the sale of nineteen types of semi-automatic assault weapons and also introduced a ten-bullet limit on gun clips.

A host of other issues—some local, some national, and some global,
and many similar, if not identical, to those that were animating the

more radical members of the Republican Party and the Christian Right at this time—also spurred the growth of the militia movement during the 1990s. Included among them were: abortion rights, states' rights, affirmative action, environmental issues, immigration policy, gay rights, taxation, border security, educational standards, the United Nations, and the negative impact of international trade agreements like NAFTA or the General Agreement on Tariffs and Trade (GATT) on the American economy. What distinguished the militias, in general terms—and not all militias were exactly alike, it's important to stress—was how they responded to these issues: their ready embrace of arms, uniforms, and paramilitary posturing; their strident and frequently violent rhetoric; and the conspiratorial framework in which their ideas and beliefs were frequently cast.

The officially stated aim of the Michigan Militia, for example, was to confront "tyranny, globalism, moral relativism, humanism and the New World Order threatening to undermine these United States of America." The group was established by a real estate agent called Ray Southwell, with the help of Baptist minister and gun store owner, the Reverend Norman Olson, following a dispute between Southwell and his local school board over the teaching of what Southwell called "socialist values." The lesson the two men drew from this experience—and from broader trends in American life—was that "you are not in control of your life, your children, your home. The government is in control." "We have to let the tyrants, the politicians, and the bureaucrats know that we're taking a stand," Southwell explained. Donning military fatigues and training at least twice a month with loaded weapons, they thus started to prepare for the coming day when "the Constitution will be suspended" and "martial law imposed."

Similarly, the Militia of Montana—formed by a retired snowmobile salesman called John Trochmann, together with his brother, David, and his nephew, Randy—spoke of the "power hungry individuals [who] have corrupted our government and are working on sabotaging our freedom by destroying the Constitution . . . in order to establish the 'New World Order.'" Linda Thompson, self-proclaimed acting adjutant general of the Unorganized Militia of the United States, argued, "We've got to throw off the tyrants, as occurred first in 1776," and saw this scenario as likely to "occur within the next 20 years." J. J. Johnson, the leader of the

Ohio Unorganized Militia and one of the few prominent African Americans in the movement, suggested to Congress, in a hearing held in the aftermath of the Oklahoma City bombing, that "the only thing standing between some of the current legislation being contemplated [in Washington] and armed conflict is time."

On other occasions, militia members could be heard mumbling darkly about sinister black government helicopters that were being used to spy on law-abiding citizens; about the building of concentration camps to house "Patriot resisters"; and of secret markings that could be found on the back of road signs to help guide future invading UN forces. Not surprisingly, then, for Kenneth Stern and many other observers of the movement, the militias were simply the latest manifestation of Richard Hofstadter's "paranoid style" in American history.

George H. W. Bush had expressed his hopes for a "new world order" of peace and security in an address to a joint session of Congress in September 1990 at the end of the Cold War, but this wasn't the sense in which militia members were using the term. On the contrary, in their view Bush and other "global elitists" were all part of an ongoing conspiracy to undermine American sovereignty in order to make the country part of a new "one-world government." The most well-known and influential proponent of this theory was actually Pat Robertson. His 1991 book *The New World Order* was a *New York Times* best seller, selling more than half a million copies. In it, Robertson outlined a vast conspiratorial web—one comparable to the work of Robert Welch and Joe McCarthy earlier in the century—of manipulative bankers, political dupes, corporate stooges, international financiers, Freemasons, Bolsheviks, and members of the Bavarian Illuminati, whose "grand design" was the creation not just of a "one-world government," but also a "one-world army, a one-world economy . . . and a world dictator served by a council of twelve faithful men." Prominent among Robertson's list of malefactors within the United States were the Trilateral Commission, the Council on Foreign Relations, the Federal Reserve, the Rockefeller and Ford Foundations, the J. P. Morgan Bank, and various individuals from Woodrow Wilson to Henry Kissinger.

In February 1995, the *New York Review of Books* ran a highly critical review of Robertson's book, noting his constant references to Jewish bankers and demonstrating his reliance on well-known anti-Semites such

as Nesta Webster and Eustace Mullins for the "evidence" he was presenting. Robertson denied that he was anti-Semitic. He did not believe that
international finance should be seen as Jewish, he said. He was a strong
supporter of Israel and blamed one of his researchers for coming up with
the material from Webster and Mullins. Nor, he added, did he "embrace
a conspiracy theory of history."

Militias too were accused of anti-Semitism and also of racism. Concerns about the similarity of many of their anti-government views to
those of explicitly racist groups such as the Aryan Nations and Posse
Comitatus; the often indiscriminate circulation of various forms of racist or anti-Semitic propaganda to be found at militia meetings, on their
websites, or at gun shows; and the vulnerability of the movement to infiltration by racists and other extremists who were looking to "present a
'patriotic' face to the public and the media," in the words of the SPLC,
were all frequently expressed. Most informed observers agreed that the
movement as a whole was not being driven by racism or anti-Semitism,
but this did little to quell the widespread public and political anxiety that
surrounded it. These fears were encapsulated by Montana state senator
and director of the Montana Human Rights Network, Ken Toole, who
described the movement as being like a "funnel moving through space":

> At the front end, it's picking up lots and lots of people by hitting on
> issues that have wide appeal, like gun control and environmental re-
> strictions, which enrage many people here in the West. Then you go
> a little bit further into the funnel, and it's about ideology, about the
> oppressiveness of the federal government. Then further in you get the
> belief systems. The conspiracy. The Illuminati. The Freemasons. Then
> it's about the anti-Semitic conspiracy. Finally, at the narrowest end of
> the funnel, you've drawn in the hard core, where you get someone like
> Tim McVeigh popping out.

The worry for Toole and others who monitored the far right was that
the "bigger the front end of the tunnel is, the bigger the number that get
to the core."

Militia members and others on the margins of American society were
not the only ones prone to inflammatory anti-government rhetoric in the
mid-1990s, however. For example, on April 13, 1995, Wayne LaPierre,
executive vice president of the 3.5 million-strong gun rights' advocacy

group the National Rifle Association (NRA), wrote a highly charged six-page fund-raising letter to his members. Specifically referencing the events at Ruby Ridge and Waco, as well as the more recent ban on semi-automatic weapons, he warned of "our freedoms slowly slipping away when jack-booted government thugs, wearing black, armed to the teeth, break down a door, open fire . . . and kill or maim law-abiding citizens." ("In Clinton's administration," he continued, "if you have a badge, you have the government's go-ahead to harass, intimidate, *even murder*" [emphasis in original].) The popular right-wing talk-show host Rush Limbaugh, whose daily broadcasts reached an estimated twenty million Americans, could also be heard speculating about the possibility of a "second violent American revolution" over the issue of property rights. "I got my fingers about a quarter of an inch apart," he told his radio audience early in 1994. The revolution was "just about that far away," he said, because people "are sick and tired of a bunch of bureaucrats in Washington driving into town and telling them what they can and can't do with their land." G. Gordon Liddy, the disgraced former Watergate burglar and talk radio's "host of the year" for 1995, went even further still. Having already described the cardboard cut-outs of Bill and Hillary Clinton that he used for target practice, he offered his listeners some very practical advice on what to do when the "brutal thugs" of the ATF came "smashing" into their homes. "Head shots, head shots," he advised. "Kill the sons of bitches!"

Newt Gingrich's description of the Democrats as "enemies of normal Americans," or new House majority leader Dick Armey's taunting of his congressional opponents by referring to Clinton as "*your* president" or calling Hillary Clinton a "Marxist," seemed tame in comparison. Although there was also Jesse Helms's suggestion that the president "better have a bodyguard," should he decide to visit any military bases in the senator's home state of North Carolina—Helms said it was an "offhand remark," one that hadn't been intended to be taken literally. Clinton clearly had all of this in mind when he started warning that people "should examine the consequences of what they say and the kinds of emotions they're trying to inflame" in the aftermath of the Oklahoma City bombing.

The president incorporated this concern into his politics of "triangulation," part of his fight back against the House Republicans, whom he

increasingly tarred with the brush of extremism. Believing that Gingrich
and his allies were out of touch with the values of ordinary Americans—
who remained reluctant to give up the services and entitlements that "big
government" programs afforded them (as we saw in the previous chapter)—he even began turning some of the conservatives' key phrases and
ideas against them. In August 1995, for example, he opposed proposed
Republican cuts in social spending because the "congressional majority
seems to be determined to cut back on programs that advance our family
values." "How can you talk about family values in one breath," he rea-
soned, "and in the next, take Head Start away from 50,000 poor children
or cut back college loans and grants for students who need and deserve
them or cut back workers' training for people who are unemployed?"

Things came to a head in the bitter fight over the federal budget. From
the beginning of the fiscal year, on October 1, 1995, the government
had been operating on the basis of a series of continuing resolutions—
essentially temporary authorizations to spend funds—the first of which
was due to come to an end in mid-November. On November 10, the

President Bill Clinton delivers his 1995 State of the Union address as his arch
Republican adversary Newt Gingrich and Vice President Al Gore watch on.
Library of Congress Prints & Photographs Division, Roll Call Photograph Collec-
tion, LC-RC05-1995-5015.

Republicans delivered their budget proposal to the White House, but Clinton refused to approve it, resulting in a partial shutdown of government services that lasted for six days. In December, the Republicans returned with another budget, which included deep cuts in Medicare funding—intended to save $270 billion over five years—and a plan to shift much of the responsibility for the program from the federal government to the states—where it was assumed that further cuts would take place—as well as a large tax cut for the wealthy (worth $245 billion). Medicare would "wither on the vine," Gingrich predicted. "This is the largest domestic decision we have made since 1933 . . . a fundamental change in the direction of government." Calculating—correctly—that the Republicans would get the blame, Clinton vetoed the budget bill, as well as an additional continuing resolution, and another government shutdown began on December 16. This one lasted for three weeks, as eight hundred thousand federal workers were sent home, national parks and museums were closed, and all nonessential government services were suspended. In early January, Gingrich and the Republicans backed down, and the government reopened.

All the elements of Clinton's strategy were on display during his State of the Union address to Congress on January 23, 1996. Continuing with the practice that had been initiated by Ronald Reagan in 1982, the president had invited a number of notable Americans to sit in the public gallery as his guests during the speech. One of them was Richard Dean, a Vietnam veteran and civil servant, who had been working inside the Murrah Building when it was bombed. As Clinton noted in his address, after the explosion Dean had "reentered that building four times" and saved the lives of three women. "But Richard Dean's story doesn't end there," the president went on. "This last November, he was forced out of his office when the government shut down. And the second time the government shut down he continued helping Social Security recipients, but he was working without pay." On behalf of Dean, his family, and "all the other people who are out there working every day doing a good job for the American people," Clinton then issued a challenge to "all of you in this chamber: Never, ever shut the federal government down again!"

Clinton had not only given a human face to the "tyrannical bureaucracy" that was supposedly intent on ruining the country—reminding Americans of the essential work that government workers did on their behalf—he had also skillfully linked the government shutdown to the Oklahoma City bombing and tied everything in with the Republican right. It was a strategy that would serve him well in the upcoming presidential election. Yet the address also revealed just how much the politics of triangulation at root often simply meant acknowledging the continuing conservative drift of much of American life, as Clinton called for "sweeping welfare reform" that would "really move people from welfare to work"; encouraged the introduction of "V-chips" that would enable parents to block "inappropriate" television programs; and promised to "take our streets back from crime and gangs and drugs." "The era of big government is over," he declared, sounding more like Ronald Reagan than either FDR or JFK. "We know . . . government does not have all the answers. We know there's not a program for every problem."

Clinton's opponent in 1996 was the Senate majority leader, Bob Dole from Kansas. A fiscal conservative, who had opposed Reagan's supply-side tax cuts as irresponsible and who was also highly critical of Gingrich—he once described his colleague as a "one-man-band who rarely took advice"—Dole had to see off the challenge of both Pat Buchanan and the millionaire publisher Steve Forbes in the primaries. On February 26, he visited the eighty-seven-year-old Barry Goldwater at his home in Arizona in order to receive the blessing of the former standard-bearer of the radical right. His host duly vouched for Dole as the heir apparent to the "Barry Goldwater, Ronald Reagan legacy of conservatism." But as the conversation turned to the current state of the GOP—to Gingrich, Buchanan, and the like—the Arizonian was forced to admit that he and Dole had somehow become "the new liberals of the Republican Party." "Can you imagine that?" he asked his guest ruefully. It was a telling acknowledgment of just how much the U.S. political scene was changing.

Despite the philosophical differences between them—not to mention the high level of personal animosity—the Clinton campaign linked Dole and Gingrich together as much as possible. "If Dole wins and Gingrich runs Congress, there'll be nobody there to stop them," as one of the Democrats' ads had it. ("In my run for the presidency in 1996 the Democrats greeted me with a number of negative TV ads, and in every one of them Newt was in the ad. He was very unpopular," was how Dole himself recalled the campaign in 2012.) The government shutdown, the fallout from the Oklahoma bombing, and increasing public dissatisfaction with the "Gingrich revolution"—58 percent of respondents expressed their disapproval of the job Congress was doing in September 1995, for example—all undoubtedly contributed to Clinton's victory. But the most decisive factor, as it had been in 1992, was the state of the American economy, which was starting to boom: GDP was running at 3 percent per year by 1996, the unemployment rate had fallen to 5.3 percent (it had been 7.3 percent four years earlier), the inflation rate was below 3 percent, and significant steps had also been taken to reduce the federal deficit (which stood at $140 billion in 1996; down from $290 billion in 1992).

Clinton defeated Dole with 49.2 percent of the popular vote (47.4 million votes) to 40.7 percent (39.1 million), and in the Electoral College by 379 votes to 159. But the Republicans maintained their control of both houses of Congress—losing four House seats and gaining three in the Senate. Divided government would therefore continue, and overall the results provided further evidence of just how competitive the two main parties were against each other. At the same time, the eight million votes that Ross Perot—running this time on a Reform Party ticket—received in 1996 (8.4 percent of the total), although down considerably from 1992, demonstrated that there was also a significant portion of the electorate for whom traditional parties and traditional candidates continued to offer very little appeal.

Clinton's second term was dominated by the impeachment proceedings against him. Hillary Clinton was widely ridiculed for suggesting, during an interview on the *Today* program on January 27, 1998—as the allegations and investigations came close to fever pitch—that there was a "vast right-wing conspiracy that has been conspiring against my husband since the day he announced for president." But there was a great deal of truth in what the first lady said. The former head of the Little Rock Citizens' Council, Jim Johnson, had kicked things off in 1992 by encouraging the right-wing political activist Floyd Brown, founder of the political action committee Citizens United, to publish a book detailing Clinton's alleged character defects. Its title—which swiftly caught on as a general term of abuse of the president—was *"Slick Willie": Why America Cannot Trust Bill Clinton*. By 1994, Jerry Falwell, who had returned to politics in 1991 with a new organization called Liberty Alliance, claimed to have sold more than sixty thousand copies of an anti-Clinton video called *The*

Clinton Chronicles that outlined the president's "involvement" in a host of nefarious activities including murder, drug running, prostitution, and money laundering. (The video was actually the work of Pat Matrisciana's Christian Right production company, Jeremiah Films. There was also an accompanying book.) And Richard Mellon Scaife alone was believed to have spent more than $2 million, between 1994 and 1997, on what was euphemistically called the "Arkansas project"—basically, an attempt to uncover as many unsavory details about Clinton's past as possible.

The results of Scaife's digging were published most often in the archly conservative *American Spectator* magazine, but the right-wing media more broadly joined in with what, at times, seemed an almost relentless attack against the president. This included talk radio hosts like Rush Limbaugh; newspapers including the *Washington Times*, the *New York Post*, and the *Wall Street Journal*; new website-based sources such as *The Drudge Report*; and the up-and-coming cable news channel, Fox News. Funded by the Australian-born billionaire media mogul Rupert Murdoch, Fox began broadcasting in October 1996, and under the direction of Roger Ailes—who had masterminded George Bush's 1988 presidential campaign—it swiftly established a significant audience for its determinedly conservative approach (although "fair and balanced" was its official slogan). By 2000 it was available in fifty-six million American homes. The growth of this right-wing media network had been facilitated both by the deregulation of the cable industry in 1996 and the Reagan administration's earlier abandonment of the "fairness doctrine" in 1987, which since 1949 had required radio and television stations to provide contrasting views representing all sides of an issue in matters of public interest.

The impeachment proceedings themselves grew out of two different legal problems involving the president, both of which eventually became entangled with his sexual relationship with a twenty-three-year-old White House intern called Monica Lewinsky. The first of these problems was a sexual harassment case that had been filed by a former Arkansas state employee called Paula Jones in May 1994. It alleged that Clinton had propositioned and lewdly exposed himself to her in a Little Rock hotel room when he was still governor. Jones's case was being financed and supported by a range of conservative groups, including the Landmark Legal Foundation, the Independent Women's Forum, and the

Federalist Society—all three of which had received generous funding from Richard Scaife. Things turned difficult for Clinton on May 27, 1997, when the Supreme Court ruled that there was no reason for the lawsuit to be deferred until after he left office; that testifying in the case would not "place unacceptable burdens on the President that will hamper the performance of his official duties"; and that there was no serious risk of exposing the presidency to "politically motivated harassing and frivolous litigation."

The second legal problem facing Clinton went back to a failed land development project in northwest Arkansas called Whitewater, which both he and his wife had borrowed money to invest in during the 1980s. Among other issues, questions had arisen over whether money had been illegally diverted from the project to pay for Bill Clinton's gubernatorial election campaign in 1984 and whether Hillary Clinton, then a partner in the Rose Law Firm, had a conflict of interest in the deal because she was the official state regulator of the bank from which the Clintons had borrowed the money—through a shady businessman called James McDougal—which subsequently went bust. The whole affair became a major cause célèbre following the suicide of White House deputy counsel and close friend of the Clintons, Vincent Foster, in July 1993. Under considerable pressure, especially from the right-wing press, Clinton agreed to the appointment of a special counsel called Robert Fiske Jr. to investigate matters in January 1994. Fiske found nothing to incriminate the Clintons, but in August he was replaced by Kenneth Starr, a Texas-born Washington lawyer who had served as solicitor general in the Bush administration. Starr was a pious, conservative Republican. He had been educated at the Church of Christ–affiliated Harding College, in Searcy, Arkansas—one of the bastions of the anti-communist radical right during the 1960s, as we saw in chapter 2—before moving on to George Washington University and Duke Law School and clerking for Chief Justice Warren Burger. Making matters even murkier, before his appointment as independent counsel, Starr had also provided free legal advice to Paula Jones as a member of the conservative Federalist Society.

Clinton's relationship with Lewinsky began in November 1995, during the first government shutdown, and was still ongoing in April the following year when she was transferred to the Pentagon. There she met a woman called Linda Tripp, who secretly recorded her speaking about her intimate dealings with the president. Tripp then passed these tapes on to the legal team of Paula Jones, which was diligently searching for all the evidence of extramarital affairs carried on by Clinton that it could find. On December 19, 1997, Jones's attorneys subpoenaed Lewinsky, and on January 7, 1998, she signed an affidavit denying that she had any sexual relationship with the president. Starr, whose four-year investigation into the Whitewater affair was going nowhere, was tipped off about Lewinsky's testimony and supplied with his own copies of Tripp's tapes. Believing that he now had evidence to charge Clinton with suborning perjury and obstructing justice, Starr presented his findings to a panel of federal judges that oversaw the activities of all independent counsels and received its authorization to widen the scope of his inquires beyond the original Arkansas land deal.

Clinton finally testified in the Paula Jones's case on January 17, 1998. Asked about Lewinsky, the president denied they had had sex. He did the same thing in public, in the White House, on January 26, with his wife and Vice President Al Gore by his side; by now the allegations were all out in the open and a media frenzy had ensued. "I did not have sexual relations with that woman, Ms. Lewinsky," he declared. "I never told anyone to lie, not a single time—never. These allegations are false. And I need to go back to work for the American people." Clinton was basing his denials on the credibility-stretching grounds that oral sex, among other activities, did not constitute "sexual relations" or "sex," as he understood the terms. Jones's case was halted in April 1998 because she had been unable to prove that she had suffered any damages. In November, Clinton agreed to pay her $850,000, albeit without any apology or admission of guilt, if she would drop her appeal of the Arkansas court's decision.

The Starr investigation, meanwhile, continued on. Over the summer of 1998, Lewinsky agreed to testify to a federal grand jury in return for immunity from prosecution. She also produced a navy-blue dress stained with the president's semen—as ignominious DNA tests later proved (Linda Tripp had persuaded Lewinsky not to have the dress dry-cleaned). On September 9, Starr delivered his graphically detailed 445-page report to the House of Representatives, which would have to determine whether there were sufficient grounds to impeach the president for "high crimes and misdemeanors" as the Constitution required. Saying next to nothing about the Whitewater land deal, the report did offer abundant information about the nine sexual encounters and fifteen phone-sex conversations that had taken place between Clinton and Lewinsky, as well as all the lies and obfuscations that had resulted from their affair.

Gingrich and the House Republican right were gleeful. Unable to defeat Clinton at the ballot box, Starr had seemingly provided them with an alternative means of removing the president from the White House. Clinton's behavior—his moral laxity and basic unfitness for public office—was also made the centerpiece of the Republican campaign for the upcoming midterm elections. Indeed, back in April, Gingrich had already promised to refer to the Lewinsky scandal in every speech he gave between then and election day. That Gingrich was himself having an illicit affair with one of his own employees throughout this time— a young woman also in her twenties, as many in the Republican Party leadership knew—had not deflected the GOP from its strategy. The House Speaker confidently predicted major gains for the Republicans in November—anywhere between ten and forty seats, depending on how "everything breaks," as Gingrich told the *Atlanta Journal*. But it didn't happen. It was the Democrats that added to their seats in the House— they won five, thereby reducing the overall Republican majority to ten (222 to 212); the first time since 1934 that the party controlling the White House had actually improved its position in an off-year election. (There was no change in the balance of the Senate.)

In their partisan zeal, the Republican right had fundamentally misjudged the mood of the country. Opinion polls showed that a significant majority of Americans—about 60 percent—made a clear distinction between Clinton's personal conduct and his job performance as president. The continuing strength of the American economy certainly helped in this respect: by 1998, the government was actually running a budget *surplus* of $70 billion, and it would be more than double that by the time Clinton left office. But it was also the case that the "cultural issues" and "family values"—including attitudes toward sex—that so animated the political and religious right held much less resonance for many other Americans. This was also reflected in the considerable level of animosity that was directed toward Starr, who was widely seen as engaging in a vindictive, moralistic, and highly personal crusade against the president—only 19 percent of Americans approved of what he was doing, according to opinion polls, while 43 percent disapproved.

Three days after the midterm election results, Gingrich announced that he was resigning both from his position as speaker of the House and from Congress itself. What is particularly noteworthy about this, especially given the direction American politics would increasingly take in the twenty-first century, was that Gingrich was pushed out by his House colleagues—even his closest supporters let him know that it was time for him to step aside—not because they regarded him to be too extreme but because they regarded him as too *moderate*. They were disappointed by Gingrich's willingness to work with the Clinton administration after the government shutdowns in 1995–1996 and for helping to secure the passage of NAFTA, for example. In fact, Gingrich had only just survived a coup against him in 1997 that had been led by Dick Armey and the ultra-conservative House majority whip, Tom DeLay (TX).

It now fell to Armey, DeLay, and the chairman of the House Judiciary Committee, Henry Hyde (IL), to see the impeachment proceedings through to their dénouement. On December 19, the House passed two articles of impeachment against Clinton for perjury and obstruction of justice, the first president to be sanctioned in this way since Andrew Johnson in 1868. On February 12, 1999—after a trial lasting thirty-seven days—the Senate rejected the perjury charge by a vote of fifty-five to forty-five and the obstruction of justice charge on a fifty-fifty vote. Clinton had survived. (As set out in Article 2, Section 4 of the Constitution, a successful conviction required a two-thirds majority, or sixty-seven votes. Given that the Republicans only controlled fifty-five seats, in truth, for all the drama, the final result was never really in doubt.)

Looking back, and despite Clinton's electoral successes, the 1990s were important years in the development of the American right, both within Congress and outside of it. During this time, as we have seen, the more "moderate" form of conservative Republicanism associated with George H. W. Bush—and even Ronald Reagan—was largely displaced by the obstructionist and confrontational radicalism of Newt Gingrich—and those who came after him—as the "southernization" of the GOP continued apace. The Christian Right also underwent a major revival, picking itself up from the disappointments of the previous decade and increasingly tying itself to the Republican Party, as evidenced by the rise of Pat Robertson and Ralph Reed's Christian Coalition. The bitter partisanship of the Clinton years, culminating in the unsavory spectacle—on a host of levels—of the president's unsuccessful impeachment, also did little to restore faith in the efficacy and trustworthiness of politicians or politics more broadly. Nor too did the conspiracies—both real and imagined— that swirled around the presidency.

As for the militia movement, the decade did not end well. The "Y2K" catastrophe that many militia groups had been predicting as 1999 turned into the year 2000 did not take place (the fear, which was by no means confined to militia members, was that the world's computer system would not be able to cope with the changeover into the new millennium); and for most observers the execution of Timothy McVeigh on June 11, 2001, brought the movement to at least a symbolic close. In August 2009, however, the SPLC issued a new report about a "second wave" of militia activity, which it attributed to the Great Recession of 2008–2009 and the election of a new liberal administration headed by the nation's first black president, Barack Obama. A reenergized militia movement was also attempting to associate itself with the burgeoning Tea Party movement in the United States, the report noted.

It is the Tea Party and the subsequent rise of Donald J. Trump to the presidency of the United States that we now turn to examine.

6

Tea Parties and Trumpism

The Radical Right in the Twenty-First Century

TO MANY AMERICANS THE ELECTION of Barack Obama in 2008 seemed to herald a new liberal ascendency in the United States. After all, not only did Obama win the presidency with a greater share of the popular vote than any Democratic Party candidate since Lyndon Johnson in 1964, but he came into office with a Democratic majority in both the House and the Senate and with his party having won seven governorships and in firm control of twenty-seven state legislatures. The nation's first African-American president, he was young, confident, and charismatic, with a clearly articulated progressive political agenda. There was even talk of his victory being the beginning of a "post racial America." It would not come to pass. Opposition to Obama, especially from the radical right, was both swift and extensive, including from the newly formed Tea Party movement. This chapter examines the rise and influence of the Tea Party, focusing particularly on its relationship with the Republican Party, right-wing media, and its enormously wealthy, ultra-conservative backers. It also considers the connection between the appearance of the Tea Party and perhaps the most stunning development in recent American political history, the election of Donald Trump to the White House in 2016—as clear a repudiation of the Obama presidency as it is possible to imagine. How did this happen? Where did Donald Trump come from? And does his election represent a continuation of the politics of the radical right, as we have been examining them in this book, or something different? These are some of the questions addressed in this chapter. We begin, though, with the Tea Party.

The Tea Party emerged on the American political scene spectacularly, and seemingly out of nowhere, in early 2009. Claiming inspiration from the nation's revolutionary founding fathers, especially the "Boston Tea Party" of 1773, when Samuel Adams and his Sons of Liberty dumped tea in Boston's harbor to protest both Britain's taxation policies and American colonists' lack of representation in Parliament, members of the Tea Party were just ordinary citizens, they said, people who were fed up with big government, who were "Taxed Enough Already," and who wanted to take their country back. But the Tea Party wasn't just composed of local activists in groups such as the Jefferson Area Tea Party Patriots of Virginia; the Pink Slip Patriots of Tempe, Arizona; or the Southwest Metro Tea Party of Chanhassen, Minnesota. (Theda Skocpol and Vanessa Williamson identified approximately eight hundred active local Tea Party groups in the summer of 2011, with a total membership in the region of 160,000 to 200,000. Other researchers put the number of Tea Party activists closer to 350,000.) It was also supported and encouraged—sometimes to a considerable extent—by a range of free-market, right-wing lobbying groups and their wealthy corporate backers, together with the conservative media, most notably Fox News. This led to widespread accusations from the Tea Party's opponents that it was really an "Astroturf" movement rather than a genuinely grassroots one. As we shall see, there was certainly some truth to this, as there was to the other main criticism of the movement, which was that much of its vehemently expressed opposition to the Obama administration seemed motivated, at least in part, by the new president's race.

Yet it is also important to recognize just how extensive support for the Tea Party was (albeit within certain readily identifiable demographic limits). Opinion polls and surveys revealed that approximately 20 percent of American adults—or forty-five million people—considered themselves to be Tea Party supporters. These supporters were predominantly white, male, middle-aged or older, well-educated—with a college degree or higher—and comfortably middle class. They also tended to be regular churchgoers—mostly at evangelical churches—and were overwhelmingly conservative and Republican in their politics. Tea Party supporters could be found in all fifty states, although Tea Party groups often had a higher membership in the South. In these terms, then, as political scientists Christopher Parker and Matt Barreto have pointed out, support for the Tea Party came from a very similar constituency to that which has supported other right-wing groups in American history, including both the John Birch Society (JBS) in the 1960s and the Ku Klux Klan in the 1920s.

Nor were the key motivating ideas and beliefs of the Tea Party especially new. Although deeply impacted by the combined—and profoundly jolting—experience of the Great Recession of 2008 and the subsequent election of Barack Obama to the White House, at root the demands of the Tea Party, at both the elite and grassroots levels, remained very much those that had been emanating from the radical right ever since the passing of the New Deal: for limited government and lower taxation, for fewer government regulations and a curtailing of the welfare state, for restrictions on organized labor and greater economic freedom for business, and for a return to a strict construction of the Constitution and "traditional" American values. This is not to say that all members of the Tea Party were in complete agreement on all these issues—they were not—nor that there weren't contradictions and tensions to be found within the Tea Party philosophy—there definitely were—but the apparent novelty of thousands of modern, middle-aged Americans donning tricorn hats and waving revolutionary-era "Don't Tread on Me" flags should not detract from the essential familiarity and long standing continuity of the movement's cris de coeur. Be that as it may, though, the impact of the Tea Party on American politics and on American life was both considerable and dramatic. It undermined the Obama presidency. It pushed both the Republican Party and the whole national political debate to the right. And it arguably did much to lay the groundwork for the even more startling—and even more dramatic—election of Donald Trump to the presidency in 2016.

Although it would not manifest itself until after Obama's victory, disillusionment with the GOP was a major factor in the rise of the Tea Party. Bookended by the devastating terrorist attacks of September 11, 2001, and the economic crisis that started to engulf the nation in the fall of 2008, the presidency of George W. Bush in particular had been a major disappointment to many conservatives. Despite instituting massive tax cuts for the wealthy and businesses and reducing government regulations in the energy sector and with respect to the environment, overall the former Texas governor (the son of George H. W. Bush) had presided over a considerable growth in both the government's size and its spending during his two terms in office. In the process Bush had turned a $236 billion budget surplus into a $485 billion deficit and almost doubled the size of the national debt to $10.7 trillion. He had launched two extremely costly—both financially and in terms of lives lost—overseas invasions in Afghanistan and Iraq as part of an ill-defined "war on terror," conflicts that also resulted in the considerable growth of the national security bureaucracy under the auspices of the newly established Department of Homeland Security. Domestically, he had also overseen the introduction of both a major new Medicare prescription drug benefit and the expansion of the federal government's powers over the nation's schools as part of his No Child Left Behind law. In addition, the Christian Right was disappointed by the inadequacies of Bush's much trumpeted faith-based initiatives program, which in David Kuo's insider critique, *Tempting Faith: The Inside Story of Political Seduction* (2006), was portrayed as little more than a cynical charade designed to shore up evangelical votes.

Worse still—indeed, most heinously of all in the eyes of future Tea Partiers—on October 3, 2008, in an attempt to stabilize the economy in the wake of the collapse of Lehman Brothers and other financial institutions as a result of the sub-prime mortgage crisis, Bush "bailed out" the banking industry to the tune of $700 billion as part of the administration's Troubled Asset Relief Program (TARP). Two months later, Bush allocated $17.4 billion to General Motors and Chrysler, initiating a bailout of the auto industry that would become even more extensive under the Obama administration. So much for the self-correcting majesty of the free market. As E. J. Dionne writes, "A conservative president was forced to turn to big government to save the banking system and the economy."

The Republican Party presidential candidate in 2008 was the Arizona senator John McCain. His reputation as a congressional maverick who supported immigration reform, health care reform, and campaign finance reform—and his apparent willingness to work with Democrats to achieve these ends—made him suspect in the eyes of many conservatives, and his resounding defeat to Obama merely compounded the problems inside the GOP, creating both a leadership vacuum and a sense of drift that the Tea Party was quick to exploit. (Recruiting the governor of

Alaska Sarah Palin to his self-described "team of mavericks" had a more positive impact. With her plain-speaking and folksy "mama grizzly" charm, she quickly became a Tea Party favorite.) McCain lost to Obama by 59.9 million votes to 69.5 million (45.7 percent to 52.9 percent), and by 175 votes to 365 in the Electoral College, as the Democrats, as previously noted, took control of both the House and the Senate.

Obama came into office on the promise of "hope" and "change." He campaigned on a progressive agenda to revive the economy, create jobs, reform the tax system, and regulate Wall Street. He wanted to provide affordable and accessible health care to all Americans, to tackle climate change and promote "clean energy," to strengthen public education, to protect the Social Security system, and to end the war in Iraq. And although facing the worst economic crisis since the Great Depression, he thought—naively perhaps—that he could do all this while bringing the country together, overcoming the bitter partisanship that had marked Washington for so many years. As he put it in his inaugural address on January 20, 2009, before a crowd of approximately 1.8 million people on the National Mall, the largest such gathering in U.S. history: "On this day, we gather because we have chosen hope over fear, unity of purpose over conflict and discord. On this day, we come to proclaim an end to the petty grievances and false promises, the recriminations and worn-out dogmas that for far too long have strangled our politics." In less than a month, the Tea Party protests began.

On February 10, 2009, an unemployed auto worker called Mary Rakovich organized a protest against Obama's proposed $787 billion stimulus bill at a town hall meeting in Fort Myers, Florida, which the president was attending with the state's Republican Governor Charlie Crist. Six days later, a thirty-year-old conservative blogger called Keli Carender, who wrote under the pen name "Liberty Belle," organized what she called an "Anti-Porkulus Protest" in Seattle, with the aid of the syndicated columnist and political commentator Michelle Malkin. The term "porkulus" was borrowed from the conservative radio host Rush Limbaugh, who used it derogatively to describe the Obama stimulus plan, which he saw as a socialistically inclined example of traditional "pork barrel politics" that would do nothing to create new jobs. But both the Fort Myers and the Seattle events were very much local protests, small in size and impact. What really galvanized the incipient Tea Party

Presidential candidate Barack Obama addresses the Democratic National Convention in Denver, Colorado, on August 28, 2008. The first African American to occupy the White House, Obama's presidency would spur both the growth of the Tea Party and the election of Donald Trump in 2016. Library of Congress Prints & Photographs Division, Carol M. Highsmith Archive, LC-DIG-highsm-03844.

was a televised rant by the CNBC financial reporter Rick Santelli on the floor of the Chicago Mercantile Exchange on February 19.

With cheering commodities traders urging him on in the background, Santelli railed against both the Obama stimulus plan and the more recently announced Homeowner Affordability and Retirement Act, which was intended to help struggling homeowners refinance their mortgages. The Obama administration was rewarding "bad behavior" by subsidizing "the losers' mortgages," he said. "This is America! How many of you people want to pay your neighbor's mortgage that has an extra bathroom and can't pay their bills." "We're thinking of having a Chicago Tea Party in July," he continued. "All you capitalists that want to show up to Lake Michigan, I'm gonna start organizing."

Santelli's rant—"the rant heard round the world," as it became known—was quickly picked up by conservative bloggers and websites such as *The Drudge Report*; excerpts from it were broadcast repeatedly on Fox News; and it received millions of viewings on YouTube. As Lee Fang has noted, within just a few hours of Santelli speaking, the right-wing lobbying groups Americans for Prosperity (AFP) and the Sam Adams Alliance had registered TaxDayTeaParty.com and TaxPayerTeaParty. com as new website domains, and a new Facebook page encouraging anti-Obama Tea Party protests across the country went live. The free market advocacy group FreedomWorks, headed by former Republican majority leader Dick Armey, also moved to promote the movement. On February 20, following a conference call of fifty online activists, an organization called the National Tea Party Coalition was established. Other would-be national coordinating groups soon followed, including 1776 Tea Party, Tea Party Patriots, Tea Party Nation, Tea Party Express, and ResistNet. All this activity raised suspicion that Santelli's outburst had been much less spontaneous than it had first seemed, but whether or not this was the case—and the allegation has never been proved—the effect was no less startling.

About thirty thousand Americans in fifty-one cities took part in the first "official" Tea Party protests on February 27, 2009. By April 15—"Tax Day"—there were demonstrations in more than 750 towns and cities across the country. Similar numbers of protests followed on July 4. Contentious congressional town hall events occurred throughout August, as Tea Partiers—some openly carrying guns—disrupted, challenged, and heckled their elected representatives in opposition to Obama's Affordable Health Care proposals. And on September 12, 2009, the first national Tea Party rally took place in Washington, D.C. Attended by seventy thousand people, it was a noisy and colorful affair, one that marked both the increasing significance of the movement and its increasing controversy. Protestors carried signs denouncing big government, the bailouts, high taxes, and Obama's health care plans. But they also carried signs depicting the president as an African witch doctor, with a Hitler moustache, or as Heath Ledger's Joker from the film *The Dark Knight* above the legend "Socialism." There were signs reading "Defend the Constitution," "I'll Keep My Guns, Freedom, and Money. You Can Keep the 'Change,'" and "Impeach the Spoiled Brat" and others suggesting that Obama was a Muslim or a communist.

The Washington rally and other Tea Party events had all been heavily promoted by the Fox News network, including by its most prominent figures: Bill O'Reilly, Sean Hannity, Neil Cavuto, and Greta Van Susteren.

Fox, it is important to stress, was the most watched cable news network in the country, and its relationship with its audience was extremely strong. According to a CBS/*New York Times* poll in 2010, for example, fully 63 percent of Tea Party supporters watched the network, most getting their news from nowhere else. Nobody played a more important role in generating early support for the Tea Party at Fox—and within the right-wing mediasphere more broadly—than Glenn Beck. The conspiracy-minded former disc jockey and Mormon convert was its biggest draw, reaching three million viewers a day at his peak; and this despite his resolutely old school, low-tech, chalkboard approach and mawkish tendency to break down in tears during broadcasts.

Beck did not just promote Tea Party events on air. He attended them, spoke at them, and even created his own grassroots, Tea Party–aligned groups under the auspices of his 9-12 Project. The aim of the project, he explained, was to reestablish the sense of unity of purpose that the country had experienced in the days after the terrorist attacks of 9/11: "to bring us all back to the place we were on September 12," when "we were united as Americans, standing together to protect the values and principles of the greatest nation ever created." That was not all, though. "9-12" also referred to the "nine founding principles and twelve eternal values" that Beck claimed the nation's founding fathers had used to establish the United States. Principle number one was "America is good." Principle number seven was "I work hard for what I have and I will share it with who I want. Government cannot force me to be charitable."

Along with FreedomWorks—which, it was later revealed, was secretly paying the broadcaster $1 million a year to read "embedded content" written by its staff on his shows—Beck's 9-12 Project was one of the co-sponsors of the September 12 Washington rally. In August the following year, with Sarah Palin as one of the keynote speakers, Beck drew one hundred thousand protestors back to the nation's capital for a "Restore Honor" rally. Over half of the eight hundred local Tea Parties identified by Skocpol and Williamson in their national survey of the movement in 2011 referred to Beck's 9-12 project on their websites, and 115 included a reference to it in their names (the Wyoming 9-12 Coalition and Daytona 9-12, for example).

If Beck was the most public of the Tea Party's boosters, Charles and David Koch, the multibillionaire owners of Koch Industries, a multinational petrochemical and manufacturing conglomerate, were its most secretive, at least initially—their role in backing both the Tea Party and opposition to the Obama administration more widely was exposed in an article by Jane Mayer in *The New Yorker* in August 2010, as well as in a subsequent book. The Koch family had a long history of supporting right-wing causes, going back, as we have seen, to Fred Koch's involvement in establishing the JBS in the 1950s and his sons' financial backing of various organizations during the rise of the New Right, including the Center for Liberation Studies, the Institute for Humane Studies, the Heritage Foundation, and the Cato Institute. Both the Heritage Foundation and the Cato Institute would go on to support the Tea Party as well.

In 1980 David Koch had stood as the Libertarian Party's vice-presidential candidate, but it was a chastening experience. Despite spending $2 million on the campaign, he and his running mate, Ed Clark, received only 1 percent of the votes. This convinced the Koch brothers that their energies—and their money—would be better spent behind-the-scenes—on think tanks, in academia, through front groups—in order to create a much more receptive environment for their anti-government, ultra-free-market ideas. Dispersing more than $100 million over the next thirty years, the expansive result of these efforts would eventually become known as "the Kochtopus."

Citizens for a Sound Economy, which was established in 1984 and which worked concertedly against the Clinton administration during the 1990s, was one tentacle of the Kochtopus, but it split apart in 2003. Its two successor organizations, Americans for Prosperity and Freedom-Works, both played critical roles in the development of the Tea Party. AFP continued to receive its money directly from the Kochs, but the Armey-led FreedomWorks sought out alternative sources of corporate funding, including from the Philip Morris tobacco company, the insurance giant MetLife, and billionaire Richard Mellon Scaife. Other wealthy backers of the anti-Obama revolt, whom David Frum, the former speechwriter for George W. Bush, criticized as "the radical rich" in an article in *Foreign Affairs*, included the venture capitalist Tom Perkins; financier Stephen Schwartzman; the co-founder of Home Depot Kenneth Langone; and Randy and Earl "Ken" Kendrick, the latter the founder of the software company Datatel and co-owner of the Arizona Diamondbacks baseball team.

The official motto of FreedomWorks is: "Lower Taxes. Less Government. More Freedom." Both it and AFP—along with other right-wing lobby groups—provided the Tea Party with a wide range of support, including training for new activists, advice on recruitment, speakers for rallies, press releases, media talking points, and even transportation to and from protests. FreedomWorks's website contained useful tips on "How to Organize Your Own 'Tea Party' Protest," including using homemade signs with "BIG LETTERS" and picking a good location with "lots of traffic." Armey and the president of FreedomWorks, Matt Kibbe, also teamed up to write their own mission statement for the movement called *Give Us Liberty: A Tea Party Manifesto* (2010).

This support was not always welcomed by members of the Tea Party, though. In part, this was because it obviously made the movement easier to dismiss as simply the creation of corporate interests and the wealthy— a "grassroots citizens' movement brought to you by a bunch of oil billionaires," as David Axlerod, one of President Obama's most senior advisors put it. In April 2010, for example, the Tea Party Patriots issued a press release disassociating itself from the Tea Party Express, the creation of a pre-existing, pro-McCain political action committee called Our Country Deserves Better, which was funded by the California political consultant Sal Russo, accusing the Express of draining money from genuine "local grassroots tea party organizers." There was also resentment that people like Dick Armey and the South Carolina senator Jim DeMint were setting themselves up as self-appointed national spokesmen for the movement. But it was also because the views of ordinary Tea Partiers and those of their billionaire backers were not always totally aligned. Ultra-free-market advocates like those in FreedomWorks and AFP pushed for the complete privatization of Medicare and Social Security, for example, but surveys and opinion polls consistently showed that grassroots Tea Partiers remained overwhelmingly in favor of these quintessential "big government" programs.

The apparent contradiction in the views of these Tea Party members—pointedly illustrated by signs reading "Keep Your Government Hands Off My Medicare" at rallies opposing the Affordable Health Care Act—seemed to offer further confirmation of the oft-made claim that Americans were "ideologically conservative" but "operationally liberal" in much of their politics. (We saw this dynamic at work in previous chapters with respect to both the Reagan and Gingrich "revolutions," for example.) Yet as the historian Ronald Formisano has pointed out, such positions also reflected a heartfelt philosophy of "producerism," one that could trace its roots back to the Populist Party of the 1890s. This philosophy made a clear distinction between those who had "earned" their benefits and rewards through hard work and "non-producers" who were simply "freeloading" off the system. In the case of the Tea Party, it was the young, those on low incomes, and illegal immigrants who were most often cast in the nonproducing role. Other tensions within the Tea Party could be found between those who wanted the movement to remain focused on economic issues, such as wasteful government spending or the size of the national debt, and those for whom social issues, such as abortion or gay marriage, were equally important animating concerns. Then there was the issue of race.

Tea Partiers bitterly resented the characterization of their movement as being motivated by racism, yet there was clearly evidence to support the accusation, and not just in the offensive images of President Obama depicted as an African witch doctor. Research conducted in 2010 by scholars at the University of Washington on the attitudes of Tea Party supporters across seven states revealed that Tea Partiers were less favorably disposed towards African Americans and Hispanics than most Americans, regarding them as less hardworking, less intelligent, and less trustworthy than other racial groups, for example. Similarly, the CBS/ *New York Times* survey mentioned earlier found that 52 percent of Tea Party supporters were of the view that "too much had been made of the problems facing black people" in America in recent years, compared to 28 percent of non–Tea Party respondents. The support of many Tea Partiers for the Birther movement's conspiratorial contention that Obama was not even an American citizen (discussed further below, with specific reference to Donald Trump's championing of the cause) also seemed to indicate a troubling racial dimension to their opposition to the administration. Indeed, in the view of Parker and Barreto, the Tea Party could be best understood as another manifestation of the counter-subversive tradition in American history, with Obama and his big-government, progressive politics symbolically representing everything that was "going wrong" in the country: a subversive force—alien, foreign, "other"—that was taking the United States away from "real Americans" (i.e., white, mostly male, middle-class, middle-aged, heterosexual Christians).

The Republican Party found itself in a difficult position with respect to the rise of the Tea Party. On the one hand, the movement provided some much-needed energy and activism in the wake of McCain's resounding defeat in the 2008 presidential election. The Party's leadership hoped that it could harness this energy and utilize the abundance of new money flowing into the movement to help revive its own fortunes and also achieve its overriding aim of making Obama a "one-term president." On the other hand, both grassroots activists and elite-level Tea Partiers such as Dick Armey spoke openly about "taking over the GOP," pushing it even further to the right than it already was. They derided Republicans who failed to share the Tea Party's aims as RINOs—"Republican In Name Only"—and regarded those self-same party leaders—people like Senate minority leader Mitch McConnell (KY) and House minority leader John Boehner (OH)—as part of the problem rather than the solution: as "establishment Republicans."

The extraordinary impact of the Tea Party on both the Republican Party and the nation as a whole was made clear in the 2010 midterm elections. The Tea Party made its intentions clear during the GOP primaries by running scores of candidates against those they considered to be too moderate. To be sure not all of these candidates won, but significant numbers of them did, including in Alaska, Colorado, Delaware, Nevada, New York, South Carolina, and Utah. And even if some of these Tea Partiers were subsequently defeated in the general election because they were considered to be too extreme or too inexperienced, as was the case most notably with Christine O'Donnell in Delaware and Sharron Angle in Nevada, the campaigns themselves could still be celebrated for their ideological purity and insurgent promise. Overall, the Republicans gained sixty-three seats in 2010, forty-two of which went to Tea Party–aligned candidates. The GOP regained control of the House by 242 to 193—their biggest turnaround since the elections of 1948—and also picked up six seats in the Senate to reduce the Democrats' majority to just four. In addition, the Republican Party gained 675 seats in state legislatures and added six new governorships, with Scott Walker in Wisconsin, Rick Scott in Florida, and John Kasich in Ohio particularly identified with the Tea Party. All in all, it was a remarkable victory. As Obama himself noted, the Democrats had taken a "shellacking."

Why? In part, it was because of the Tea Party's efforts. In part, it was because of the ongoing economic crisis (more than fifteen million Americans were still out of work). But mostly, it was because large numbers of those voters who had propelled Obama to the White House just two years earlier—the young, Hispanics, and African Americans—had stayed away from the polls. The indirect role played by the Supreme Court should not be discounted either, however. On January 21, 2010, in *Citizens United v. Federal Election Commission*, the Court had ruled that no limits could be placed on the amount of money that corporations, unions, and other groups could spend on the election of political candidates, provided that such money was not given to candidates directly. Banning such expenditure placed an unwarranted restriction on the freedom of speech of such groups under the First Amendment, the Court believed—albeit by the narrow margin of five to four. In theory, liberal and conservative donors were free to spend in equal measure, but in practice it was the radical right that took most advantage of the decision, with the 2010 midterms functioning as their first testing ground. According to Jane Mayer, for example, the Kochs' donor network alone "spent at least $130.7 million on winning a Republican majority" in the House in 2010. (By the 2012 election cycle, the Kochs' political expenditure had grown to $412 million, and in 2016 it reached a colossal $889 million.)

Driven on by the Tea Party Caucus, which had been created by the Minnesota congresswoman Michelle Bachmann in July 2010, radical House Republicans wasted little time in flexing their newly acquired political muscles during the 112th Congress. They cut funding to government programs such as Head Start, which provides educational support for low-income children and their families. They slashed the budgets of federal agencies such as the Environmental Protection Agency, the National Endowment for the Arts, and the Corporation for Public Broadcasting. They forced the Obama administration to extend the Bush-era tax cuts for another two years (the price of securing a thirteen-month extension of unemployment benefits, among other things). And they pushed the nation to the brink of default—much to the chagrin of the party leadership—on the formally routine matter of raising the debt ceiling. They also voted again and again—thirty-five times in total—to repeal the Affordable Care Act, which Obama had finally signed into law in March 2010.

The ambition of the Republican right was evidenced in Chairman of the House Budget Committee Paul Ryan's (WI) "Path to Prosperity" budget proposal for 2012. Clearly reflecting the influence of right-wing lobbying groups such as the Heritage Foundation and the AFP—whose Wisconsin branch had given Ryan its "Defender of the American Dream" award for 2008—the plan aimed to reduce government spending by $5.8 trillion over ten years, mostly by replacing the Medicare system with private insurance and by making deep cuts in Medicaid, education funding, and social safety-net programs such as Food Stamps. It also called for $2 trillion in tax cuts, including reducing the top rate of income tax from 35 percent to 25 percent; tax rates not seen in the United States since the 1920s. The proposal passed the House by 235 to 193—only four Republicans voted against it while all the Democrats did—but it was defeated in the Senate by 57 to 40. Although he later recanted his criticism, even Newt Gingrich was moved to reject the radicalism of Ryan's budget, describing it as an unwelcome example of "right-wing social engineering."

The 2012 presidential election illustrated the continuing influence of the Tea Party on the Republican Party and also the ongoing volatility of the American electorate. A number of Tea Party–backed candidates—each seeming to reflect different parts of the overall coalition—competed in the primaries, including Gingrich, Michelle Bachmann, the Texas governor Rick Perry, the business executive Herman Cain, the Pennsylvania senator Rick Santorum, and the Texas congressman Ron Paul. They all lost to the former Massachusetts governor Mitt Romney, the extremely wealthy former head of the private equity firm Bain Capital and a member of the Church for Latter-Day Saints. Romney was by no means a Tea Party favorite, but he veered hard to the right during the campaign as he attempted to court the movement's support: opposing immigration reform; proposing wholesale cuts in taxes and government spending; and denouncing "Obamacare" even though it was based, in part, on health care reforms he had overseen in Massachusetts.

Having won the nomination, and appointed Paul Ryan as his vice-presidential running mate, Romney also gave clear voice to the "producerist" philosophy that was so central to the Tea Party. "There are 47 percent of the people who will vote for the president no matter what," he explained to donors who had paid $50,000 a head to listen to him during a lunch in Boca Raton, Florida, on May 17, 2012.

> Forty-seven percent who are with him, who are dependent upon government, who believe that they are victims, who believe that government has responsibility to care for them, who believe that they are entitled to health care, to food, to housing, to you name it. That's an entitlement. And the government should give it to them. . . . These are people who pay no income tax. Forty-seven percent of American people pay no income tax. . . . And my job is not to worry about these people—I'll never convince them that they should take personal responsibility and care for their lives.

Admittedly, the speech was supposed to have been private—it was made public by a reporter from *Mother Jones* magazine in September—but there was no reason to doubt the sincerity of Romney's views.

Romney's comments hurt him in November, as did his suggestion that the problem of illegal immigration could be solved by "self-deportation." Obama won comfortably by 69.9 million votes to 60.9 million (51.1 percent to 47.2 percent) and by 332 to 206 in the Electoral College, as those members of his constituency who had stayed away from the polls in 2010 returned once again to the Democratic fold. The Democrats also gained eight seats in the House and two in the Senate, although they lost the governorship of North Carolina to the Republicans.

Obama's second term was marked by the same level of obstruction and unwillingness to compromise on the part of the Republican Party and its Tea Party confrères that had been evident throughout his first, although this time the loudest voice for Tea Party obstructionism often came from the newly elected senator for Texas, Ted Cruz, rather than anyone in the House. As result, despite the killing of twenty children and six staff members at the Sandy Hook Elementary School, in Newtown, Connecticut, there would be no overhaul of the nation's gun laws. Nor would there be comprehensive immigration reform, with a "path to citizenship" for the nation's eleven million illegal immigrants. (There would, though, be the Deferred Action for Childhood Arrivals program [DACA], created by executive order to offer protection for some of those who had been brought into the United States as children.) The Tea Party also managed to engineer a shutdown of the government from October

1 through October 17, 2013, as it tried once again to defund the Affordable Care Act. The 2014 midterms hardly helped Obama either, as the Republicans increased their majority in the House and also took control of the Senate. Sounding a very familiar tune, on election night the victorious incoming Senate majority leader, Mitch McConnell, declared that "this experiment in big government has lasted long enough."

This is not to say that Obama was without his successes during this time. But they were mostly in the sphere of foreign affairs—reopening diplomatic relations with Cuba, entering into the Paris climate accord, and securing an agreement with Iran to halt the development of its nuclear weapons program—or where, as with DACA, he could act through executive orders—such as raising the minimum wage and introducing new limitations on carbon emissions. Overall, however, the gridlock and bitter partisanship that increasingly seemed to be the hallmark of American political life continued largely unabated during his second four years in office. It was something the election of Donald Trump in 2016 would do very little to change.

Donald J. Trump was born in Queens, New York, on June 14, 1946, the fourth of five children to Mary Anne MacLoed, who had emigrated from Scotland in 1930, and Frederick "Fred" C. Trump, a successful property developer of German ancestry—Fred had inherited the business after the death of his father, Frederich, in the great flu epidemic of 1918. Driven by a fierce work ethic, Fred both indulged his children and instilled a firm sense of discipline and competiveness in them. This was especially the case for Donald, who was regularly told that he was "a king" but also that he needed to become "a killer." Donald began his schooling at the Kew-Forest School in Queens, but after some disciplinary problems—he would later claim that he had given a teacher a black eye "because I didn't think he knew anything about music"—and following his father's discovery of a knife collection that he and a friend had been acquiring during secret weekend excursions to Manhattan, in the fall of 1959 he was sent away to the New York Military Academy (NYMA) in upstate New York. Although no academic star, Trump thrived in the school's hierarchical and relentlessly competitive environment, especially because of his basketball and baseball skills. Indeed, during his junior year at the academy, the latter earned him his first newspaper headline—"Trump Wins Game for NYMA"—an initial "brush with fame [that] could be seen as the spark of the fire that would eventually light all of Trump's life," as one of his biographers, Michael D'Antonio, puts it. He was also named the official "ladies' man" of his class in the school's yearbook.

In May 1964 Trump went to college, first to Fordham University in the Bronx and then, in 1966, to the University of Pennsylvania's Wharton School, where he majored in real estate. He received four educational draft deferments from the Vietnam War during this time. On completion of his degree in 1968, he was deemed medically unfit for service except in the case of a national emergency, apparently because of bone spurs in his heels. Throughout his education, Trump had worked with his father during weekends and holidays. After graduating from Wharton, he finally joined the family business full-time, helping to manage the company's extensive—and lucrative—portfolio of middle-class and low-income residential housing rentals located predominantly in Brooklyn, Queens, and Staten Island. While eyeing an expansion of the family business into Manhattan and beginning to establish his reputation as a New York "playboy," Trump also made an ill-fated attempt at becoming a Broadway producer, investing $70,000 in a play called *Paris Is Out!* in 1970, only for the show to fold after 112 performances.

In 1973 Trump and his father were sued by the federal government for discriminating against African-American tenants in contravention of the Fair Housing Act of 1968. This was not the first allegation of racism against Fred. In 1927, aged twenty-one, he had been arrested following a disturbance that broke out during a Memorial Day parade by the Ku Klux Klan through Queens, although it was not clear whether he was taking part in the march, protesting it, or simply observing it. And in the 1950s, the noted folk singer Woody Guthrie, who lived in a Trump-owned apartment in Brooklyn, rewrote one of his most famous dust-bowl ballads, "I Ain't Got No Home," to castigate "Old Man Trump" and his "Beach Haven" property, "where no black ones come to roam." Rather than settling the case—which would have simply required them to promise not to discriminate in the future—the Trumps initially decided to launch a countersuit, claiming that they had suffered $100 million in damages because of the government's "irresponsible and baseless" allegations. Donald in particular had been persuaded of the merits of this strategy by the powerful New York lawyer and former right-hand man of Senator Joe McCarthy, Roy Cohn.

Trump had met Cohn at the Le Club nightclub in Manhattan, and he quickly became a significant influence on the young property developer, not just as a lawyer, but as a broader advisor, publicist, and political fixer. Trump deeply admired Cohn's toughness, combativeness, and sense of loyalty—Cohn "would kill for somebody he liked," Trump once remarked approvingly. Cohn's philosophy, which swiftly became Trump's philosophy, was never to back down. If attacked, hit back twice as hard, and if you have to fight dirty—or employ all manner of distraction—in order to win, so be it. It was an approach that would be reinforced by the former Nixon political operative Roger Stone, who also became an important advisor to Trump, after Cohn introduced the two of them while Stone was on the hunt for donations to Ronald Reagan's 1980 presidential campaign. It is somewhat ironic, then, that in 1975, after more than two years of fighting, the Trumps finally settled the Fair Housing Act case on essentially the same terms that had been available to them at the outset. Donald would later claim that the settlement "meant nothing because we never discriminated in the first place" and that he and his father never made any "admission of anything," but the terms of the agreement required them both to "thoroughly acquaint themselves" with the existing law on housing discrimination and to take out ads in the local press assuring members of minority communities that they had equal access to housing and expressly prohibited the Trumps from "discriminating against any person in the terms, conditions, or privileges of sale or rental of a dwelling."

Another, very different kind of mentor to Trump was the Reverend Norman Vincent Peale, the pastor of New York's Marble Collegiate Church, which the Trump family occasionally attended, although neither father nor son were especially religious. Peale also presided over Trump's first marriage, in 1977, to the Czech model Ivana Zelníčková Winklmayr. (The couple had three children together—Donald Jr., Ivanka, and Eric—before a very public divorce in 1992, following Trump's affair with the actress Marla Maples, with whom he would have another child, Tiffany, in 1993. Maples and Trump married the same year and divorced in 1999. Trump married for a third time to the Slovenian model Melania Knauss in 2005. Their son, Barron, was born the next year.) Peale was the author of the best-selling motivational book *The Power of Positive Thinking* (1952) and also had a popular radio show and nationally syndicated newspaper column, in which he set out his controversial if business-friendly nostrums for success, including: "Learn to pray big prayers. God will rate you according to the size of your prayers" and "I know that with God's help I can sell vacuum cleaners." "The mind can overcome any obstacle," Trump told the *New York Times* in 1983, reflecting on Peale's influence. "I never think of the negative."

Backed by his father's considerable wealth—estimated to be $100 million in 1975 and as much as $300 million by the time of his death in 1999—and also utilizing his extensive political and business connections, Donald Trump successfully entered the Manhattan real estate market in 1978, purchasing the run-down Commodore Hotel next to Grand Central Terminal and transforming it into the Grand Hyatt Hotel. This was followed by the building of the fifty-eight-story Trump Tower in midtown Manhattan in 1983, which attracted such famous residents as pop star Michael Jackson, film director Steven Spielberg, and talk show host Johnny Carson, and which quickly became Trump's signature property. Trump also expanded his operations into casinos in Atlantic City (the Trump Plaza, Trump Castle, and the Taj Mahal); a football team in the United States Football League (the New Jersey Generals); an airline (the Trump Shuttle), which flew between New York, Washington, and Boston; as well as numerous other businesses and ventures. He appeared on television programs such as *Lifestyles of the Rich and Famous* and in 1987 published his first book, the best-selling *Trump: The Art of the Deal*.

In the book, the future president clearly set out his media strategy, albeit through his ghostwriter, Tony Schwartz:

> One thing I've learned about the press is that they're always hungry for a good story, and the more sensational the better. . . . The point is that if you are a little different, or a little outrageous, or if you do things that are bold or controversial, the press is going to write about you. . . .
>
> The funny thing is that even a critical story, which may be hurtful personally, can be very valuable to your business. . . . I play to people's fantasies. People may not think big themselves, but they can still get very excited about those who do. That's why a little hyperbole never hurts. People want to believe that something is the biggest and the greatest and the most spectacular.
>
> I call it truthful hyperbole. It's an innocent form of exaggeration—and it's a very effective form of promotion.

Trump's hunger for publicity was so great—"The show is Trump," he would say, "and it is sold-out performances everywhere"—that he even adopted a fake persona, John Baron (sometimes Barron), to act as his own spokesman when he didn't want to engage with reporters directly. Schwartz came to regret writing *The Art of the Deal* for Trump, speaking out publicly against him in 2016, after it became clear that his former employer was a serious contender to win the presidency. "I put lipstick on a pig," he told *The New Yorker*. "I feel a deep sense of remorse that I contributed to presenting Trump in a way that brought him wider attention and made him more appealing than he is."

Overextended and saddled with enormous amounts of debt, the Trump business empire underwent a series of reversals during the early 1990s, the luster that had previously attached to the Trump name beginning to fade. According to Michael Kranish and Marc Fisher in their book *Trump Revealed: An American Journey of Ambition, Ego, Money and Power* (2016), the Trump Organization was $3.2 billion in debt in the spring of 1990, with both the Trump Shuttle and the Atlantic City casinos in considerable financial trouble. Trump was able to avoid personal bankruptcy, however, as Kranish and Fisher recount, because the major financial institutions that had lent money to him—including Citibank and Chase Manhattan—had just as much to lose if his businesses went under as Trump himself did, perhaps more. As a result, a deal was reached to restructure Trump's loans, with the banks deferring interest payments on almost $1 billion for up to five years, and providing a further $65 million in financing, while taking control of various Trump assets including his three casinos, private plane, and yacht. Trump himself was given a personal spending limit of $450,000 a month, dropping to $300,000 within two years. (Trump still needed to present a positive and successful public image if he was to effectively dispose of his assets and repay his debts, the banks reasoned.) Nonetheless, the Taj Mahal still went bankrupt in 1991, as did the Trump Plaza Hotel and Casino, the Trump Castle Hotel and Casino, and the famed Plaza Hotel in New York in 1992 (Trump had paid $407 million for the hotel only four years earlier). Two more bankruptcies followed: Trump Hotels and Casino Resorts in 2004 and Trump Entertainment Resorts in 2009.

Yet Trump rebounded. By 1996 *Forbes* estimated his net worth to be $450 million and by 2000 that figure was $1.7 billion. (Trump put his own worth at more than $5 billion in 2000. The true size of his wealth is currently impossible to determine, although its "accurate" public articulation remains a source of considerable concern to Trump himself. In 2004, for example, he unsuccessfully sued the writer Timothy O'Brien for suggesting that he might "only" be worth $150 to $250 million.) Capitalizing on his return to good fortune, in 1997 Trump published *Trump: The Art of the Comeback*, written with Kate Bohner, but he attained a whole new level of fame and notoriety in 2004 when he agreed to take part in a new reality TV show called *The Apprentice* on NBC. The show saw sixteen contestants competing in a series of tasks for the chance to win a one-year, $250,000 job with the Trump Organization. Each episode culminated in a showdown of that week's worst-performing contestants with Trump and his advisors, often including his children, in a fake boardroom seemingly located high up in Trump Tower. "The Donald," as he was now widely known, would dismiss the loser with the show's catchphrase, "You're fired!" Twenty million Americans tuned in for the show's opening episode, rising to twenty-seven million for the season finale, thereby making it one of the top ten television programs of the year. The show and its spinoff, *The Celebrity Apprentice*, would run for fourteen seasons, providing Trump with invaluable publicity, as he appeared, week after week, as a dynamic, decisive, and supremely confident decision maker. *The Apprentice* was "mythmaking on steroids," noted Timothy O'Brien, drawing a "straight line" from the *Art of the Deal* to the show to the 2016 presidential campaign.

What, though, of Trump's actual politics? Both father and son had been Goldwater Republicans in 1964, but in truth neither was especially ideological. They would donate to both political parties, if it would help to facilitate their business deals—as it often did, especially at the local level. Donald contributed to both Jimmy Carter's and Ronald Reagan's presidential campaigns in 1980, for example, and spent at least $3.1 million on various political candidates at all levels of the political system between 1995 and 2016. His official party registration also shuttled back and forth between the Republican and Democratic parties during this time, although he claimed to have always voted for the Republican candidate for president. That said, he was also a strong supporter of Bill Clinton, describing him as "terrific" and praising him for doing "an amazing job" in 1997, and a vocal critic of George W. Bush and the "disaster" of the war in Iraq, despite having been initially in favor of it.

Beyond these largely transactional practices, Trump's first more sub-stantive engagement with politics came in September 1987, when he paid $95,000 to place an open letter addressed to the "American people" in the *New York Times*, the *Boston Globe*, and the *Washington Post*. Although seeming to prefigure some of the themes of his 2016 presidential cam-paign—arguing that the United States "should stop paying to defend countries that can afford to defend themselves," like Japan and Saudi Arabia, for example, and complaining that "our great country" was being "laughed at"—the letter was really a publicity stunt dreamt up by Roger Stone, intended to promote *The Art of the Deal*. Encouraged by a Republican activist from New Hampshire called Michael Dunbar, in October Trump also made a fly-by visit to the Granite State, home to the nation's first primary, as part of Dunbar's speculative—and, from Trump's perspective, hardly serious—"Draft Trump" campaign for the upcoming 1988 presidential election. "I'm not here because I'm running for president," Trump declared during his forty-minute address at the Portsmouth Rotary Club, somewhat anticlimactically. "I'm here because I'm tired of our country being kicked around and I want to get my ideas across." "If the right man doesn't get into office, you're going to see a catastrophe in this country in the next four years like you're never going to believe," he asserted, melodramatically if characteristically, "and then you'll be begging for the right man."

Trump flirted with the presidency again in 2000, this time as a mem-ber of the Reform Party. Again, Roger Stone was involved, although Stone's motivation, in addition to promoting the Trump brand, seemed also to stem from his desire to prevent the Reform Party (perhaps led by Pat Buchanan) from splitting the Republican vote, as Stone believed had happened in 1992 and 1996, when it was led by another businessmen and political outsider, Ross Perot—which is to say, that the Machiavellian Stone was looking for someone who could be relied upon to sabotage the very party he was purporting to lead. (The Reform Party was an attrac-tive proposition, whether for a serious political campaign or simply for publicity purposes, because it was eligible for $12 million in federal fund-ing as a result of Perot's previous performances.) Just as Perot had done, Trump announced his intention to "explore" the possibility of becoming president live on the *Larry King* show; he also suggested to his host that Oprah Winfrey might make an ideal running mate. Trump characterized himself as a conservative, but many of his policy positions suggested otherwise: he was in favor of universal health care, for example; wanted gay soldiers to be able to serve openly in the military; supported abortion; and proposed a onetime tax on the wealthy in order to protect the Social Security system. In February 2000, Trump went back on television and wrote an op-ed in the *New York Times* to explain that he was ending his exploratory campaign because "the Reform Party is a total mess." The experience, however, had been the "greatest civics lesson that a private citizen can have," he said.

Back in April 1989, Trump had bought full-page ads in four New York newspapers—the *New York Times*, the *New York Post*, the *Daily News*, and *Newsday*—so that he could comment on the brutal rape and beating of a young white investment banker called Trisha Meili, who had been attacked while jogging in Central Park. Five youths, aged between fourteen and sixteen, were arrested and charged with the crime. Four were black and one was Hispanic. Denouncing what he called the "roving bands of wild criminals" loose in the city, Trump wanted to "bring back the death penalty" and to "bring back our police," he said. He also attacked New York's mayor, Ed Koch, with whom he had been having a long-running feud because of Koch's comments that New Yorkers should not indulge in hatred and rancor over the incident. "I do not think so," Trump wrote. "I want to hate these muggers and murderers. They should be forced to suffer and when they kill they should be executed for their crimes." Trump denied that he was being racist, arguing that he was merely giving voice to what most people really thought but were too afraid to say. Three years later, the five men were cleared of the crime and released from prison after another man confessed to carrying out the attack, which was confirmed by DNA evidence. The city paid $41 million to settle the five men's wrongful imprisonment suit, as it became clear that their original confessions had been coerced. Still Trump refused to apologize. He called the settlement a "disgrace," argued that the men did "not exactly have the pasts of angels," and suggested that they owed "the taxpayers of the City of New York an apology for taking money out of their pockets like candy from a baby."

Concerns about Trump's racial attitudes surfaced again in 2011, amid fresh speculation that he might run for the presidency, when he became one of the leading voices of the so-called Birther movement, which was questioning whether Barack Obama was actually born in the United States and therefore a "legitimate" president. The conspiracy theory, which was also popular among certain sections of the Tea Party, contended that Obama had really been born in Kenya, where his father was from, and not Hawaii, as his birth certificate showed. (Obama had released a short form of his birth certificate in 2008, but this had failed to put the rumors and speculation to rest.) At the Conservative Political Action Conference in Orlando, Florida, in February 2011, Trump noted: "Our current president came out of nowhere. Came out of nowhere. In fact, I'll go a step further. The people that went to school with him never saw him; they don't know who he is. Crazy!" He appeared on Fox News with Bill O'Reilly, wondering if the reason that Obama wouldn't release his birth certificate—despite the fact that he already had—was that it showed that the president was a Muslim. And he told NBC that he had dispatched a team of investigators to Hawaii to uncover the "truth" and that "they cannot believe what they're finding," although he did not reveal what it was that they had found.

On April 27, 2011, the White House released Obama's long-form birth certificate in an attempt to bring an end to what the president called "this silliness." A few days later, Trump attended the annual White House Correspondents' Dinner as a guest of the *Washington Post*. He was ridiculed both by the host, comedian Seth Meyers, and by Obama directly. "I know he's taken some flack lately. But no one is happier, no one is prouder to put this birth certificate matter to rest than The Donald," the president said. "And that's because he can finally get back to focusing on the issues that matter—like, did we fake the moon landing? What really happened in Roswell? And where are Biggie and Tupac?" Trump would only finally abandon his Birther theories in September 2016: "President Barack Obama was born in the United States, period. Now, we all want to get back to making America strong and great again," he said, during a campaign event in Washington, D.C. But even then, he tried to blame Hillary Clinton for starting the controversy, while also seeking credit for his role in "finishing" it.

Because of Trump's history—his involvement with the Birthers, his high-profile business and media career, his seemingly insatiable hunger for publicity, and his previous unconvincing dalliances in politics—it was hardly surprising that very few observers took him seriously on

June 16, 2015, when, in the lobby of Trump Tower, he announced that he was seeking to become the next Republican president of the United States. From the outset, it was clear that Trump wasn't going to be a conventional candidate and that he would not be running a conventional campaign. In the aftermath of Romney's defeat to Obama in 2012, the chairman of the Republican National Committee, Reince Priebus—who would go on to become Trump's first chief of staff—had undertaken a detailed analysis of what the party needed to do to win the next election. Officially called the Growth and Opportunity Project but better known more colloquially as the "autopsy report," the one-hundred-page document stressed the need to make the GOP more inclusive, for it to reach out to the young, to women, to Hispanics, and to African Americans, to create "a more welcoming conservatism." This would not be Trump's approach. Instead, during his largely unscripted opening campaign address, Trump highlighted what he saw as America's profound decline—"The American Dream is dead," he noted at one point—and he focused especially on the issue of illegal immigration, with Mexico identified as a particular problem. "When Mexico sends its people, these aren't the best and the finest," he lamented. "They're not sending you. . . . They're sending people that have lots of problems, and they're bringing those problems with us [*sic*]. They're bringing drugs. They're bringing crime. They're rapists. And some, I assume, are good people."

Trump's solution to this problem was to "build a great, great wall on our southern border" and to have Mexico pay for it. He also promised to repeal the Affordable Care Act and to replace it with "something much better for everybody." He would bring an end to injurious trade deals, he said; create "the strongest military that we've ever had"; rebuild the nation's infrastructure; defeat ISIS; defend the Second Amendment; reform the tax system; save Medicare, Medicaid, and Social Security "without cuts"; and be "the greatest jobs president God ever created." The speech may have been light on policy details—and Trump would do little to add in those details in the ensuing sixteen months—but the broad themes of his campaign—"Make America Great Again," which he borrowed from Ronald Reagan, but which sounded a lot like the Tea Party rallying cry of "Take America Back"; and "America First," with its echo, whether conscious or not, of Lindbergh and the isolationists of the 1930s—clearly struck a nerve, especially among white, working-class voters.

Just as important in explaining Trump's appeal, though, was his style and approach. He was the outspoken outsider, the commonsense truth-teller, someone who was unafraid to breach the conventions of political correctness, someone who knew "how the game was played" but who because of his great personal wealth would not be beholden to the lobbyists and the special interests. He promised to "drain the Washington swamp," mocked those Republican nominees who sought funding from the Koch brothers as "puppets"—although the Kochs would later play a key role in the staffing of his administration—and routinely ridiculed politicians of both parties as "all talk and no action." He was a billionaire populist, a friend to the "forgotten men and women of our country," and only he could fix what was wrong with America.

In the absence of a traditional organizational structure, Trump conducted his campaign largely in the media, on Twitter, and through large, raucous public rallies where he was, by turns, angry, scolding, confrontational, digressive, humorous, and reassuring. He was a regular on Fox News and an enormous ratings draw on all the TV networks, receiving $2 billion in "free" media exposure during the primary campaign alone—a figure calculated on the basis of how much he would have had to pay in advertising rates for the news coverage he received—three times as much as the next three major Republican candidates combined. He assigned unflattering nicknames to many of his Republican opponents—there were sixteen of them at the outset, including the former Florida governor "Low-Energy" Jeb Bush, the Florida senator "Little" Marco Rubio, and his Texas colleague "Lyin'" Ted Cruz—and became embroiled in numerous controversies: accusing George W. Bush of deliberately misleading the American people into the Iraq War; mocking the disabled; feuding with the Pope; embracing torture; retweeting the views of neo-Nazis; suggesting that Ted Cruz's father had been involved in the JFK assassination; calling for a complete ban on Muslims entering the United States; and seeming to encourage violence against protestors who attended his rallies—"I'd like to punch him in the face," he said on one occasion; "Knock the crap out of him," on another.

With the Republican establishment increasingly concerned that Trump might actually win the party's nomination, on March 3, 2016, Mitt

Romney, the party's standard-bearer only four years before, launched an unprecedented attack on the current GOP front-runner. "Donald Trump is a phony, a fraud," Romney said, in a speech at the University of Utah. "His promises are as worthless as a degree from Trump University. He's playing members of the American public for suckers." There were even suggestions that the party might engineer a contested convention in order to stop the New Yorker. Trump's response was to suggest that there would be "riots" if that happened. "I think you would have problems like you've never seen before. I think bad things would happen," he said, although he himself "wouldn't lead" such efforts, he made clear. In the end Trump won the nomination with a record-breaking 13.3 million votes in the primaries, eclipsing George W. Bush's total from 2000 by 1.8 million (although it was also true that he received more votes against him, more than 15 million, than any other previous Republican candidate). The Indiana governor Mike Pence, a staunch social conservative and former Tea Party–supporting congressman, was named his running mate.

Trump's Democratic opponent in the general election was Hillary Clinton, Obama's secretary of state, a former New York senator, and the wife of Bill Clinton, who had seen off her own insurgent challenger in the form of the Vermont senator and "Democratic socialist" Bernie Sanders. It was a contentious and bruising campaign, as Trump continued with the tactics that had served him so well in the primaries. He labeled Clinton "Crooked Hillary" to highlight her alleged corruption; led chants of "Lock Her Up!" at his rallies in reference to her use of a private e-mail server during her tenure as secretary of state, which was being investigated by the FBI; and claimed that she and Obama were the "founders" of ISIS. But he also went further. During a campaign address in Wilmington, North Carolina, on August 9, 2016, he seemed to make a thinly veiled assassination threat against his opponent during a discourse on Clinton's likely Supreme Court nominees and her supposed desire to abolish Americans' right to bear arms: "If she gets to pick her judges, nothing you can do, folks. Although the Second Amendment people— maybe there is, I don't know. But I'll tell you what, that would be a horrible day." And in an extraordinary speech at West Palm Beach, Florida, on October 13, he placed Clinton at the center of an enormous global conspiracy. "Hillary Clinton meets in secret with international banks to plot the destruction of U.S. sovereignty in order to enrich . . . global financial powers, her special interest friends, and her donors," he said:

> This election will determine if we are a free nation or whether we have only the illusion of democracy, but are in fact controlled by a small handful of global special interests rigging the system, and our system *is* rigged. . . .
>
> Our corrupt political establishment, that is the greatest power behind the efforts at radical globalization and the disenfranchisement of working people [*sic*]. Their financial resources are virtually unlimited, their political resources are unlimited, their media resources are unmatched.

Just a few days earlier, on October 7, the same day that it was revealed that Russia was behind a series of cyberattacks on the Democratic National Committee, the *Washington Post* released a tape recording from a 2005 *Access Hollywood* show in which Trump could be heard boasting about using his celebrity to sexually assault women. Speaking to the show's host, Billy Bush, a cousin of George and Jeb Bush, in what he believed to be a private conversation, Trump recounted how he was "automatically attracted to beautiful women." "I just start kissing them," he said. "It's like a magnet. Just kiss. I don't even wait . . . and when you're a star they let you do it. You can do anything. . . . Grab them by the pussy. You can do anything." Condemnation was immediate and widespread, including from dozens of prominent Republicans such as Paul Ryan and Mitch McConnell (although neither officially withdrew their endorsements of the GOP candidate). Indeed, the outcry was such that Trump was forced to issue an apology for his remarks, although in typical Roy Cohn style, he also attempted to strike back. "I've said some foolish things," he admitted in a ninety-second video, "but there is a big difference between the words and the actions of other people. Bill Clinton has actually abused women and Hillary has bullied, attacked, shamed, and intimidated his victims."

As election day approached, and with opinion polls and surveys indicating that he was running behind Clinton, Trump began to question the legitimacy of the whole electoral process. "The election is absolutely being rigged by the dishonest and distorted media pushing Crooked Hillary—but also at many polling stations—SAD," he wrote in one tweet. And during the final debate between the two candidates on October 19, he refused to say that he would accept the results of the election if he lost—"I will look at it at the time," he said. Concerns about Trump's commitment to democracy, suggestions that he was really an authoritarian demagogue or even a fascist, had been voiced with increasing regularity ever since Trump transformed himself from a joke candidate into a serious contender during the Republican primaries. These concerns came not just from liberals or progressives but from conservatives as well. Robert Kagan, a senior fellow at the Brookings Institution, published an article in the *Washington Post* entitled "This Is How Fascism Comes to America," and David Frum wrote in the *Atlantic* on "How to Build an Autocracy," for example. "No American demagogue—not Huey Long, not Joseph McCarthy, not George Wallace—has ever reached such proximity to national power," was how the liberal editor of the *New Yorker*, David Remnick, put it in March 2016.

The appointment of Steve Bannon, a former Goldman Sachs banker, onetime Hollywood film producer, and the then head of the ultra-conservative website Breitbart News, as the CEO of the Trump campaign in August 2016 did little to allay these concerns. (Bannon, who would go on to become Trump's chief strategist in the White House, took over the running of the campaign from Paul Manafort, who resigned as campaign manager shortly after Bannon's appointment.) A self-described "economic nationalist," Bannon regarded Breitbart as a "platform for the alt-right," an amorphous term, that, as the academic George Michael has written, encompasses a whole range of "rightist activists and intellectuals . . . including those who believe in libertarianism, men's rights, cultural conservatism, isolationism and populism," but which is also embraced by Klansmen, neo-Nazis, and other white nationalists. Prominent members of the alt-right include Richard Spencer and his National Policy Institute think tank; Jared Taylor, the founder and editor of *American Renaissance* magazine; and neo-Confederate and neo-fascist groups such as the League of the South and the National Socialist Movement of America.

In a speech in Reno, Nevada, on August 25, 2016, Hillary Clinton excoriated Trump for building his campaign on "prejudice and paranoia," for his racism, for his conspiracy theories, and for "taking hate groups mainstream." She took particular aim at what she called the "de facto merger" between Breitbart and the Trump campaign. "This is not conservatism as we have known it. This is not Republicanism as we have known it," she argued. "These are race-baiting ideas, anti-Muslim and anti-immigrant ideas, anti-woman—all key tenets making up an emerging racist ideology known as the 'Alt-Right.'" "Of course, there has always been a paranoid fringe in our politics, a lot of it rising from racial resentment," she went on. "But it's never had the nominee of a major party stoking it, encouraging it, and giving it a national megaphone—until now."

Remarkably, despite all the controversies and all the vitriol, all the condemnation and all the outrage, Donald Trump won the 2016 presidential election. It was close. In fact, Trump lost the popular vote by 62.9 million votes to 65.8 million (46.1 percent to 48.2 percent)—the fifth president in American history to do so—but he won comfortably in the Electoral College by 304 votes to Clinton's 227, largely by taking the key states of Pennsylvania, Wisconsin, and Michigan, albeit by a margin of just over one hundred thousand in each of them. True to form, Trump suggested, with no evidence to support the claim, that Clinton had only won the popular vote because of the "millions of people who voted illegally" and once in office established a Voter Fraud Commission to investigate the matter. In Congress, the Republicans lost six seats in the House and two seats in the Senate, reducing their majority over the Democrats to 241 to 194, and 52 to 46, respectively.

Many explanations were provided to explain Trump's unlikely victory, especially from those opposed to him. The media was blamed because of the extensive coverage it had provided the billionaire and for not being critical or probing enough of his candidacy during its earliest stages. The GOP leadership was blamed for its failure to stop Trump at the outset and for its seeming inability to look beyond partisan politics to broader moral and ethical considerations. Hillary Clinton was blamed for being an uninspiring candidate, for being too unpopular and having too much "baggage" attached to her. In her post-election memoir, *What Happened* (2017), Clinton herself blamed ongoing misogyny and sexism, as well as FBI director James Comey for reopening the investigation into her use of a private e-mail server on October 28, 2016—just eleven days before polling day—only to close it again nine days later. Yet it also has to be acknowledged how effective a campaigner Trump proved to be, how adroitly he navigated both the media and the political landscape, exploiting both the ongoing resentments against the Obama administration—whether racially motivated or otherwise—and the widespread disillusionment that

Portrait of President-elect Donald Trump, December 15, 2016. Trump's election victory was one of the most surprising events in recent American history. Library of Congress Prints & Photographs Division, LC-DIG-ppbd-00607.

many Republicans had with their own party and with politics in general (as the rise of the Tea Party had already demonstrated). In this respect, Clinton's experience and apparent preparedness for the White House— "There has never been a man or a woman . . . more qualified than Hillary Clinton to serve as the president of the United States," eulogized Obama during the Democratic convention in Philadelphia—was less an asset and more of a liability, at least for a certain portion of the electorate.

There was some hope that Trump would be more "presidential" in office than he had been as a candidate. In fact during the election campaign Trump himself had suggested that it was "easy to act presidential" and that, with notable the exception of Abraham Lincoln, he would be "more presidential than any president who's ever held this office." His first year in the White House, though, was very much as chaotic, combative, and controversial as his campaign had been. In his Inaugural Address, he spoke of the "American carnage" that he saw around him and then had his press secretary, Sean Spicer, claim falsely that Trump's was "the largest audience to ever witness an inauguration—period—both in person and around the globe." He routinely attacked the media for providing what he called "fake news," even going so far as to label organizations such the *New York Times*, NBC News, and CNN "the enemy of the American people." He accused his predecessor President Obama of secretly ordering a wiretap of Trump's offices in New York before the election. He seemed to defend neo-Nazis and other members of the alt-right after violence broke out at a far-right rally in Charlottesville, Virginia, in August 2017, suggesting that there were "very fine people on both sides" in the confrontation. And he continued to rely on Twitter as one of his primary means of communication, using it to get into Twitter wars with everyone from the rapper Snoop Dogg, the actress Meryl Streep, and the National Football League, to members of his own party, including Mitch McConnell, John McCain, and the chairman of the Senate Foreign Relations Committee, Bob Corker (TN), as well as foreign leaders such as Kim Jong-un, whom Trump derisively referred to as "Little Rocket Man," in reference to the North Korean's nuclear weapons program.

Nor, with the significant exception of major tax cuts—directed mostly toward the wealthy and corporations—were there many legislative achievements during Trump's first year. No repeal and replacement of Obamacare. No infrastructure bill. No building of "the wall," for example. Instead, Trump relied on a flurry of executive orders to achieve his policy goals—allowing more extensive offshore drilling for oil and gas, preventing transgender Americans from serving in the military, scaling back restrictions on carbon emissions, and ending the DACA program—although many of these orders also seemed designed simply to undo Obama-era regulations. In a similar vein, Trump threatened to pull the United States out of the Paris climate accord and to decertify the landmark Joint Comprehensive Plan of Action intended to restrict Iran's ability to develop nuclear weapons. A ban preventing travelers from several predominantly Muslim countries from entering the United States was introduced, although it had to be repeatedly modified following legal challenges over its constitutionality, and the administration did successfully nominate Neil Gorsuch to the Supreme Court.

Overall, it was hardly the record of "winning" that Trump had promised on the campaign trail. And, overshadowing it all, was the specter of several investigations—by the FBI, in Congress, and by special counsel Robert Mueller—into the Russian government's interference in the 2016 presidential election and the question of whether members of the Trump campaign had "colluded" in that interference. Trump called the investigations the "greatest witch-hunt in political history," but his firing of FBI director James Comey on May 9, 2017, apparently because of his frustration with Comey's role in the inquiries, did little to allay the concerns. Indeed, it set off a whole series of new ones, over whether the president might be attempting to obstruct justice. In October 2017, the first charges arising from Mueller's investigation were brought forth. Trump's former campaign manager Paul Manafort and his business associate Rick Gates, who had also worked on the Trump campaign, were accused of various crimes including money laundering, tax evasion, and "conspiracy against the United States." In addition, the former Trump foreign policy advisor George Papadopoulos admitted to making false statements to the FBI when he was questioned about his attempts to make contact with the Russian government during the election.

It is obviously tempting to regard Donald Trump as sui generis— and there is certainly much truth in this characterization. But we also need to see his candidacy and his presidency, even at this early stage, as a continuation and, to some extent, a culmination of deeper historical trends and developments, many of them closely related to the history of the American radical right. Trump, for example, both actively courted the Tea Party—"The Tea Party people are incredible people. These are people who work hard and love the country, and they get beat up all the time by the media," he said, during a campaign rally in

Nashville, for example—and also skillfully, if cynically, rode the wave of discontent and disillusionment that the movement represented. Indeed, as this chapter has shown, both the Great Recession of 2008 and the subsequent Obama presidency, for different but also connected reasons, form the essential backdrop for understanding both the rise of the Tea Party and that of Trump. It is also the case, however, that Trump utilized and built upon strategies and practices that had been integral to the more radical elements of the Republican Party—as well as the conservative mediasphere—for more than forty years: intransigence, belligerence, dog-whistle politics, demonization of "the Other," and a generalized assault on Washington and the very utility of government itself, key among them. Trumpism as a political philosophy may be difficult to pin down because of the ever-shifting positions, attention-seeking showmanship, and underlying narcissism of its chief articulator, but its origins, energies, resentments, and motivations are much more readily identifiable.

Conclusion

NUMEROUS EXPLANATIONS HAVE BEEN OFFERED to explain Donald Trump's startling election victory in 2016. Many of these have emphasized worldwide trends and developments: the negative impact of globalization and neoliberalism; the lingering effects of the Great Recession; a widespread loss of faith in democracy; the appeal of authoritarian leaders—the proverbial "strong men"—in places such as Russia, Turkey, and Hungary; the broader reemergence of virulent anti-immigrant sentiment, evident, for example, in France, Holland, and Germany; fears about terrorism; surging nationalism; and a distrust of "experts." There is certainly some truth to be found in many of these explanations—to what the writer Pankaj Mishra has characterized as our current "age of anger"—but, ultimately, as we have seen in this book, Trump's victory can only really be understood by placing it within the context of recent U.S. history, especially the history of the American radical right.

For all his particularities and idiosyncrasies, Trump's underlying aims, in most respects, remain the same ones that have been animating the radical right ever since the 1930s: lower taxes, smaller government, less bureaucracy, and fewer regulations. A glance at Trump's cabinet— the wealthiest ever assembled—demonstrates this clearly enough, with the former CEO of ExxonMobil, Rex Tillerson, as secretary of state; Steve Mnuchin, a former investment banker and hedge fund manager, as secretary of the treasury; and the billionaire investor Wilbur Smith as secretary of commerce. Other Trump appointments—like some of those in the Reagan years or during the presidency of George W. Bush—seem to have been made because the person chosen is either fundamentally opposed to, or profoundly ignorant of, the mission of the government agencies they preside over: Betsy DeVos at the Department of Education, Tom Price at the Department of Health and Human Services, Scott Pruitt at the Environmental Protection Agency, Rick Perry at the Energy Department, and Ben Carson at the Department of Housing and Urban Development, for example.

During a question-and-answer session at the February 2017 Conservative Political Action Conference in Oxon Hill, Maryland, Steve Bannon, still then the president's chief strategist—he left his position by "mutual consent" in August—was explicit about what he called "the deconstruction of the administrative state." As he explained: "If you look at these cabinet appointments, they were selected for a reason and that is the deconstruction [of the administrative state]. The way the progressive left runs is if they can't get it passed, they're just going to put in some sort of regulation in an agency. That's all going to be deconstructed and I think that's why this regulatory thing is so important." It is true that Bannon's motivations may well be different from Trump's—with the former having a more intellectual and ideological intent, and the latter more interested in unleashing entrepreneurship and the "majesty" of the free market—but the effect is the same.

The second way that Trump can be seen as connected to, and expressive of, the history of the modern American radical right is through the manner of his politics and his style: in his proclivity for the conspiratorial and appeal to the populist; in his extreme rhetoric and reliance on the strategy of "Multiple Untruth" (à la Senator McCarthy); in his tendency toward the demagogic and his subtle—and not so subtle—racism; in his apparent contempt for the normal rules of democratic politics; and in his desire to turn back the clock in order to "Make America Great Again." To be sure, there are ways that the Trump agenda seems to run counter to long-standing conservative ideas and values—calling for massive infrastructure spending, promising to save Medicare and Social Security in its current form, threatening to undo international free trade agreements—but overall, both in spirit and in substance, Trumpism is much closer to the philosophy of the radical right than any other American ideology. (Critics of Trump have also pointed to his support for increased military spending and the expansion of the anti-immigrant bureaucracy as examples of his inconsistent attitude toward "big government," but this is to ignore the fact that defense of the nation and the necessity for "law and order" have always been exempted from the right's anti-statist beliefs.)

What, then, of the broader history of the radical right in the United States since the 1930s? How can we best characterize and understand this period of American history?

As we have seen, from the outset a very close relationship has existed between American business and the radical right. From the creation of the American Liberty Lobby in 1934, through the establishment of the John Birch Society in 1959 and support for the New Right in the 1970s and 1980s, and on to the emergence of the Tea Party in the early 2000s, corporate interests, wealthy businessmen, and their private foundations have provided critical backing not just for specific groups but also for a wide range of think tanks, lobbyists, political action committees, and other organizations as they endeavored to capture the "marketplace of ideas," undermine confidence in the federal government, and shift the nation rightward. In Donald Trump, there is an actual businessman in the White House, of course. He is not the first—Warren Harding was a newspaper publisher; Herbert Hoover, a mine owner; Harry Truman ran a haberdashery; Jimmy Carter was a peanut farmer; George H. W. Bush was an oilman; as was his son George W. Bush, also the managing partner of the Texas Rangers baseball team—but he is the first to have entered the White House without any additional professional political or military experience. (With the exception of Truman, none of these for-mer businessmen were regarded as particularly effective stewards of the economy, one might note, however.) For the ultra-free-market advocates of the "radical rich," such as the Koch brothers, Bob and Rebekah Mer-cer, and Richard Mellon Scaife, it is tempting to suggest that their ulti-mate aim is really the establishment of a plutocracy in the United States.

Corporations and the wealthy have also sought to extend their influ-ence through the Republican Party, as have other members of the radi-cal right, including vocal anti-communists, the advocates of massive resistance, members of the John Birch Society, evangelical Christians, other components of the New Right, and, most recently, the Tea Party. The GOP itself has moved markedly and decisively to the right during the period covered in this book. Indeed, from Goldwater in the 1960s, through Reagan in the 1980s, and on, most especially, to the Republican right of the 1990s and 2000s—with their attempts to impeach Bill Clinton, repeated shutdowns of the government, and wholesale obstruction of the presidency of Barack Obama—in many respects the modern Republican Party has *become* the radical right. This is evident in the anti-government "litmus tests" that are increasingly placed on Republican candidates for public office and in the widespread fear of "moderate" or "establishment"

Republicans that they will be "primaried" from the (even further) right if they fail to show sufficient ideological zeal. In fact, the very term "moderate Republican"—which, as Geoffrey Kabaservice has shown in his recent book on the subject, has a deep and rich history—is now close to being an oxymoron. Steve Bannon's threat to oust Republicans who fail to get behind Donald Trump's agenda is another example of the trend.

Since the 1930s, the American radical right has encompassed such varying groups and individuals as Father Coughlin; Gerald Winrod's Defenders of the Christian Faith; Dr. Fred Schwartz's Christian Anti-Communism Crusade; Citizens' Councils; Governor George Wallace and his American Independence Party; Richard Viguerie; Phyllis Schlafly and her Stop ERA campaign; Pat Robertson and Ralph Reed's Christian Coalition; militia groups; right-wing media figures like Rush Limbaugh and Glenn Beck; the Tea Party; assorted senators and congressmen including Martin Dies, Joe McCarthy, Strom Thurmond, James Eastland, Newt Gingrich, Dick Armey, and Ted Cruz; and arguably two presidents in Ronald Reagan and Donald Trump. As this list suggests, the radical right is not a monolithic movement. There have been differences of approach and differences of emphasis. Some groups have been elite driven and some have arisen from the grassroots. Some have been marginalized and some have been embraced by the political mainstream. Throughout, though, certain themes, ideas, and modes of expression have repeatedly come to fore, including a reverence for the Constitution and an embrace of the nation's founding fathers; a fear of subversion and a tendency toward conspiracy theories; a defense of "traditional" values and a concern that some Americans—civil rights activists, liberals, immigrants—may not share those values; and, above all, a deeply rooted hostility toward the interventionist state and "big government."

The radical right emerged initially in response to the New Deal and liberalism's apparent ascendency in the United States, but it has continued to develop as the nation itself has developed, forced to react to changing times and to changing conditions—to the Cold War, the rise of the civil rights movement, the expansion of the welfare state, declining economic growth, and the election of the country's first African-American president, for example. In doing so, it has embraced new—and often highly confrontational—forms of politics, as well as new forms of media, as it has tried—and often succeeded—to get its anti-government message out to the American people. As we have seen, members of the radical right have frequently courted controversy. They have been attacked for their extremism, for their racism, and for their manipulative populism and demagogic tendencies. They have been seen as a threat to democracy, even as harbingers of American fascism. In sum, the impact of the radical right on the United States since the passing of the New Deal has been considerable. It is a long way—in many different ways—from FDR to Donald Trump.

A Note on Sources

GENERAL SOURCES

For an overview of much of the broader history covered in this book, there is no better place to begin than with James T. Paterson's *Grand Expectations: The United States, 1945–1974* (New York: Oxford University Press, 1996), together with its follow-up *Restless Giant: The United States from Watergate to* Bush v. Gore (New York: Oxford University Press, 2005). Readers looking for a more provocative and partial interpretation of this same period might wish to consult Oliver Stone and Peter Kuznick's *The Untold History of the United States* (New York: Gallery Books, 2012) or watch the accompanying ten-part documentary series. In terms of the specific history of the radical right since the 1930s, David H. Bennett's *The Party of Fear: The American Far Right from Nativism to the Militia Movement*, rev. ed. (New York: Vintage, 1995) and Seymour Martin Lipset and Earl Raab's *The Politics of Unreason: Right-Wing Extremism in America, 1790–1977*, 2nd ed. (Chicago: Chicago University Press, 1978) are essential starting points, along with Chip Berlet and Matthew Lyon's *Right-Wing Populism in America: Too Close for Comfort* (New York: The Guildford Press, 2000) and Sara Diamond's *Roads to Dominion: Right-Wing Movements and Political Power in the United States* (New York: Guilford Press, 1995). In addition, Nicole Hemmer's *Messengers of the Right: Conservative Media and the Transformation of American Politics* (Philadelphia: University of Pennsylvania Press, 2016) is a superb account of the crucial role played by various forms of media—radio, television, magazines, book clubs—in the development of conservatism, including the radical right, since the late 1940s.

INTRODUCTION

The essays in Daniel Bell's edited collection *The Radical Right: "The New American Right," Expanded and Updated* (Garden City: Doubleday,

1963) were critical in establishing our initial understanding of the radical right. But no work was more influential than Richard Hofstadter's "The Paranoid Style in American Politics," which can be found in *The Paranoid Style in American Politics and Other Essays* (Cambridge:, MA Harvard University Press, 1965). I have provided a detailed analysis and critique both of Seymour Martin Lipset's and Hofstadter's approach to the subject in *American Extremism: History, Politics and the Militia Movement* (New York: Routledge, 2004), 17–33. Timothy Patrick McCarthy and John McMillan provide an excellent introduction to the history of the radical left in the United States in *The Radical Reader: A Documentary History of the American Radical Tradition* (New York: New Press, 2003), which begins with the American Revolution and ends with the anti-war protests against George W. Bush in 2003.

A wide-ranging and thoughtful discussion of the nature of demagoguery is provided by Michael Singer in *Demagogue: The Fight to Save Democracy from its Worst Enemies* (New York: Palgrave Macmillan, 2009). On the nature of populism and its development not just in the United States but around the world, see John B. Judis's *The Populist Explosion: How the Great Recession Transformed American and European Politics* (New York: Columbia Global Reports, 2016) and Jan-Werner Muller's *What is Populism?* (Philadelphia: University of Pennsylvania Press, 2016). Michael Kazin offers a richly fascinating account of the phenomenon in the U.S. in *The Populist Persuasion: An American History* (New York: Basic Books, 1995).

On the "counter-subversive tradition" in American history, see David Brion Davis's *The Fear of Conspiracy: Images of Un-American Subversion from the Revolution to the Present* (Ithaca, NY: Cornell University Press, 1971); Richard O. Curry and Thomas M. Brown, eds., *Conspiracy: The Fear of Subversion in American History* (New York: Holt, Rinehart & Winston, 1972); and Michael Paul Rogin, *"Ronald Reagan, The Movie" and Other Episodes in Political Demonology* (Berkeley: University of California Press, 1988). Robert Alan Goldberg provides a highly readable account of American conspiracy theories and conspiracy culture more broadly in *Enemies Within: The Culture of Conspiracy in Modern America* (New Haven, CT: Yale University Press, 2001). Kathryn S. Olmsted's *Real Enemies: Conspiracy Theories and American Democracy, World War I to 9/11* (New York: Oxford University Press, 2009) is also highly recommended.

CHAPTER 1:
BIG GOVERNMENT ON THE MARCH

There are an enormous number of books on the Great Depression and
the New Deal. Among the best are: David M. Kennedy, *Freedom from
Fear: The American People in Depression and War, 1929–1945* (New York:
Oxford University Press, 1999); William E. Leuchtenberg, *Franklin D.
Roosevelt and the New Deal, 1932–1940* (New York: Harper & Row, 1963);
Alan Brinkley, *The End of Reform: New Deal Liberalism in Recession and
War* (New York: Vintage, 1983); Steve Fraser and Gary Gerstle, eds., *The
Rise and Fall of the New Deal Order* (Princeton, NJ: Princeton University
Press, 1989); Ira Katznelson, *Fear Itself: The New Deal and the Origins of
Our Time* (New York: W. W. Norton, 2013); Studs Terkel, *Hard Times:
An Oral History of the Great Depression* (New York: Pantheon, 1970); and
Morris Dickstein, *A Cultural History of the Great Depression* (New York:
W. W. Norton, 2009). Jefferson Cowie provides a relatively brief but
extremely thoughtful examination of the New Deal and its impact on
the United States in *The Great Exception: The New Deal and the Limits of
American Politics* (Princeton, NJ: Princeton University Press, 2016).

The best accounts of the history of the American Liberty League
remain G. Wofskill's *The Revolt of the Conservatives: A History of the
American Liberty League, 1934–1940* (Boston: Houghton Mifflin, 1962)
and Frederick Randolph's "The American Liberty League, 1934–1940,"
American Historical Review 561, no. 1 (Oct. 1950): 19–33. On the wider
history of American business's opposition to "big government," readers
should consult Kim Phillips-Fein's *Invisible Hands: The Making of the
Conservative Movement from the New Deal to Reagan* (New York: W. W.
Norton, 2009) and Kathryn S. Olmsted's more narrowly focused *Right
Out of California: The 1930s and the Big Business Roots of Modern Conservatism* (New York: The New Press, 2015).

T. Harry Williams's magisterial *Huey Long* (New York: Alfred A.
Knopf, 1969) is still the best account we have of the "Kingfish" and his life,
although readers looking for a shorter version of Williams's arguments
should consider "The Gentleman from Louisiana: Demagogue or Democrat" in the *Journal of Southern History* 26 (Feb. 1960): 3–21. The most
recent biography of Father Coughlin is Donald Warren's *Radio Priest:
Charles Coughlin, the Father of Hate Radio* (New York: Simon & Schuster,

1996), but David Bennett's *Demagogues in the Depression: American Radicals and the Union Party* (New Brunswick, NJ: Rutgers University Press, 1969) is still important to read. Better still, though, is Alan Brinkley's combined biography of Long and Coughlin, *Voices of Protest: Huey Long, Father Coughlin and the Great Depression* (New York, Vintage, 1983), particularly his discussion of the "dissident ideology" in chapter 7.

Leo P. Ribuffo's *The Old Christian Right: The Far Right from the Great Depression to the Cold War* (Philadelphia: Temple University Press, 1983) is essential on the radical right in the 1930s and the "Brown Scare." Important too are Geoffrey S. Smith's *To Save a Nation: American "Extremism," the New Deal and the Coming of World War II* (Chicago: Ivan R. Dee, 1992) and Alex Goodall's more recent *Loyalty and Liberty: American Countersubversion from World War I to the McCarthy Era* (Urbana: University of Illinois Press, 2013). On the fascists and "quasi-fascists" of this time, see Scott Beekman, *William Dudley Pelley: A Life in Right-Wing Extremism and the Occult* (Syracuse, NY: Syracuse University Press, 2005); Peter H. Amann, "A 'Dog in the Nighttime' Problem: American Fascism in the 1930s," *The History Teacher* 19, no. 4 (Aug. 1986): 559–584, and "Vigilante Fascism: The Black Legion as an American Hybrid," *Comparative Studies in Society and History* 25, no. 3 (July 1983): 490–524; and Leland Bell, "The Failure of Nazism in America: The German-American Bund, 1936–1941," *Political Science Quarterly* 85, no. 4 (Dec. 1970): 585–599.

For readers looking for more on America's entry into the Second World War and the "Great Debate" between the isolationists and the interventionist that took place during this time, Robert A. Divine's *The Reluctant Belligerent: American Entry into World War II* (New York: McGraw-Hill, 1979) still provides an excellent introduction, although Lynne Olson certainly offers a more exciting and evocative account of the same events in *Those Angry Days: Roosevelt, Lindbergh, and America's Fight Over World War II, 1939–1941* (New York: Random House, 2014). Wayne S. Cole's *America First: The Battle Against Intervention, 1940–1941* (New York: Octagon Books, 1971) and Marc C. Johnson's "Franklin D. Roosevelt, Burton K. Wheeler, and the Great Debate: A Montana Senator's Crusade for Non-Intervention before World War II," *Montana: The Magazine of Western History*, 62, no. 4 (Winter 2012): 3–22, are also useful. On the development of the national security state, see James T. Sparrow,

Warfare State: World War II Americans and the Age of Big Government (New York: Oxford University Press, 2011).

CHAPTER 2:
WRESTLING THE OCTOPUS

On the broad sweep and often devastating effect of the Second Red Scare on American life, see David Caute, *The Great Fear: The Anti-Communist Purge Under Truman and Eisenhower* (New York: Simon and Schuster, 1978); Ellen Schrecker, *Many Are the Crimes: McCarthyism in America* (Boston: Little Brown, 1998); Richard Fried, *Nightmare in Red: The McCarthy Era in Perspective* (New York: Oxford University Press, 1990); and Ted Morgan, *Reds: McCarthyism in Twentieth-Century America* (New York: Random House, 2003).

Richard Gid Powers provides a detailed and remarkably evenhanded account of the complex history of American anti-communism in *Not Without Honor: The History of American Anticommunism* (New York: Free Press, 1995). Michael J. Heale's *American Anticommunism: Combating the Enemy Within* (Baltimore: Johns Hopkins University Press, 1990) is another important work on the subject. Susan Jacoby expertly assesses the significance of the Hiss case in *Alger Hiss and the Battle for History* (New Haven, CT: Yale University Press, 2009). For more details on HUAC and the FBI's role in the anti-communist network, readers should consult Walter Goodman's *The Committee: The Extraordinary Career of the House Committee on Un-American Activities* (New York: Farrar, Straus and Giroux, 1968); Kenneth O'Reilly's *Hoover and the Un-Americans: The FBI, HUAC, and the Red Menace* (Philadelphia: Temple University Press, 1983); Athan Theoharis and John Stuart Cox's *The Boss: J. Edgar Hoover and the Great America Inquisition* (Philadelphia: Temple University Press, 1988); and Tim Weiner, *Enemies: A History of the FBI* (New York: Random House, 2012). The wider historical context is examined in Robert Goldstein, *Political Repression in Modern America: From 1879 to 1976* (Urbana: University of Illinois Press, 2001). Landon R. Y. Storr's *The Second Red Scare and the Unmaking of the New Deal Left* (Princeton, NJ: Princeton University Press, 2013) offers a detailed analysis of the various loyalty investigations of the 1940s and

1950s, demonstrating how these investigations were used to attack and discredit the legacy of the New Deal.

On the actual history of American communist activity from the late forties through to the midsixties, readers should begin with Theodore Draper's *American Communism and Soviet Russia* (New Brunswick, NJ: Transaction Publishers, 1960, 2003); Harvey Klehr and John Earl Hayes's *The American Communist Movement: Storming Heaven Itself* (New York: Twayne, 1992); and Harvey Klehr, John Earl Haynes, and Fridrikh Igorevich's *The Secret World of American Communism* (New Haven, CT: Yale University Press, 1995).

The best biography of Senator McCarthy is David M. Oshinsky's *A Conspiracy So Immense: The World of Joe McCarthy* (New York: Oxford University Press, 2005). Readers looking for a more concise but still insightful account of McCarthy's life should consider Tom Wicker's *Shooting Star: The Brief Arc of Joe McCarthy* (Orlando, FL: Harcourt, 2006). The older biographies—Richard H. Rovere's *Senator Joe McCarthy* (New York: Harcourt, Brace, Jovanovich, 1959) and Thomas Reeves's *The Life and Times of Joe McCarthy* (New York: Stein and Day, 1982)—should not be discounted, however. A spirited if largely unconvincing revisionist defense of the senator from an avowedly conservative perspective is provided by M. Stanton Evans in *Blacklisted by History: The Untold Story of Senator Joe McCarthy* (New York: Three Rivers Press, 2007).

Moving beyond the man to the "ism," other important works include: Earl Latham's *The Communist Controversy in Washington: From the New Deal to McCarthy* (Cambridge, MA: Harvard University Press, 1966); Michael Paul Rogin's *The Intellectuals and McCarthy: The Radical Specter* (Cambridge, MA: MIT Press, 1967); Robert Griffith's *The Politics of Fear: Joseph R. McCarthy and the Senate*, 2nd ed. (Amherst: University of Massachusetts Press, 1987); Athan Theoharis, *Seeds of Repression: Harry S. Truman and the Origins of McCarthyism* (Chicago: Quadrangle Books, 1971); and Thomas Doherty's engrossing *Cold War, Cool Medium: Television, McCarthyism, and American Culture* (New York: Columbia University Press, 2003).

In addition to Lipset and Hofstadter's essays, early assessments of the John Birch Society and the wider radical right of the 1960s can be found in J. Allen Broyles's *The John Birch Society: Anatomy of a Protest* (Boston: Beacon Press, 1964); Benjamin R. Epstein and Arnold Foster's

The Radical Right: Report on the John Birch Society and Its Allies (New York: Vintage, 1967); and George Thayer's *The Farther Shores of Politics: The American Political Fringe Today*, 2nd ed. (New York: Clarion, 1968). Much of this section of the book drew on my own research into the Society, published as *The World of the John Birch Society: Conspiracy, Conservatism and the Cold War* (Nashville: Vanderbilt University Press, 2014). Terry Lauz's *John Birch: A Life* (New York: Oxford University Press, 2016), although focused on the Baptist missionary who gave the Society its name, contains much insightful commentary on the organization. Claire Conner, whose parents forced her to join the JBS when she was just thirteen, also provides a compelling account of the Society from the "inside" in *Wrapped in the Flag: A Personal History of America's Radical Right* (Boston: Beacon Press, 2013). The various essays in David Farber and Jeff Roche's *The Conservative Sixties* (New York: Peter Lang, 2003) are also important to consider.

CHAPTER 3:
RESISTING THE TIDE

There is a vast and rich historiography on the civil rights movement. I can only give a small sampling of the important work that has been done in this area, but readers who want to further their knowledge, both of the specific events discussed in this chapter and the broader story of the African American freedom struggle, would do well to consult the following: C. Vann Woodward, *The Strange Career of Jim Crow* (New York: Oxford University Press, 1955, 2003); Michael J. Klarman, *From Jim Crow to Civil Rights: The Supreme Court and the Struggle for Racial Equality* (New York: Oxford University Press, 2006); Leon F. Litwack, *Trouble in Mind: Black Southerners in the Age of Jim Crow* (New York: Vintage, 1999); John Dittmer, *Local People: The Struggle for Civil Rights in Mississippi* (Urbana: University Press of Illinois, 1994); William Doyle, *An American Insurrection: The Battle of Oxford, Mississippi, 1962* (New York: Doubleday, 2001); Timothy B. Tyson, *The Blood of Emmett Till* (New York: Simon and Schuster, 2017); and Clayborne Carson, *In Struggle: SNCC and the Black Awakening of the 1960s* (Cambridge, MA: Harvard University Press, 1981, 1995). Perhaps the best single-volume history of the civil rights movement is Adam Fairclough's *Better Day Coming: Blacks and Equality, 1890–2000* (London: Penguin, 2001). The fullest account of the key period between 1954 and 1968 is Taylor Branch's magnificent three-volume series: *Parting the Waters: America in the King Years, 1954–63* (New York: Simon and Schuster, 1988), *Pillar of Fire: America in the King Years, 1963–65* (New York: Simon and Schuster, 1998), and *At Canaan's Edge: America in the King Years, 1965–68* (New York: Simon and Schuster, 2006). Mary L. Dudziak's *Cold War Civil Rights: Race and the Image of American Democracy* (Princeton, NJ: Princeton University Press, 2000) is also extremely illuminating on the interconnections between the Cold War and the civil rights struggle.

On the radical right's "massive resistance" to the civil rights movement, the initial groundbreaking work was done by Numan V. Bartley in *The Rise of Massive Resistance: Race and Politics in the South During the 1950s* (Baton Rouge: Louisiana State University Press, 1969); Neil R. McMillen in *Citizens' Councils: Organized Resistance to the Second Reconstruction, 1954–64* (Urbana: University of Illinois Press, 1971, 1994); and Francis M. Wilhoit in *The Politics of Massive Resistance* (New York: George Braziller, 1973). Their work has been extended and deepened by George Lewis's *The White South and the Red Menace: Segregationists, Anticommunism, and Massive Resistance, 1945–1965* (Gainesville: University Press of Florida, 2004) and *Massive Resistance: The White Response to the Civil Rights Movement* (London: Hodder Arnold, 2006), as well as the collected essays in Clive Webb's *Massive Resistance: Southern Opposition to the Second Reconstruction* (New York: Oxford University Press, 2005).

The States' Rights Democratic Party is expertly covered in Kari Fredrickson's *The Dixiecrat Revolt and the End of the Solid South* (Chapel Hill: University of North Carolina Press, 2001), and John Kyle Day provides a compelling analysis of the importance of the congressional Southern Manifesto in *The Southern Manifesto: Massive Resistance and the Fight to Preserve Segregation* (Jackson: University Press of Mississippi, 2014). A detailed study of the desegregation process in Virginia's schools can be found in the essays in Matthew D. Lassiter and Andrew B. Lewis's *The Moderates Dilemma: Massive Resistance to School Desegregation in Virginia* (Charlottesville: University of Virginia Press, 1998). The importance of local dynamics is also evident in Karen Anderson's probing account of the events at Little Rock, Arkansas, in *Little Rock:*

Race and Resistance at Central High School (Princeton, NJ: Princeton University Press, 2013). Joseph Crespino's *Strom Thurmond's America* (New York: Hill and Wang, 2012) is a riveting study of the man and his times, which connects the Dixiecrat not just with the radical right and the anti-communist movement, but also with the postwar conservative movement as a whole. Readers should also consult Michael J. Klarmen's "How *Brown* Changed Race Relations: The Backlash Thesis," *Journal of American History* 81, no. 1 (June 1994): 81–118, which argues, persuasively, that the "backlash" to the Supreme Court's decision in *Brown v. Board of Education* was actually more important in bringing about substantive reform than the decision itself.

For more on the Ku Klux Klan and the efforts of other violent extremists such as J. B. Stoner, see David M. Chalmers's *Hooded Americanism, The First Century of the Ku Klux Klan: 1865 to the Present* (New York: Doubleday, 1965); Wyn Craig Wade's *The Fiery Cross: The Ku Klux Klan in America* (New York: Simon and Schuster, 1987); and especially Clive Webb's *Rabble Rousers: The American Far Right in the Civil Rights Era* (Athens: University of Georgia Press, 2010). Webb also discusses the role played by General Walker and other military officers such as Rear Admiral John Crommelin in resisting racial reform. I discuss Walker and the John Birch Society's attitudes to civil rights in *The World of the John Birch Society: Conspiracy, Conservatism and the Cold War* (Nashville: Vanderbilt University Press, 2014); as does Jonathan Schoenwald in his excellent book *A Time for Choosing: The Rise of Modern American Conservatism* (New York: Oxford University Press, 2001).

The importance of race, the southern strategy, and "dog-whistle politics" to the Republican Party from Barry Goldwater's failed 1964 presidential campaign onward is addressed in various works including: Rick Perlstein, *Before the Storm: Barry Goldwater and the Unmaking of the American Consensus* (New York: Hill and Wang, 2001) and its follow-up *Nixonland: The Rise of a President and the Fracturing of America* (New York: Scribner, 2009); Kevin Philips, *The Emerging Republican Majority* (New York: Anchor Books, 1970); Thomas Edsell and Mary Edsell, *Chain Reaction: The Impact of Race, Rights and Taxes on American Politics* (New York: W. W. Norton, 1992); Joseph E. Lowndes, *From the New Deal to the New Right: Race and the Southern Origins of Modern Conservatism* (New Haven, CT: Yale University Press, 2009); Timothy N. Thurber, *Republicans and*

Race: The GOP's Frayed Relationship with African Americans, 1945–1974 (Lawrence: University Press of Kansas, 2012); Ian Haney-López, *Dog Whistle Politics: How Coded Racial Appeals Have Reinvented Racism and Wrecked the Middle Class* (New York: Oxford University Press, 2015); and Matthew F. Delmont, *Why Busing Failed: Race, Media, and the National Resistance to School Desegregation* (Berkeley: University of California Press, 2016).

Readers looking for a biography of Goldwater should turn to Alan Goldberg's *Barry Goldwater* (New Haven, CT: Yale University Press, 1995). The complex figure of George Wallace is best captured in Dan T. Carter's *The Politics of Rage: George Wallace, the Origins of New Conservatism and the Transformation of American Politics* (Baton Rouge: Louisiana State University Press, 1996), but Stephen Lesher's *George Wallace: An American Populist* (Reading, MA: Addison-Wesley, 1994) also contains useful insights. The significance of the 1968 election to modern American politics is captured nicely in Michael Cohen's *American Maelstrom: The 1968 Election and the Politics of Division* (New York: Oxford University Press, 2016).

CHAPTER 4:
OUT OF THE WILDERNESS

Excellent overviews of the New Right can be found in Lisa McGirr's *Suburban Warriors: The Origins of the New American Right* (Princeton, NJ: Princeton University Press, 2001); Bruce J. Schulman and Julian E. Zeizer's *Rightward Bound: Making America Conservative in the 1970s* (Cambridge, MA: Harvard University Press, 2008); Allan J. Lichtman's *White Protestant Nation: The Rise of the American Conservative Movement* (New York: Atlantic Monthly Press, 2008); Laura Kalman's *Right Star Rising: A New Politics, 1974–1980* (New York: Norton, 2010); and Michael Stewart Foley, *Front Porch Politics: The Forgotten Heyday of American Activism in the 1970s and 1980s* (New York: Hill and Wang, 2013).

On the enormously significant role played by big business and the wealthy in building the New Right in the 1970s and 1980s, readers should consult both David Vogel's *Fluctuating Fortunes: The Political Power of Business in America* (New York: Basic Books, 1989) and Kim Phillips-

Fein's *Invisible Hands: The Making of the Conservative Movement from the New Deal to Reagan* (New York: Norton, 2009). Jason Stahl has provided a much-needed history of right-wing think tanks in *Right Moves: The Conservative Think Tank in American Political Culture since 1945* (Chapel Hill: University of North Carolina Press, 2016).

One of the leading figures of the New Right, Richard Viguerie, offers his own account of the rise of the movement in *The New Right: We're Ready to Lead* (Falls Church, VA: Viguerie Co., 1981). Interested readers should also seek out his later, more polemical, *The Establishment v. The People: Is a New Populist Revolt on the Way?* (Chicago: Regnery Gateway, 1983). Alan Crawford, a disillusioned member of the New Right coalition—he was an assistant editor of Vigureie's *Conservative Digest* magazine—is highly critical of its activities and politics in *Thunder on the Right: The "New Right" and the Politics of Resentment* (New York: Pantheon Books, 1980). Another critical account is provided by John S. Saloma III's *Ominous Politics: The New Conservative Labyrinth* (New York: Hill and Wang, 1984). Much more sympathetic is William A. Rusher in *The Rise of the Right* (New York: Morrow, 1984). More academic analyses of the movement are provided in Rebecca E. Klatch's *A Generation Divided: The New Left, the New Right, and the 1960s* (Berkeley: University of California Press, 1999); Jean Hardisty's *Mobilizing Resentment: Conservative Resurgence from the John Birch Society to the Promise Keepers* (Boston: Beacon Press, 1999); and Pamela Johnston Conover and Virginia Gray's *Feminism and the New Right: Conflict Over the American Family* (New York: Praeger, 1983). Donald T. Critchlow's *Phyllis Schlafly and Grassroots Conservatism: A Woman's Crusade* (Princeton, NJ: Princeton University Press, 2005) is also an important resource.

The rise of the religious right in the 1970s and 1980s has also generated an extensive literature. Among the best studies are William Martin's *With God on Our Side: The Rise of the Religious Right in America* (New York: Broadway Books, 1996); Sara Diamond's *Not by Politics Alone: The Enduring Influence of the Religious Right* (New York: Guilford Press, 1998); Darren Dochuk's *From Bible Belt to Sun Belt: Plain-Folk Religion, Grassroots Politics, and the Rise of Evangelical Conservatism* (New York: Norton, 2011); Alex R. Schäfer's *Countercultural Conservatives: American Evangelicalism from the Postwar Revival to the*

New Christian Right (Madison: University of Wisconsin Press, 2011); and, most recently, Francis Fitzgerald's *The Evangelicals: The Struggle to Shape America* (New York: Simon and Schuster, 2017). On the lives and careers of Jerry Falwell and Pat Robertson, I found Susan Friend Hardings's *The Book of Jerry Falwell: Fundamentalist Language and Politics* (Princeton, NJ: Princeton University Press, 2000) and David Marley's *Pat Robertson: An American Life* (Lanham, MD: Rowman & Littlefield, 2007) to be most useful. James Hunter's *Culture Wars: The Struggle to Define America* (New York: Basic Books, 1991) also provides invaluable context on the period.

On the "malaise" of the Carter years, readers should seek out Meg Jacobs's *Panic at the Pump: The Energy Crisis and the Transformation of American politics in the 1970s* (New York: Hill and Wang, 2016) and Burton I. Kaufman's *The Presidency of James Earl Carter Jr.* (Lawrence: University of Press of Kansas, 1993, 2006) as starting points. From the vast range of sources on the remarkable life and presidency of Ronald Reagan, a number stand out, including: Lou Cannon's *Governor Reagan: His Rise to Power* (New York: Public Affairs, 2003) and *President Reagan: The Role of a Lifetime* (New York: Public Affairs, 2000); Garry Wills's *Reagan's America: Innocents at Home* (New York: Doubleday, 1987); Matthew Dallek's *The Right Moment: Ronald Reagan's First Victory and the Decisive Turning Point in American Politics* (New York: Free Press, 2000); Gil Troy's *Morning in America: How Ronald Reagan Invented the 1980s* (Princeton, NJ: Princeton University Press, 2005); and Sean Wilentz's *The Age of Reagan: A History, 1974–2000* (New York: HarperCollins, 2008). The best short history is Jules Tygiel's *Ronald Reagan and the Triumph of American Conservatism*, 2nd ed. (New York: Pearson, 2006). Seth Rosenfeld's *Subversives: The FBI's War on Student Radicals and Reagan's Rise to Power* (New York: Farrar, Straus and Giroux, 2012) and Rick Perlstein's *The Invisible Bridge: The Fall of Nixon and the Rise of Ronald Reagan* (New York: Simon and Schuster, 2014) are also worth pursuing. Reagan's own account of his life can be found in *Where's the Rest of Me? Ronald Reagan Tells His Own Story* (New York: Meredith Press, 1965), written with Richard C. Hubler, and *An American Life* (New York: Simon and Schuster, 1990).

Finally, the document collections *The Rise of Conservatism in America, 1945–2000: A Brief History with Documents* (Boston: Bedford/St. Martin's,

2008), by Ronald Story and Bruce Laurie, and *Conservatives in Power: The Reagan Years, 1981–1989: A Brief History with Documents* (Boston: Bedford/St. Martin's, 2011), by Meg Jacobs and Julian E. Zelizer, are not only extremely rich in primary-source material. They also contain excellent introductory essays.

CHAPTER 5:
RADICALISM RISING

For an overview of the presidency of George H. W. Bush, the best place to start is with Michael Duffy and Dan Goodgame's *Marching in Place: The Status-Quo Presidency of George Bush* (New York: Simon & Schuster, 1992) or John Greene's *The Presidency of George Bush* (Lawrence: University Press of Kansas, 2000). Timothy Stanley has written an informative account of Pat Buchanan's long and controversial career in *The Crusader: The Life and Tumultuous Times of Pat Buchanan* (New York: Thomas Dunne Books, 2012). Ross Perot, another populist political outsider, is still in need of a really first-rate biography. The best to date is Ken Gross's *Ross Perot: The Man Behind the Myth* (New York: Random House, 1992).

There a number of very good analyses of Bill Clinton's years in the White House, including Joe Klein's *The Natural: The Misunderstood Presidency of Bill Clinton* (New York: Broadway Books. 2002); William C. Berman's *From the Center to the Edge: The Politics and Policies of the Clinton Presidency* (Lanham, MD: Rowman and Littlefield, 2001); and, most recently, Gil Troy's *The Age of Clinton: America in the 1990s* (New York: Thomas Dunne Books, 2015). Readers interested in Clinton's own assessment of his presidency should consult his exhaustive—if often exhausting—autobiography, *My Life* (New York: Vintage, 2004).

The rise of the radical Republican right during this time is covered well in Sean Wilentz's *The Age of Reagan: A History, 1974–2000* (New York: HarperCollins, 2008); Allan J. Lichtman's *White Protestant Nation: The Rise of the American Conservative Movement* (New York: Atlantic Monthly Press, 2008); and E. J. Dionne Jr.'s *Why the Right Went Wrong: Conservatism—From Goldwater to the Tea Party and Beyond* (New York: Simon & Schuster, 2016). For more detail on Newt Gingrich and his Contract with

America, see Elizabeth Drew, *Showdown: The Struggle Between the Gingrich Congress and the Clinton White House* (New York: Simon and Schuster, 1997); Evan Thomas et al., *Back from the Dead: How Clinton Survived the Republican Revolution* (New York: Atlantic Monthly Press, 1997); Major Garret, *The Enduring Revolution: How the Contract With America Continues to Shape the Nation* (New York: Crown Forum, 2005); and Steven M. Gillon, *The Pact: Newt Gingrich, Bill Clinton and the Rivalry that Defined a Generation* (New York: Oxford University Press, 2008). Gingrich's own insights can be found in *To Renew America* (New York: HarperCollins, 1995) and *Lessons Learned the Hard Way: A Personal Report* (New York: HarperCollins, 1998). Dan T. Carter traces the connections between the "Republican Revolution" of the mid-1990s and the southern strategy of the early 1960s in *From George Wallace to Newt Gingrich: Race in the Conservative Counterrevolution, 1963–1994* (Baton Rouge: Louisiana State University Press, 1996).

The British journalist Gavin Esler provides a compelling outsider's account of the rising tide of anti-government sentiment during the 1990s in *The United States of Anger: The People and the American Dream* (London: Penguin, 1997). The American journalist Peter Applebome's *Dixie Rising: How the South is Shaping American Values, Politics and Culture* (San Diego: Harcourt Brace, 1997) also offers fascinating insights into the period from a different, but no less important context.

On the militia movement, my own books, *Homegrown Revolutionaries: An American Militia Reader* (Norwich, UK: Arthur Miller Centre for American Studies, 1999) and *American Extremism: History, Politics and the American Militia Movement* (New York: Routledge, 2004) contain a useful selection of primary-source material and a more detailed analysis of how militia members have used and abused American history to further their goals. Kenneth S. Stern provides the best narrative account of the early years of the movement in *A Force Upon the Plain: The American Militia Movement and the Politics of Hate* (Norman: University of Oklahoma Press, 1997). Steven M. Chermak's *Searching for a Demon: The Media Construction of the Militia Movement* (Boston: Northeastern University Press, 2002) and Stuart A. Wright's *Patriots, Politics and the Oklahoma City Bombing* (Cambridge: Cambridge University Press, 2007) both offer important insights from notable academics in the field. The Southern Poverty Law Center's *The Second Wave: Return of the Militias*

(Montgomery, AL: Southern Poverty Law Center, 2009) is especially useful on the later years of the movement.

For more details on the events at Ruby Ridge, Waco, and the Oklahoma City bombing, readers should seek out Jess Walter's *Every Knee Shall Bow: The Truth and Tragedy of Ruby Ridge and the Randy Weaver Family* (New York: Regan Books, 1995); Dick J. Reavis's *The Ashes of Waco: An Investigation* (New York: Simon & Schuster, 1995); and Dan Herbeck and Lou Michaels's *American Terrorist: Timothy McVeigh and the Oklahoma City Bombing* (New York: Regan Books, 2000). Edward T. Linenthal's *The Unfinished Bombing: Oklahoma City in American Memory* (New York: Oxford University Press, 2001) offers a revealing and moving analysis of the broader impact of the bombing on American culture.

Of the many books on the impeachment of Clinton, those I found most useful in the writing of this chapter were: Floyd Brown, *"Slick Willie": Why America Cannot Trust Bill Clinton* (Annapolis, MD: Washington Book Pub., 1993); Elizabeth Drew, *The Corruption of American Politics: What Went Wrong and Why* (Seacaucus, NJ: Birch Lane, 1999); Jeffrey Toobin, *A Vast Conspiracy: The Real Story of the Sex Scandal That Nearly Brought Down a President* (New York: Random House, 2000); William J. Bennett, *The Death of Outrage: Bill Clinton and the Assault on American Ideals* (New York: Simon & Schuster, 1998); James B. Stewart, *Blood Sport: The President and His Adversaries* (New York: Simon & Schuster, 1996); Joe Conason and Gene Lyons, *The Hunting of the President: The Ten-Year Campaign to Destroy Bill and Hillary Clinton* (New York: St. Martin's Press, 2000); and Richard Posner, *An Affair of State: The Investigation, Impeachment and Trial of William Jefferson Clinton* (Cambridge, MA: Harvard University Press, 1999).

CHAPTER 6:

TEA PARTIES AND TRUMPISM

One of the first assessments of the Tea Party was Kate Zernike's *Boiling Mad: Inside Tea Party America* (New York: Times Books, 2010). It remains a must-read. Much less objective, but nonetheless useful is Will Bunch's *The Backlash: Right-Wing Radicals, High-Def Hucksters, and Paranoid Politics in the Age of Obama* (New York: Harper Collins, 2010). Jill Lepore's

The Whites of Their Eyes: The Tea Party's Revolution and the Battle Over American History (Princeton, NJ: Princeton University Press, 2010) focuses on Tea Party members' engagement with the American past. Theda Skocpol and Vanessa Williamson's *The Tea Party and the Remaking of Republican Conservatism* (New York: Oxford University Press, 2013) is a deeply detailed and informative study of the movement. Also highly recommended are Christopher S. Parker and Matt A. Barreto's *Change They Can't Believe In: The Tea Party and Reactionary Politics in America* (Princeton, NJ: Princeton University Press, 2014); Ronald P. Formisano's *The Tea Party: A Brief History* (Baltimore: John Hopkins University Press, 2012); and Lee Fang's *The Machine: A Field Guide to the Resurgent Right* (New York: The New Press, 2013). A thoughtful defense of the Tea Party is provided by Elizabeth Price Foley in *The Tea Party: Three Principles* (New York: Cambridge University Press, 2012). For an understandably more partisan perspective, see Dick Armey and Matt Kibbe's *Give Us Liberty: A Tea Party Manifesto* (New York: William Morrow, 2010).

Jane Mayer first revealed the Koch brothers' behind-the-scenes backing of the Tea Party in "Covert Operations: The Billionaire Brothers Who are Waging a War Against Obama," in the *New Yorker*, August 30, 2010. She followed this up with the much more extensive *Dark Money: The Hidden History of the Billionaires Behind the Rise of the Radical Right* (New York: Doubleday, 2016). See also Nancy MacLean's *Democracy in Chains: The Deep History of the Radical Right's Stealth Plan for America* (New York: Viking, 2017), which tells the story of how the Noble Prize–winning historian James McGill Buchanan originated many of the ideas that would be developed by the Koch brothers, initially as an attempt to preserve the power of white elites in response to the Supreme Court's decision in *Brown v. Board of Education*. Jeff Nesbit's *Poison Tea: How Big Oil and Big Tobacco Invented the Tea Party and Captured the GOP* (New York: Thomas Dunne Books, 2016) should also be consulted. Robert Draper provides a compelling account of the impact of the Tea Party during the 112th Congress in *When The Tea Party Came to Town* (New York: Simon & Schuster, 2012), and E. J. Dionne Jr. skillfully explores how it pushed the Republican Party further to the right in *When the Right Went Wrong: Conservatism—From Goldwater to the Tea Party and Beyond* (New York: Simon & Schuster, 2016).

For more on Fox News and Glenn Beck, see Gabriel Sherman's *The Loudest Voice in the Room: How the Brilliant, Bombastic Roger Ailes Built Fox News—and Divided a Country* (New York: Random House, 2014) and Dana Milbank's *Tears of a Clown: Glenn Beck and the Tea Bagging of America* (New York: Doubleday, 2010). Other important articles and reports include: Sean Wilentz, "Confounding Fathers: The Tea Party's Cold War Roots," the *New Yorker*, October 18, 2010; David Frum, "Crashing the Party: Why the GOP Must Modernize to Win," *Foreign Affairs* 93, no. 5 (September/October 2014): 37–46; The Anti-Defamation League, *Rage Grows in America: Anti-Government Conspiracies* (New York: Anti-Defamation League, 2009); Devin Burghart and Leonard Zeskind, *Tea Party Nationalism: A Critical Examination of the Tea Party Movement and the Size, Scope, and Focus of Its National Factions* (Kansas City: Institute for Research and Education on Human Rights, 2010); and Mark Lilla, "The Tea Party Jacobins," the *New York Review of Books*, May 27, 2010.

For overviews and analyses of the presidencies of George W. Bush and Barack Obama, readers are encouraged to examine the essays in Julian E. Zelizer's *The Presidency of George W. Bush: A First Historical Assessment* (Princeton, NJ: Princeton University Press, 2010); David Kuo's *Tempting Faith: The Inside Story of Political Seduction* (New York: Free Press, 2006); Michael Grunwald's *The New New Deal: The Hidden Story of Change in the Obama Era* (New York: Simon & Schuster, 2012); Jonathan Alter's *The Promise: President Obama Year One* (New York: Simon & Schuster, 2011) and *The Center Holds: Obama and His Enemies* ((New York: Simon & Schuster, 2013); Dan Balz's *Collision 2012: Obama vs. Romney and the Future of Elections in America* (New York: Viking, 2013); and Jeremi Suri, *The Impossible Presidency: The Rise and Fall of America's Highest Office* (New York: Basic Books, 2017).

Given that the history of the Trump presidency is still ongoing, for this section I utilized a range of journalistic sources including from the *New York Times*, the *New York Review of Books*, the *New Yorker*, the *Washington Post*, the *(London) Guardian*, *Foreign Affairs*, CNN, and Fox News. Some of the articles I found most useful were: David Frum, "How to Build an Autocracy," the *Atlantic*, March 2017; Robert Kagan, "This is How Fascism Comes to America," the *Washington Post*, May 18, 2016;

David Remnick, "American Demagogue," the *New Yorker*, March 14, 2016; Robert O. Paxton, "American Duce: Is Donald Trump a Fascist or a Plutocrat?" *Harper's Magazine*, May 2017; Walter Russell Mead, "The Jacksonian Revolt: American Populism and the Liberal Order," *Foreign Affairs* 96, no. 2 (March/April 2017): 2–7; Andrew Marantz, "Trolling the Press Corps: The Trump Administration Disrupts the Daily Briefing," the *New Yorker*, March 20, 2017; Michael Tomasky, "The Dangerous Election," the *New York Review of Books*, March 24, 2016; Elizabeth Drew, "Terrifying Trump," the *New York Review of Books*, March 9, 2017; Mark Danner, "The Real Trump," the *New York Review of Books*, December 22, 2016; Jane Mayer, "Trump's Boswell Speaks," the *New Yorker*, July 25, 2016; Martin Amis, "Don the Realtor: The Rise of Trump," *Harper's Magazine*, August 2016; Emily Nussbaum, "Guilty Pleasure: How TV Created Donald Trump," the *New Yorker*, July 31, 2017; Connie Bruck, "A Hollywood Story: Did the Movies Really Make Steve Bannon," the *New Yorker*, May 1, 2017; and George Michael, "The Rise of the Alt-Right and the Politics of Polarization in America," *Skeptic Magazine* 22, no. 2 (2017): 9–17.

Trump's early career was first covered by Wayne Barrett in *Trump: The Deals and the Downfall* (New York: HarperCollins, 1992). Gwenda Blair's *The Trumps: Three Generations of Builders and a Presidential Candidate* (New York: Simon & Schuster, 2000, 2016) is also an excellent resource. Other biographies include Timothy L. O'Brien's *Trump Nation: The Art of Being The Donald* (New York: Grand Central Publishing, 2005, 2016); David Clay Johnson's highly critical *The Making of Donald Trump* (Brooklyn: Melville House, 2016); Michael D'Antonio's excellent *The Truth About Trump* (New York: Thomas Dunne, 2016); and Michael Kranish and Marc Fisher persuasive and informative *Trump Revealed: An American Journey of Ambition, Ego, Money and Power* (New York: Scribner, 2016). Interested readers may also wish to consider Trump's own books, including *Trump: The Art of the Deal* (New York: Ballantine Books, 1987), written with Tony Schwartz; *Trump: The Art of the Comeback* (New York: Crown Business, 1997) written with Kate Bohner; and his recent campaign manifesto, *Crippled America: How to Make America Great Again* (New York: Threshold Editions, 2016).

Joshua Green's *Devil's Bargain: Steve Bannon, Donald Trump, and the Storming of the Presidency* (New York: Penguin Press, 2017) is highly revealing on the contentious relationship between the two men. On the alt-right more broadly, readers should consult David Neiwert's *Alt-America: The Rise of the Radical Right in the Age of Trump* (New York: Verso: 2017). Much more detail on the 2016 presidential campaign can be found in Jonathan Allen's *Shattered: Inside Hillary Clinton's Doomed Campaign* (New York: Crown 2017) and Hillary Clinton's memoir, *What Happened* (New York: Simon & Schuster, 2017). On the tumultuous first year of Trump's presidency, see also Michael Wolff's *Fire and Fury: Inside the Trump White House* (New York: Henry Holt and Co., 2018).

CONCLUSION

Pankaj Mishra provides a fascinating analysis for the worldwide context for Trump's appeal in *Age of Anger: A History of the Present* (New York: Farrar, Straus and Giroux, 2017). Geoffrey Kabaservice offers a detailed and engaging history of the rise of radicalism within the GOP in *Rule and Ruin: The Downfall of Moderation and the Destruction of the Republican Party from Eisenhower to the Tea Party* (New York: Oxford University Press, 2012).

Index

About the Author

D. J. Mulloy is chair and professor of history at Wilfrid Laurier University, where he specializes in the study of post-1945 U.S. history. He is the author of *American Extremism: History, Politics, and the Militia Movement* (2004) and *The World of the John Birch Society: Conspiracy, Conservatism, and the Cold War* (2014).